Multilingual Education Yearbook

Series Editor

Indika Liyanage, School of Education, Deakin University, Burwood, VIC, Australia

Advisory Editorial Board

Bob Adamson, Department of International Education and Lifelong Learning, The Education University of Hong Kong, Tai Po, Hong Kong SAR, Hong Kong

Suresh Canagarajah, Department of Applied Linguistics and English, Pennsylvania State University, University Park, PA, USA

Andy Kirkpatrick, Department of Humanities, Languages and Social Science, Griffith University, Nathan, QLD, Australia

Parlo Singh, Griffith Institute for Educational Research, Griffith University, Mt. Gravatt Campus, Mount Gravatt, QLD, Australia

The *Multilingual Education Yearbook* publishes high-quality empirical research on education in multilingual societies. It publishes research findings that in addition to providing descriptions of language learning, development and use in language contact and multilingual contexts, will shape language education policy and practices in multilingual societies.

The *Multilingual Education Yearbook* is highly relevant to researchers in language and education, language education professionals, and policy makers, covering topics such as:

- The effects of multilingual education and literacy education on the maintenance and development of multilingualism.
- The effects of the introduction of English as a curriculum subject and/or medium of instruction upon multilingual and literacy education.
- The respective role(s) of vernaculars and 'local' languages, national languages and English in education, especially where the languages are of different language families, and scripts are different or languages lack an orthography.
- The role in multilingual education of other major languages such as Arabic, French, Hindi, Mandarin and Spanish.
- The effects of multilingual and/or English language education on school drop out and retention rates.
- The effects of the 'internationalization' of universities worldwide, potential privileging of the English language and of knowledge published in English.
- Bilingual/multilingual acquisition of non-cognate and 'different-script' languages.
- Takeholder attitudes toward notions of multilingualism and related notions of linguistic proficiency, standards, models and varieties.
- Critical evaluations of language policy and its implementation.

More information about this series at http://www.springer.com/series/15827

Indika Liyanage · Tony Walker
Editors

Multilingual Education Yearbook 2019

Media of Instruction & Multilingual Settings

Editors
Indika Liyanage
School of Education
Deakin University
Burwood, VIC, Australia

Tony Walker
School of Education
Deakin University
Burwood, VIC, Australia

ISSN 2522-5421　　　　　　　ISSN 2522-543X　(electronic)
Multilingual Education Yearbook
ISBN 978-3-030-14385-5　　　ISBN 978-3-030-14386-2　(eBook)
https://doi.org/10.1007/978-3-030-14386-2

Library of Congress Control Number: 2019932834

© Springer Nature Switzerland AG 2019
This work is subject to copyright. All rights are reserved by the Publisher, whether the whole or part of the material is concerned, specifically the rights of translation, reprinting, reuse of illustrations, recitation, broadcasting, reproduction on microfilms or in any other physical way, and transmission or information storage and retrieval, electronic adaptation, computer software, or by similar or dissimilar methodology now known or hereafter developed.
The use of general descriptive names, registered names, trademarks, service marks, etc. in this publication does not imply, even in the absence of a specific statement, that such names are exempt from the relevant protective laws and regulations and therefore free for general use.
The publisher, the authors and the editors are safe to assume that the advice and information in this book are believed to be true and accurate at the date of publication. Neither the publisher nor the authors or the editors give a warranty, express or implied, with respect to the material contained herein or for any errors or omissions that may have been made. The publisher remains neutral with regard to jurisdictional claims in published maps and institutional affiliations.

This Springer imprint is published by the registered company Springer Nature Switzerland AG
The registered company address is: Gewerbestrasse 11, 6330 Cham, Switzerland

Contents

Medium of Instruction and Multilingual Contexts: Unravelling the Questions and Unpacking the Challenges 1
Indika Liyanage and Tony Walker

Language Alternation as an Interactional Practice in the Foreign Language Classroom 25
Anna Filipi

Multilingualism and Language Mixing Among Singapore University Students 43
Kingsley Bolton and Werner Botha

Educational Globalization and the Creation of Split Identities 63
François Victor Tochon

Bilingual Education Classrooms in Sri Lankan Schools: A Social Space for Ethnolinguistic Reconciliation 81
Harsha Dulari Wijesekera and Jennifer Alford

CLIL for Who? Commodification of English-Medium Courses in Japan's Higher Education 103
Kayoko Hashimoto and Gregory Paul Glasgow

Benefits of Translanguaging and Transculturation Exchanges Between International Higher Degree Research Students and English Medium Research Supervisors 121
Minglin Li and Beryl Exley

Trilingualism and Medium of Instruction Models in Minority Schools in Qinghai Province, China 137
Ma Fu

Children's Views and Strategies for Making Friends in Linguistically Diverse English Medium Instruction Settings 151
Maryanne Theobald, Gillian Busch and Megan Laraghy

English in a Mongolian Ethnic Minority Primary School 175
Yayuan Yi and Bob Adamson

Scrutinising Critical Thinking (CT) in Chinese Higher Education: Perceptions of Chinese Academics 189
Anhui Wang, Indika Liyanage and Tony Walker

Media of Instruction in Indonesia: Implications for Bi/Multilingual Education 209
Tony Walker, Indika Liyanage, Suwarsih Madya and Sari Hidayati

Medium of Instruction and Multilingual Contexts: Unravelling the Questions and Unpacking the Challenges

Indika Liyanage and Tony Walker

Abstract In times and contexts where multilingual classrooms and educational settings are the norm, attention to medium of instruction (MOI), and to practices around language use in teaching and learning, is unavoidable. Prioritising one language as the MOI over others arguably has a profound impact on all languages and their various stakeholders in multilingual contexts. MOI policy decisions, their enactments, and how these realise broader geopolitical and socio-political agendas in multilingual contexts present another layer of complexity in questions regarding MOI in multilingual education. MOI is deployed as policy and promoted as practice to pursue diverse objectives, but enactment in classrooms often provokes unexpected outcomes and multilingual practices that illustrate the creativity and resourcefulness of language users. As language users—teaching practitioners and their students—respond to fluidity and complexity in language ecologies of the current multilingualism (Aronin in Learning and using multiple languages: current findings from research on multilingualism. Cambridge Scholars Publishing, Newcastle upon Tyne, UK, pp 1–28, 2015), researchers are in turn responding to investigate and analyse rich sources of data that can reveal the realities of moment-to-moment practices and that can offer new or alternative approaches and responses to the needs of diverse stakeholders. This chapter foregrounds how these challenges and complexities interact in relation to choices, implementations, and enactments of MOI in multilingual settings. It also explores how they impact on educational processes, developments and outcomes, as well as broader social and (geo)political agendas, and contributions researchers make to understand these.

Keywords Media of instruction · MOI policy · English as MOI · MOI & local languages · Multilingual classrooms

---

I. Liyanage (✉) · T. Walker
School of Education, Deakin University, Geelong, Australia
e-mail: indika.liyanage@deakin.edu.au

T. Walker
e-mail: t.walker@deakin.edu.au

1 Media of Instruction & Education

Multilinguality is not a new feature of human social interaction in the sphere of education, but today "the use of multiple languages is distinct from the forms, patterns, and nature of multilingualism arrangements of the past" (Aronin, 2015, p. 3). Movements of people, products, and information have led not only to the spread of dominant language practices in education, but also to the dispersal of multiple other languages, creating complex and fluid classroom language ecologies. This new linguistic dispensation (Aronin & Singleton, 2008) so permeates the enterprise of education that the demand for and/or use of multiple languages is integral to its conduct across the globe (Liyanage, 2018a). In such circumstances, a focus on medium/media of instruction (MOI) is unavoidable. Classrooms in which the language practices used in instruction differ from the language background of at least some of the students are the norm, not the exception (García & Kleyn, 2013). Although MOI alone does not determine success or failure for individuals or educational programs, there is consensus that it plays a crucial role (Cummins, 2009; Heugh, 2011), and that learning is most successful when a student is "taught and assessed in a language s/he understands and speaks well" (Benson, 2016, p. 3). This is true at least during primary education because of "the critical role played by the language (or languages) of instruction in beginning literacy and learning" (Walter & Benson, 2012, p. 278), although it must be acknowledging that without adequate written development and suitability to pedagogic demands, language/s cannot be used productively as MOI to create an effective foundation for further education, including transfer to an additional language (Trudell, 2016).

Most prosperous economically developed 'Western' states use the dominant language/s, the mother tongue/s, of the majority of their populations, and achieve outcomes that reflect the benefits of doing so (Walter & Benson, 2012). Similarly, South Korea, relying predominantly on the national language as MOI, has achieved outstanding international rankings in school education (Coleman, 2009). Yet among less prosperous states, many associate the educational success of these wealthy developed economies with the particular language used in school instruction, particularly English, and import MOIs or use those introduced by former European colonial powers but which are not the home languages of the majority of the population. If we accept, then, that MOI makes a difference in education, the estimation that nearly 40% of the world's population is unable to access education in the language spoken at home (Walter & Benson, 2012) means MOI policies have the potential to affect negatively vast numbers of individuals, communities, and nations across the world.

There is another important dimension to multilingual education—it would be a rare education system that does not include classrooms dedicated to language learning and the development of bi/multilingualism in students, and in these classrooms also MOI is a focus of the opportunities for successful learning. Within these two broad circumstances there are diverse multilingual education arrangements (see Cenoz & Gorter, 2010) across all sectors from early childhood classrooms to postgraduate study, of which perhaps the most central, and arguably the most contested, is medium of instruction (MOI). Contrarily, using a dominant or powerful language as MOI in multilingual settings is cast as a threat to the survival of non-dominant languages and to multilinguality, yet MOI is also accorded a key role in discussions of language teaching and learning aimed at development of multilingualism.

2 MOI in Multilingual Education

MOI policy decisions, their enactments, and how these realise broader geopolitical and socio-political agendas in multilingual contexts (see Walter & Benson, 2012), complicate questions of MOI in multilingual education. Given the respective role(s), perceptions, and statuses of vernacular, local and dominant languages—particularly English—in multilingual contexts, prioritising one language as and/or in MOI over others is frequently argued to have a profound impact on all languages and their various stakeholders. But clearly the nature of these impacts varies given the possible relations between the environment, the languages, and the language users (Aronin, 2015) in education settings. In many of the world's most socio-linguistically diverse regions, state objectives of economic development, or participation in the global knowledge economy, or of national identity, can drive decisions about MOI policy that make scant acknowledgement of the language backgrounds and needs of many learners and their teachers.

But while MOI is regularly deployed as a policy instrument with agendas other than educational objectives, it is also promoted in one guise or another by educators as a dimension of classroom instruction integral to successful teaching and learning. In classrooms with students of differing language backgrounds, and in classrooms dedicated to language teaching, pedagogies built on the premise that classrooms should be sites of multilingual practices, and thus of the judicious and productive use of the available linguistic resources of teachers and students as MOI, are supplanting monolingual approaches. Against these general characteristics of current multilingualism and MOI, we must remember to acknowledge that every multilingual community is multilingual "in their own way" (Aronin, 2015, p. 12), and that these diverse purposes of selection and use of MOI intersect in pedagogies, practices, and conventions that play out in the lived experiences of teachers, learners, and communities.

Enactment of language policy or pedagogic approach in institutions and classrooms often provokes unexpected outcomes and multilingual practices that illustrate the creativity and resourcefulness of language users. As language users—teaching practitioners and their students—respond to fluidity and complexity in language ecologies of the "current multilingualism" (Aronin, 2015), researchers are in turn responding to investigate and analyse rich sources of data that can reveal the realities of moment-to-moment practices and that can offer new or alternative approaches and responses to the needs of diverse stakeholders. This chapter foregrounds how the various challenges and complexities introduced above interact in relation to choices, implementations, and enactments of MOI in multilingual settings, and looks in more detail at selected contexts in which they impact on educational processes, developments and outcomes, and at the contribution that researchers make to understanding these processes.

3 MOI Policy in a Global Context

It is almost passé to remark upon the multitudinous dimensions of globalization, mobility, and communication technologies, and the super diversity that has ensued accompanied by consideration of languages as social practices that are (re)constituted in the context of use rather than as "bounded systems linked with bounded communities" (Blommaert & Rampton, 2011, p. 10). Yet across the globe policy and institutional approaches to MOI continue to be premised upon nation-state thinking that is "increasingly anachronistic … in the field of language in society" (Blommaert, 2015). In those (monolingual) terms, the default policy objective for MOI across the world is convergence on dominant or official national language/s. In most prosperous developed states, usually grouped as the West, the dominant/official language/s used as MOI align with the home language practices of the numerical majority of the population (Walter & Benson, 2012). In Australia, for example, a nation of immigrants, the 2016 census found in excess of 300 languages in use. Whilst Australia has no official language, the dominant language, English, is the only language used in the home by around 75% of the population. The non-dominant language most used in the home, by only 2.5% of the population, is Mandarin (although this could include any other dialect of Han Chinese, such as Cantonese) (Australian Bureau of Statistics, 2017). In the absence of an official language or prescribed MOI, national curriculum documents identify Standard Australian English as "the variety of spoken and written English language in Australia used in more formal settings, such as for official or public purposes, … recognised as the 'common language' of Australians" (Australian Curriculum Assessment and Reporting Authority, 2011, p. 4). Any student—including indigenous students—commencing or entering schooling and assessed to have a language other than English as the dominant home language is provided with intensive English instruction delivered by specialist English as an Additional Language (EAL) teachers for between 6 and 18 months, depending upon prior schooling history and assessed need (Liyanage, in-press). It is policy for transition to English-medium mainstream classrooms to be supported by EAL specialists, and EAL resources adapted to content areas and contexts of use are included in National Curriculum materials. Transition is a difficult process, however, and without adequate support in adaptation of EAL materials, "monolingual practices are the norm and generally uncontested" (Turner & Cross, 2016, p. 292). The very limited number of bilingual programs offered in primary schools, the isolated examples of bilingual and late language immersion programs in secondary schools, and language learning classrooms that adopt use of the target language as MOI, are all focussed on objectives of additional language learning (Liyanage, in-press) rather than the educational needs of EAL students. In higher education, despite the indispensability of multilingualism to the functioning of internationalized universities that recruit students and staff from diverse non-Anglophone backgrounds, institutions demand control of a prestigious variety of standard English and in the process problematize and devalue (multi)linguistic capital (Preece, 2011; Wang, Liyanage, & Walker, 2019). The MOI, apart from language programs, is exclusively English, and entry of students with language backgrounds other than English is regulated by stringent English language proficiency requirements of academic and disciplinary literacies. As higher education comes to terms with the new linguistic dispensation, however, there is some evidence that at research higher degree level, at least, MOI are becoming more permeable to pedagogies that "harness the languages, culture and theoretical knowledge" (Li & Exley, 2019, p. 122) that students from other language backgrounds and academic traditions bring to their research (Díaz, 2018).

In the most linguistically diverse regions of the world, by contrast, the aftermath of colonialism has left many less-prosperous peoples with linguistic legacies complicated by globalization and socio-economic tensions originating in the differing status and power associated with dominant 'foreign' languages, such as English, and local languages. Attempts by states to use MOI policies to balance desires for national identity, unity of diverse communities, and development opportunities associated with a dominant language, against a background of powerful global supra-state actors and imperatives, can prove intractable given limited resources at their disposal. In most instances, the home language/s of a majority of the population are languages other than the dominant/official language/s used as MOI. This is particularly evident in Indonesia where more than 700 languages are in use, but the national language and MOI from Grade One, bahasa Indonesia, is the home language of only around 10% of the population (Fillmore & Handayani, 2018; Simons & Fennig, 2018b; Walker, Liyanage, Madya, & Hidayati, 2019).

4 Local Languages & MOI

Although there are attempts on varying scales to replace dominant or imported languages with local language/s as MOI in regions such as South-East Asia and Eastern and Southern Africa (for state by state details see Kosonen, 2017a; Trudell, 2016), the mismatch between home language and the language of education remains a significant problem. First, the linguistic ecologies of the areas under state policy jurisdictions are frequently so complex that even when several local languages are approved for use as MOI many students, in principle, still begin schooling confronted with a language of instruction that is unfamiliar to them. Second, there is evidence (see Trudell, 2016) to indicate that in practice policy is frequently not implemented and that dominant local vernacular/s or the European languages of former colonizers, in some instances used in the home by as few as 5% of the population, are sometimes used from as early as Grade One. Third, the model applied almost universally to the use of local vernaculars is an early-exit transitional model, where a second/additional language, invariably a dominant national/official language to be used exclusively as the MOI in continuing education, is introduced around Grades Three or Four. Critics (Cummins, 2009; Heugh, 2011) argue this does not provide the optimum five to seven years (Benson, 2016) required for development of academic literacy in the first language before the cognitively and linguistically demanding task of transitioning to learn in only the additional language. These problems of early-exit transition can be alleviated to some extent by continued learning and development of L1 literacy until at least the end of primary school (Benson, 2016).

MOI policy is motivated by objectives other than educational alone, and every policy context is arguably unique, as the following instances demonstrate. The Philippines, for example, introduced in 2009 a model that could be instructive to policymakers in other settings, a pluralistic policy of mother tongue-based multilingual education (Benson, 2016), prompted at least in part by public pressures to address discrepancies in education outcomes (Kosonen, 2017b). The 19 languages currently used as MOIs in government schools at the commencement of schooling represent a fraction of the estimated 182 languages in use in the Philippines. The gradual introduction after Grade Three of Filipino (national & official language) and English (official language) for use alongside rather than replacing the L1 is based on the principle that "the ideal languages of teaching and learning, particularly at the level of basic education, are the languages that learners know best" (Walter & Benson, 2012, p. 278). In Cambodia, where the official language, Kmer, is the home language of 90% of the population, policy is shifting in a similar direction, although not as far as in the Philippines at this point. A Multilingual Education National Action Plan was announced in 2015 that recognized the right of ethnolinguistic minorities to use their mother tongue in the initial years of schooling, supporting introduction of bilingual education in provinces with high concentrations of non-dominant language users (Benson, 2016). Policies in the Philippines and Cambodia contrast sharply with that of Indonesia, where MOI policy has been an instrument of a broader language policy that has the objective of achieving national unity through development of a national language chosen precisely because it was not identified with any one of the several dominant local language groups (Widodo, 2016; Wright, 2016). The use of local languages until Grade Three, when they were replaced by bahasa Indonesia, has been abandoned, as has all formal teaching of local languages as subjects, and all students in government schools are instructed using the national language from the commencement of schooling (Walker et al., 2019).

A very different policy approach to local languages as MOI and national unity has emerged in post-colonial Sri Lanka (see Liyanage, 2018b, 2019). Of the seven languages in use in Sri Lanka (Simons & Fennig, 2018c), the two dominant local languages, Sinhala and Tamil, have a complex and inter-related socio-political and educational history disrupted by the introduction of European languages including, most importantly for contemporary policy-making, English. The right to education through mother tongue MOI has occupied a central place in language policy planning since independence in the middle of last century and was portrayed as "a means of asserting national identity, of upending privilege, and democratising opportunity" (Liyanage, 2019, in press) following more than a century of English MOI education that privileged the local elite. The local vernaculars continue to be used as MOI throughout schooling (Balakrishnar & Thanaraj, 2015; Coperahewa, 2009), and Sri Lanka's high rates of literacy suggest language education in the vernaculars, that is, using as MOI language/s learners know best, has been an outstanding success (Brock-Utne, 2016; Little, 2011). However, in terms of language and national unity, policymakers have turned to what they (contentiously) argue is a "culturally neutral" (Fernando, 2011, p. 4) language not identified with either of the dominant local language groups. English, which retains its prestige, is currently designated as a link language between the Sinhala and Tamil speech communities (Wijesekera & Alford, 2019). When the Ministry of Education reintroduced English MOI in 2001, it was re-badged as bilingual vernacular/English MOI (see Sect. 5, below), and the benefits of students from the two ethnic groups learning in a common language was espoused as contributing to the national political objective of unity.

The final instance provided here of the diversity of approaches and objectives of MOI policy is that of China, where language education and MOI policies and practices in multilingual settings are guided by national policies but reflect local circumstances and priorities (Adamson & Feng, 2014). There are 275 indigenous languages in use in China (Simons & Fennig, 2018a). China's national and official language, Mandarin (Putonghua), is the designated MOI in education, but functions for many, and far from all, as a lingua franca. More than 50 ethnic minorities are recognized, as are the languages they use, most linguistically distinct from Mandarin. Some, such as Tibetan, Korean and Mongolian, are designated official languages in autonomous regions. The Ministry of Education acknowledges that "30% of our nation's population does not speak Putonghua, and out of the 70% of population who possess Putonghua skills, only one in ten can speak Putonghua articulately and fluently" (Luo, 2014, p. 4). This is more pronounced in areas where ethnic minority populations are concentrated, for example, a decade ago among the ethnic minority groups in Yunnan, only 12% could communicate in Putonghua (Wang, 2016). MOI arrangements, particularly in the early years of schooling, are thus a challenge, and commitment to the place and use of minority languages during the past seventy years has "veered between neglect or destruction to appreciation and empowerment" (Adamson & Feng, 2014, p. 62). In some regions, such as Tibetan prefectures in Sichuan (Rong, 2007; Yun, 2016), or the Yanbian Korean autonomous region (Zhang, Wen, & Li, 2015), there are provisions for designated ethnic schools to use local languages for instruction, and Mandarin to be taught as an additional language. In Tibet, for example, these extend to senior secondary level supported by teaching and learning materials in the local language (Rong, 2007). Students in the Korean schools, for example, and in other areas where local languages are used as the MOI, have performed well academically (Adamson & Feng, 2014). But support for minority language MOI varies between communities and can be a source of tension or conflict within communities, and various models of bilingual education have emerged in response to local conditions and preferences (Ma, 2019; Yi & Adamson, 2019). Staffing bilingual schools that use minority language MOI, particularly at secondary levels for the teaching of subjects such as the sciences, technology, and languages, has proved to be an obstacle to effective enactment (Ma, 2019). In Tibet, for example, trilingually proficient English teachers are scarce, and for many students ELT is delivered using an additional language they are in the process of learning, Mandarin, as the MOI in a setting where neither language is used in the homes of learners or as the medium of day-to-day social interactions outside the classroom (Yun, 2016).

The dynamics of policy decision-making in the context of locally dominant and/or national languages and non-dominant languages elicits context-specific responses to frequently complex circumstances. The enormous diversity of languages both non-dominant and dominant, the presence of multiple language communities in most settings, the diverse linguistic ecologies within policy jurisdictions, and the pedagogic demands that must be satisfied if a language is to successfully used as MOI are the most obvious challenges. Little can be achieved without teachers with the necessary pedagogic and linguistic knowledge and skills, nor in the absence of suitable teaching/learning materials. The pervasiveness of multilinguality means these challenges confront educators everywhere, from the wealthiest states to the most economically disadvantaged. In Western nations, where language diversity is usually associated with high levels of immigration, although many also have a multiplicity of local indigenous languages, many children attempt to learn in classrooms through a MOI that is not their "best language … (i.e., one they) speak and understand competently enough to learn age-appropriate academic content" (Benson, 2016, p. 5).What frequently complicates questions of MOI, especially in settings outside the wealthy Anglosphere—including others wealthy but not English-dominant—is what Clegg (2009, p. 46) calls the "lure of English medium education." It is no exaggeration to claim that English medium instruction (EMI) is being adopted—or considered for adoption—at an accelerating rate across all education sectors, from pre-school to higher education, in all the regions of the world (Macaro, Curle, Pun, An, & Dearden, 2018a), and it is to EMI we turn in the next section.

5 English as Medium of Instruction

English medium instruction, although it has been defined as "the use of the English language to teach academic subjects (other than English itself) in countries or jurisdictions where the first language of the majority of the population is not English" (Macaro et al., 2018a), is of course standard practice in English-dominant settings. We note this at the outset, because dominant though English may be, the schools and universities of Anglophone countries—the USA, the UK, Australia, Canada, New Zealand—are sites of multilingualism where many students work hard to learn through what is not their 'best language'. Macaro et al. (2018a) defend their definition by pointing out that in higher education, at least, the majority of students with a language background other than English (LBOTE) have chosen to study in an EMI setting. Researchers and practitioners in the field are keen to distinguish between EMI as a means of teaching content, and pedagogic models such as content and language integrated learning (CLIL) that explicitly aim to advance both language and content knowledge. In many policy contexts, however EMI is embraced because (English) language learning is seen almost as an inevitable bonus in addition to the learning of content. For our discussion here, we regard situations usually identified with European models of CLIL, in which teachers are specifically trained as both language teachers as well as content teachers with explicit attention to linguistic pedagogic knowledge essential to content teaching in an additional language, as distinct from the learning-through-exposure assumptions of much EMI. Some researchers (Dearden, 2014; Shohamy, 2012) have argued that the systematic teaching of English as a foreign language is being replaced by EMI as a policy strategy for language teaching, despite the advice of many that "simply using a foreign language as medium of instruction does not guarantee effective learning of that language" (Benson, 2016, p. 3). However, perhaps the most important question to be asked is whether students in multilingual settings taught using the medium of an additional language, be it English or any other, are achieving content learning outcomes that are the equivalent, at least, of what they can achieve when the MOI is their L1. This points to the motivations of policymakers in adoption of EMI, whether these align with the aspirations for content and language achievement of LBOTE students who complete EMI programs or courses, and the need to examine the outcomes for all stakeholders.

6 EMI Policy in School Education

EMI policy in school education in specific multilingual settings is undoubtedly grounded in unique circumstances, and difficulties in nomenclature complicate any discussion. Terms such as EMI, CLIL, content-based instruction (CBI), dual/parallel language, and so forth are not only used interchangeably, but also with great variability from a policy perspective of what practices each term designates, let alone what practices are used in classroom enactment (see Lyster & Ballinger, 2011, for more on these models). However, some (contested) arguments and observations recur across most policy environments. The view widely held—but not supported by firm evidence (Graham, Choi, Davoodi, Razmeh, & Dixon, 2018; Macaro et al., 2018a)—that the sustained exposure in EMI to the target language will lead to improvements in English learning and proficiency is behind much policy to introduce EMI. This is arguably more so in settings where development of English proficiency is accorded a priority in national development objectives but attempts at systematic English as foreign language teaching is not delivering the outcomes desired. Likewise, the contested discourse (Pennycook, 2007; Wickramasuriya, 2005) that a population, or at least an educated elite, proficient in English is synonymous with modernity, international competitiveness, and thus with social mobility and access to prosperity identified with globalization is a powerful argument politically. This, coupled with discourses that assume inherent superiority of English as the language of advances in science, technology, medicine and so forth, associate EMI with a quality of education, and opportunities, unattainable through local language MOI. This mix of appeals to prestige and prosperity is socio-politically potent, but in non-Anglophone settings where attitudes to English can be ambivalent, the question of EMI is often highly charged—politically, socially and culturally—as some examples that follow illustrate.

The burgeoning of EMI is widely seen as inexorable (see Dearden, 2014, for a study of EMI in 55 countries), but this is not always so; there are instances of EMI policies winding back or stopping the practice. Attempts to improve the quality of education and international competitiveness in Indonesia, for example, through introduction of EMI from Grade Four—for at least Mathematics and Science subjects—in a small number of high-performing primary and secondary schools, dubbed International Standard Schools, were stopped after successful legal challenges based on the elitism and inequity of the scheme, and the fear that the national language would be marginalized in the academic domain. As well-founded as these objections might have been, there were more fundamental reasons to question the project: teachers were demonstrably unprepared for EMI in their language proficiency, pedagogy, and teaching materials; the language proficiency of many students meant they struggled to learn effectively (Walker et al., 2019). The initiative operated between 2008 and 2013, and arguably needed more time before making definitive assessments of its effectiveness, but there was no convincing evidence that either content or language learning outcomes were demonstrably better than those of students instructed using the local language as MOI. However, fed by demand from wealthier families who view an English medium education as superior, prestigious, and advantageous, increasing numbers of fee-levying local private schools offer imported 'international' EMI curricula, many commencing English medium classes in Grade One (Walker et al., 2019). Nearby Malaysia introduced a similar initiative in 2002, the universal use of EMI in Mathematics and Science classrooms from Grade One. Declining learning outcomes, particularly for students from poorer and rural backgrounds, led to the cessation of the practice in 2012, and reversion to Malay as MOI. Again, a major contributory factor to the policy reversal was the shortage of suitably qualified and English proficient teachers (Kirkpatrick, 2012), but middle class locals with aspirations of social mobility for their children who support the continuation/reintroduction of the use of EMI claim political and electoral motives were also involved (Dearden, 2014). Both instances, Malaysia and Indonesia, foreground the socio-political sensitivities and the pedagogic/educational shortcomings of introducing EMI in the early years of schooling (Kirkpatrick, 2012) in many similar settings.

From the content perspective, lack of convincing evidence that students perform as well or better under EMI conditions has prompted challenges to the orthodoxy that English is preferable as the MOI for Science and Mathematics for LBOTE students. Brock-Utne (2016) points to economically successful nations, such as Finland, Norway, Japan, or South Korea, that have relied on national languages to teach Sciences, as evidence that vernacular languages can meet not only the linguistic demands of teaching the required content, but also the pedagogic demands of interaction and dialogue integral to effective activity- and inquiry-based Sciences teaching and learning. If students "learn less than they could have, had they been taught in a language they know well" (Brock-Utne, 2016, p. 123), then the cost of using EMI as a language learning policy is arguably too high. The unfortunate geopolitical reality for many multilingual states is that rather than formulating MOI policy in consultation with key stakeholder such as teachers and teacher educators, the influence, interests, perspectives, and objectives of aid agencies, the Anglophone nations, the English-language publishing industry, and local political elites shape decisions (Brock-Utne, 2016).

Complicating this policy context even further, is the commodification of EMI by private education institutions, even more so in the tertiary sector than in schools, that is leading the move to EMI. EMI programs, or imported 'international' programs, are used by private schools and universities to differentiate their 'product' from public education. Dearden (2014, p. 32) suggests that MOI/EMI policy in the public education sector may be attempts to "catch-up" in order to provide equitable access to "quality education" for those unable to afford the fees of private schools. Some observers claim this was the motivation, in part, for the International Standard School initiative in Indonesia, and similar claims have been made about the introduction of bilingual education in Sri Lanka, where the children of wealthy privileged families attend elite English MOI private and international schools (Premarathna, Yogaraja, Medawattegedara, Senarathna, & Abdullah, 2016). Unlike Indonesia and Malaysia, where EMI in public schools has ceased, the objective of Sri Lanka's Ministry of Education remains equipping all junior and senior secondary schools with sufficient suitably-qualified teachers to enable introduction of English-medium instruction of selected subjects (Perera & Kularatne, 2014). The policy background of EMI in Sri Lanka differs, however, in some important respects. With a history of animosity towards English, a privileged local elite educating their children in private English medium schools, and forty years of limited success of a policy of universal English language learning (Liyanage, 2012), English is a marker of social status and education, and of division between wealthy and poor, urban and rural. Despite this, in the context of decades of ethnolinguistic tension and conflict between the Sinhalese majority and the Tamil minority, the reintroduction of EMI was justified in part as a strategy to promote the benefits of students from the two ethnic groups learning in a common language, English, for the political objective of national unity and harmony. Opinions on whether bilingual education has achieved this purpose are divided (see Irshad, 2018; Wijesekera & Alford, 2019). What is clearer is that considerable structural and resourcing constraints have limited availability of bilingual education and in many locations compromised the quality (Liyanage, 2019). Sri Lanka's bilingual education/EMI policy has arguably succeeded in meeting the two key criteria of EMI instruction—improved language learning outcomes and equivalent content learning outcomes—in only well-resourced elite public schools in major cities staffed by teachers with qualifications in language and content teaching pedagogy, and with the requisite (pedagogic) language proficiency. Thus, the outcomes of EMI policies in the three multilingual settings introduced here—Indonesia, Malaysia and Sri Lanka—are in some respects similar. EMI has been introduced with inadequate planning, preparation, and support, the learning outcomes for both content and language of many students are uncertain, and the position of EMI and English as markers of social divisions perpetuated.

7 EMI Policy in Higher Education

In the sphere of higher education, the motivations and objectives of EMI policymakers at both state and institutional levels respond to an additional layer of priorities. Universities in the Anglosphere, and particularly public universities, have come to depend on international LBOTE students as a source of income (Macaro et al., 2018a) and tailor marketing and programs to attract international enrolments, which are in turn used as evidence of their desirability and quality as study destinations. Despite the indispensably multilingual character of internationalized universities, English remains effectively unchallenged as the language of the academic domain (Mauranen, Hynninen, & Ranta, 2016; Preece, 2011), in teaching, research, and publication, positioning EMI as integral to the attraction of English dominant universities. Policy in these settings focuses on regulation of entry to English medium programs through language testing regimes that demand control of a prestigious and essentially inflexible variety of standard English (Hyland, 2016; Preece, 2011). For LBOTE students seeking to study in English dominant institutions, this means demonstrating their multilinguality through specified levels of English academic language proficiency in a setting where their broader multilingual resources are rarely valued. The opportunities for (multi)linguistically unique construal of reality and culturally-based knowledge structures to contribute to learning and research in EMI academic settings are only just beginning to be recognized (Cavazos, 2015; Li & Exley, 2019; Liu, 2016). It is important in this regard to remind ourselves that English-dominant contexts are home to local (multi)linguistically and culturally diverse indigenous and migrant-background students and researchers.

Outside the globally dominant institutions of the Anglosphere, introduction of EMI is "the single most significant current trend in internationalising higher education" (Chapple, 2015, p. 1). In Dearden's (2014) study of EMI in 55 non-English-dominant nations, only 11 did not have English-medium programs in public universities, and in all but three it was offered by private institutions. The use of EMI is invariably an internationalization strategy, and at institutional level is frequently equated with internationalisation (Hashimoto & Glasgow, 2019)—that is, to introduce EMI is to internationalize—and often introduced without consultation of teaching staff by either state or institutional policymakers (Macaro et al., 2018a). The urgency to internationalize of non-English dominant nations such as India (Agarwal, 2008), China (Ennew & Fujia, 2009; Fang, 2018; Huang, 2003; Li & Roberts, 2012), Japan (Lassegard, 2016) or Vietnam (Tran & Nguyen, 2018), coupled with the internationalization agendas of powerful English-dominant universities, is evident in "program and institutional mobility" (Hughes, 2008, p. 117), the direct importation of courses, or establishment of local campuses of foreign universities, and various off-shore models for on-line delivery of courses/programs, all delivered in English. Far more common are initiatives to deliver local courses/programs as 'international' on the basis of EMI. Macaro et al. (2018a, see pp. 47–50) provide a comprehensive survey of EMI in Europe, the Middle East, Africa and Asia, and the situation is remarkable. The latest available survey in Europe (Watcher & Maiworm, 2014, in Macaro et al.,

2018a) of 2637 higher education providers in 28 countries found 239% growth in programs delivered in English in the period 2007-2104. In China, policymakers have directed institutions to conduct between 10 and 20% of undergraduate courses in English, or another foreign language, as demonstration of quality teaching (Hughes, 2008), and one survey (Wu, et al., 2010, in Macaro et al., 2018a) found all but three of 135 Chinese higher education institutions in the study offered an average of 44 programs delivered in English.

The influence and impact of EMI extends beyond the multitude instances of courses and programs delivered using English medium. In the context of the competitiveness of the international higher education market, the pre-eminence of English language academia—education, research, and publication—has encouraged attempts in non-English dominant settings to adopt or incorporate the academic literacies, practices and conventions that define it in programs taught using local languages, or to demand demonstration of control of these literacies. All doctoral degrees in Indonesia, for example, are awarded conditional upon successful publication in an international journal, effectively an English-language publication, although the rigour with which this proviso is applied is uncertain (Coleman, 2016). A more widespread phenomenon is deference to what is often claimed to be missing from the academic work of LBOTE students—critical thinking, a concept bound up with perceptions of culturally different ways of thinking and assumptions that these thinking processes are not only superior but at the heart of the perceived dominance of the West in academia and the knowledge economy. The exposure of LBOTE students and academics to English medium study, literature or academic collaboration, in the context of international competitiveness, has prompted an identifiable transculturation (Zamel, 1997) in academic practices in non-English dominant settings. In China, for example, growth in teaching of courses in critical thinking in degree programs using Mandarin as the MOI for teaching and textbooks is regarded as an indicator of a move towards quality and international competitiveness (Dong, 2015). Academics are selectively appropriating ideas about critical thinking and absorbing them in transformative re-understandings of their own historical thinking and teaching practices (Wang et al., 2019). For multilingual academics, exposure to the English-dominant academic sphere, to EMI and practice of EMI in their own teaching, shapes development of thinking and identities that resituates them as global teaching practitioners (Dafouz, 2018; Tochon, 2019) in local academic and linguistic contexts.

Although there exists extensive literature on EMI courses and programs in diverse multilingual settings, much concentrates on attitudes and beliefs of stakeholders. The systematic review of EMI in higher education conducted by Macaro et al. (2018a) aimed to address the fact that, to their knowledge "no systematic review has been conducted of EMI in HE that has assessed whether the evidence exists to shed light on these (core) two products of EMI—language improvement and content learning" (p. 38). We rely on their findings here. Despite general consensus among academics and students that EMI is essential and advantageous in the current global environment—the high value accorded English internationally, frequent difficulties accessing current teaching/learning materials in local languages, and the attraction of international study/employment pathways—many of the problems that constrain implementation of EMI in school education are also identified in higher education. These include: insufficient consultation, planning and preparation, and over-hasty introduction of top-down policy decision-making; shortcomings in proficiencies of either/both academic teaching staff or/and students, compounded by inadequacies in student entry requirements and poor levels of staff training and support; and, perceptions/risks (and documented creation; see Tran & Nguyen, 2018) of elitism and socio-economic division, and majority exclusion from educational opportunities, all on the basis of multilingual capacities. What also frustrates researchers attempting to evaluate EMI is uncertainty and confusion about the models of delivery in practice, how language/s are used, and widespread absence of reliable objective data on (any) improvements or developments in English language proficiency. Dearden (2014), whose study of EMI in 55 nations aimed to begin uncovering where and how EMI is being implemented and its outcomes and effects, concluded that its top-down introduction from policymaking and administrative levels without adequate consultation means "we are quite some way from a 'global' understanding of the aims and purposes of EMI … (and) we are also quite some way from an understanding of the consequences or the outcomes of EMI" (p. 2). Numerous studies have concluded that there is no or insufficient evidence that EMI produces "optimal outcomes in both content subject learning and improvement of students' English level" (Fang, 2018, p. 36). Macaro et al. (2018a) reach the same conclusion, and identify the lack of rigorous examination of these questions as a fundamental failing in introduction of the shift to EMI in higher education in non-English dominant settings. They conclude that "current EMI implementation produces more challenges than opportunities for HE (higher education) teachers and students" (Macaro et al., 2018a, p. 68), reinforcing the view that it would be more advantageous for LBOTE students in multilingual (non-English dominant) settings to study in their first language, or the language of their home education system, and for resources to be directed to raising the quality of English language teaching.

8 MOI in Practice in Multilingual Classrooms

If the effects and outcomes of MOI policy are to be assessed, we also need investigations of policy enactments in the moment-to-moment interactions of multilingual classrooms. Teachers' language practices, and the language practices of their students, are subject to competing influences and objectives, and strategic compromises to solve communicative problems. Here we consider just a few of the multitude of contexts that emerge around MOI in multilingual classrooms, whilst pointing to the considerable variations that can exist from the outset in initial policy prescriptions, differing understandings of the various models for delivery of MOI policies, political and ideological motivations of policymakers that shape objectives and priorities, and modes and processes of implementation and evaluation.

To begin with initial education, many children across the world face commencing their education in classrooms in which the language of instruction does not match the language used at home. For many of these, what actually happens in classroom practices becomes irrelevant. According to the World Bank (2005, in Benson, 2016), half of the children around the world who do not attend school at all are faced with a mismatch between the languages of home and school. For students that do attend, their unfamiliarity with the MOI often renders them silent and passive, responding to teacher-centred techniques such as chorus teaching, 'safe talk', repetition, and memorisation and recall of language without understanding meaning for reproduction in tests (Alidou & Brock-Utne, 2011). Observations of non-mother-tongue classrooms in African countries (Rubagumya, 2003, in Alidou & Brock-Utne, 2011), in settings where teachers often also lack confident proficiency in the MOI, reveal widespread codeswitching to overcome difficulties explaining concepts, resolving learner misunderstanding, organising/managing classroom learning, and explaining tasks/assignments, as well as to develop interpersonal relations. In later schooling, when policy demands a process of transition from mother-tongue to a national language, similar strategies are utilized (Alidou & Brock-Utne, 2011). These activities contrast with much more participation in linguistic interaction in mother-tongue MOI classrooms in which both teachers' and students' language skills enabled teachers to use more learner-centred pedagogy (Alidou & Brock-Utne, 2011). In a completely different setting, a linguistically diverse Australian preschool classroom (Theobald, Busch, & Laraghy, 2019), where the default MOI was English and the teachers were not multilingual, the approach adopted was to endorse and value code-switching, and to legitimize the range of languages used by the children by planned use of spoken and written texts in multiple languages. Activities that relied on non-verbal participation encouraged interaction and spontaneous mother tongue language use, and children were introduced to strategies that facilitated interactions when a language was not shared. These and other examples (e.g., Brock-Utne & Alidou, 2011; Fillmore & Handayani, 2018) illustrate the significant impact of MOI on classroom discourse and participation, and how participants, students and teachers across diverse multilingual settings and variables draw on mother tongue resources to progress learning and encourage participation. Arguably, these responses also illustrate the futility of monolingual MOI policies that do not account for language practices in multilingual settings.

The research evidence indicates enactment of EMI in multilingual classrooms varies enormously in relation to contextual features, such as geographical location, stage of schooling, and so on. The key focus is the extent and nature of target language use, and by extension, of first language use. In some multilingual settings with more firmly established and well-resourced language learning programs, such as European CLIL programs, teacher English proficiency is almost universally excellent and students' use of English by the time of secondary school is well established (Butzkamm, 1998, in Macaro, Tian, & Chu, 2018b). There are examples from other parts of the world, states that are ethnolinguistically diverse, such as Singapore, but where English medium education is well established throughout the entire education system. Singapore's local teachers and students in Singapore's universities, for example, are high functioning bi/multilinguals. English is the official and major language of classrooms, but one study of interest has uncovered codeswitching practices by about one third of multilingual students in discussions of academic matters in classroom group work, practical workshops and laboratory sessions (Bolton & Botha, 2019). In other settings English proficiency is an issue, and while there are pedagogically sound arguments advanced for judicious introduction of L1 by teachers and for exploiting the entirety of students' language resources in learning, much of the deviation from target language use in EMI settings does not fall into these categories. Many of the language choices made by teachers and/or students stem from shortcomings in proficiency. Hence, codeswitching is common practice, because sometimes both parties lack the language required by the demands of the content, with some classroom research indicating 60% of L1 use is common (Macaro et al. 2018b). Teachers experiencing linguistic insecurity, or aware of proficiency shortcomings, use a variety of strategies to avoid using English, such as use of bilingual textbooks, preparing written materials that allowed them to avoid speaking or writing during class, presenting materials and tasks in English but explaining them in the L1, reliance on translation software (Zacharias, 2013), and so on. Macaro et al. (2018b) cite findings that teachers use the L1 for repetition and elaboration of English utterances, to check comprehension, and to organize and manage classroom activities. Student participation can be constrained by lack of confidence in using English, or gaps in the academic content language needed for discussion or questioning at conceptual levels. When both teachers and students are struggling with the academic language of a content area, or teachers are pitching their language choices to a lower level of proficiency, the complexities of challenging content can be lost. Hu and Duan (2018, p. 1) analysed teacher questions and student answers in EMI classes at a Chinese university and found that "an overwhelming majority of teacher questions and student responses were cognitively and linguistically simple."

In classroom settings where the primary objective is focussed explicitly on language learning and the development of bi/multilingualism, views on role of MOI have shifted, from a belief that language acquisition was facilitated by exclusion of learners' other language/s from classroom interaction, to advocacy of the systematic and judicious use of learners' L1 by teachers and of recognition of learners' L1 knowledge as a resource for learning (Cook, 2001; Cummins, 2007). In some situations, teachers and learners do not share the learner's L1, but the broad principle of L1 having a legitimate place in language learning classroom remains. We do not intend to detail the arguments that were used to support the case for avoidance of the L1 in the language classroom; these are clearly outlined by, among others, Cook (2001), and Cummins (2007). A number of reasons are proposed for the shift in approach (Macaro et al., 2018b), but among the most compelling were recognition that switching or shuttling between languages was an everyday practice in bi/multilingual interaction, that it was a language practice in many classrooms, even when teachers aimed to avoid and discourage it, and that learners themselves treated their L1 knowledge as a learning resource. These shifts were in accord with parallel post-monolingual reconceptualizations of languages as social practices that are (re)constituted in the context of use rather than as "bounded systems linked with bounded communities" (Blommaert & Rampton, 2011, p. 10). In language classrooms, rethinking the notion of languages as (un)bounded aligned with learners using L1 knowledge to construct target language knowledge, the cross-lingual transfer of literacy-related knowledge and skills, and the cognitive advantages of 'multi-competence' (Cummins, 2007). While this shift does not mean teachers should abandon the objective of including as much target language as they can in the classroom, it has legitimized the considered use of L1 by teachers for a variety of purposes when appropriate, and recognized the positive contribution its use by learners can make. Studies of classroom interaction have identified a variety of purposes for moving between target language and L1, including various iterations of "establishing constructive social relationships, communicating complex meanings to ensure understanding and/or save time, and maintaining control over the classroom environment" (Littlewood & Yu, 2011, p. 68; see also Forman, 2012). Although some researchers prefer to continue to refer to practices of shifting between target language and L1 as codeswitching (Macaro, 2009) or language mixing (Bolton & Botha, 2019), some embrace the concept of translanguaging as indicative of a wider set of discursive practices (García & Kleyn, 2013). In conversation analysis the idea of language alternation is used to capture the nature of the practice in the overall organization of episodes of classroom interaction and reflect the view of a speaker's languages "as part of a repertoire invoked and (re)negotiated in concert with others to achieve some interactional purpose" (Filipi, 2019, p. 27). Significantly, against this flexible and contingent approach to MOI in multilingual classrooms, based on current understandings of classroom language practices, MOI/EMI policymakers are positioned as among the few proponents of exclusion or avoidance of L1 in the language classroom, despite much of the research evidence on policy implementation confirming the futility of monolingually-based policy approaches.

9 Conclusion

It is not long ago that the 'Welsh not' was in general use in the UK. Cummins (1997) describes how it

> …came into existence after the 1870 Education Act in Britain as a means of eradicating the Welsh language. Any child heard speaking Welsh in school had a heavy wooden placard attached to rope placed over his or her shoulders. The placard reached to the child's shins and would bump them when the child walked. If that child heard another child speaking Welsh, he or she could transfer the 'Welsh not' to the other child. The child carrying this placard at the end of the day was beaten. (Evans, 1978, in Cummins, 1997, p. 107)

Similar practices were common in colonial education if children used local languages in school, such as in this account of punishment from Kenya where

> … one of the most humiliating experiences was to be caught speaking Gikuyu in the vicinity of the school. The culprit was given corporal punishment—three to five strokes of the cane on bare buttocks—or was made to carry a metal plate around the neck with inscriptions such as I AM STUPID or I AM A DONKEY. Sometimes the culprits were fined money they could hardly afford. (Ngiigi wa Thiongo, 1986, cited in Cummins, 1997, pp. 107–108)

Practices like this appear barbaric and cruel, unacceptable today but perhaps typical of a long-gone era. Use of such coercive measures in attempts to regulate the language/s used classrooms in multilingual communities, however, are not unknown in much more recent times:

> Children who were caught speaking their mother tongue even during recess were beaten and they had to wear "a symbol" around their neck indicating their incompetence. Unfortunately, this practice continued in francophone Africa even during the post-colonial era. It was, however, prohibited by the ministries and departments of education in the early 1980s. Unfortunately, due to lack of enforcement of the policy, it is still possible to catch some frustrated teachers using such coercive measures against pupils who have difficulties expressing themselves in the official language used as language of instruction (French). (Alidou & Brock-Utne, 2011, p. 163)

These extreme examples of imposition of dominant languages as MOI in multilingual classrooms provide us with a salutary insight into the potential impact on students of mismatches between languages of home and school. The significance for learning outcomes is confronting, "criticized for decades as negatively impacting learners' access to knowledge, the quality of classroom teaching they are offered, the validity of assessment of their learning, and any future opportunities they may have for education or work" (Benson, 2016, p. 3). But the implications for learner identity of marginalization, shame and humiliation because of the language they use add impetus to the need to consider very carefully MOI policy and its implementation and enactment in multilingual settings everywhere. What is often overlooked is the shame and insecurity experienced by teachers who introduce the L1 in classrooms against the dictates of authorities and superiors. Policies in many regions have been oriented to national development and unity, and the "one nation, one language" (Benson, 2016, p. 3) ideology that imposes a national language as MOI for education from early schooling has arguably been counterproductive to achieving those goals in many instances. We cannot pretend the challenges and obstacles in the most diverse settings do not appear insurmountable, but examples of attempts at sensitive policy development based on the principle that "use of learners' own languages for literacy and learning across the curriculum provides a solid foundation for basic and continuing education and for transfer of skills and knowledge to additional languages" (Benson, 2016, p. 3) are mounting (see Kosonen, 2017a; Trudell, 2016).

Consultation with stakeholders and educators has also too often been missing in development of EMI policy, and we have outlined some of the consequences of over-hasty, under-prepared, and under-resourced of introduction of EMI in some settings. Multilingualism is indispensable in contemporary circumstances, and development of multilinguality is on the agenda of probably every nation state. However, the inclination to see EMI as an easy option for teaching English risks the standard of learning outcomes in both content and language; many argue that unless outcomes are better than those achieved through instruction using the local language, planning and resources would be more productively directed to improving the teaching and resourcing of English language teaching in curricula.

References

Adamson, B., & Feng, A. W. (2014). Multilingual education: Lessons from China. *Curriculum Perspectives, 34*(1), 61–64.

Agarwal, P. (2008). *Privatization and internationalization of higher education in the countries of South Asia: An empirical analysis*. New Delhi: Indian Council for Research on International Economic Relations.

Alidou, H., & Brock-Utne, B. (2011). Teaching practices: Teaching in a familiar language. In A. Ouane & C. Glanz (Eds.), *Optimising learning, education and publishing in Africa: The language factor: A review and analysis of theory and practice in mother-tongue and bilingual education in sub-Saharan Africa* (pp. 159–185). Hamburg: UNESCO Institute for Lifelong Learning (UIL) & Development of Education in Africa (ADEA)/African Development Bank.

Aronin, L. (2015). Current multilingualism and new developments in multilingualism research. In M. P. S. Jordà & L. P. Falomir (Eds.), *Learning and using multiple languages: Current findings from research on multilingualism* (pp. 1–28). Newcastle upon Tyne, UK: Cambridge Scholars Publishing.

Aronin, L., & Singleton, D. (2008). Multilingualism as a new linguistic dispensation. *International Journal of Multilingualism, 5*(1), 1–16. https://doi.org/10.2167/ijm072.0.

Australian Bureau of Statistics. (2017). Cultural diversity. Retrieved from http://www.abs.gov.au/ausstats/abs@.nsf/Latestproducts/2024.0Main%20Features22016.

Australian Curriculum Assessment and Reporting Authority. (2011). *English as an additional language or dialect: Teacher resource*. Retrieved from http://www.acara.edu.au/verve/_resources/EALD_Teacher_Resource_file.pdf.

Balakrishnar, J., & Thanaraj, T. (2015). Instruction in the English medium: A Sri Lankan case study. In H. Coleman (Ed.), *Language and social cohesion in the developing world (Selected proceedings of the Ninth Language and Development Conference, Colombo, Sri Lanka, 2011)* (pp. 166–177). Colombo, Sri Lanka: British Council and Deutsche Gesellschaft für Internationale Zusammenarbeit (GIZ) GmbH.

Benson, C. (2016). Addressing language of instruction issues in education: Recommendations for documenting progress (Paper commissioned for the Global Education Monitoring Report 2016, Education for people and planet: Creating sustainable futures for all). Retrieved from http://unesdoc.unesco.org/images/0024/002455/245575E.pdf.

Blommaert, J. (2015). Commentary: Superdiversity old and new. *Language & Communication, 44*, 82–88. https://doi.org/10.1016/j.langcom.2015.01.003.

Blommaert, J., & Rampton, B. (2011). Language and superdiversity. *Diversities, 13*(2), 1–22.

Bolton, K., & Botha, W. (2019). Multilingualism and language mixing among Singapore university students. In I. Liyanage & T. Walker (Eds.), *Multilingual education yearbook 2019: Media of instruction & multilingual settings* (pp. 43–61). New York: Springer.

Brock-Utne, B. (2016). English as the language of science and technology. In Z. Babaci-Wilhite (Ed.), *Human rights in language and STEM education: Science, Technology, Engineering and Mathematics* (pp. 111–128). Rotterdam: Sense Publishers.

Brock-Utne, B., & Alidou, H. (2011). Active students: Learning through a language they master. In A. Ouane & C. Glanz (Eds.), *Optimising learning, education and publishing in Africa: The language factor: A review and analysis of theory and practice in mother-tongue and bilingual education in sub-Saharan Africa* (pp. 187–215). Hamburg: UNESCO Institute for Lifelong Learning (UIL) & Development of Education in Africa (ADEA)/African Development Bank.

Cavazos, A. G. (2015). Multilingual faculty across academic disciplines: Language difference in scholarship. *Language and Education, 29*(4), 317–331. https://doi.org/10.1080/09500782.2015.1014375.

Cenoz, J., & Gorter, D. (2010). The diversity of multilingualism in education. *International Journal of the Sociology of Language, 2010*(205), 37–53. https://doi.org/10.1515/ijsl.2010.038.

Chapple, J. (2015). Teaching in English is not necessarily the teaching of English. *International Education Studies, 8*(3), 1–13. https://doi.org/10.5539/ies.v8n3p1.

Clegg, J. (2009). *The lure of English-medium education*. In P. Powell-Davies (Ed.), *Access English EBE symposium: A collection of papers* (pp. 46–62). Kuala Lumpur: British Council East Asia.

Coleman, H. (2009). *Teaching other subjects through English in two Asian nations: Teachers' responses and implications for learners*. In P. Powell-Davies (Ed.), *Access English EBE symposium: A collection of papers* (pp. 63–87). Kuala Lumpur: British Council East Asia.

Coleman, H. (2016). The English language as Naga in Indonesia. In P. Bunce, R. Phillipson, V. Rapatahana, & R. Tupas (Eds.), *Why English?: Confronting the Hydra* (pp. 42–48). Bristol, UK: Multilingual Matters.

Cook, V. (2001). Using the first language in the classroom. *Canadian Modern Language Review, 57*(3), 402–423. https://doi.org/10.3138/cmlr.57.3.402.

Coperahewa, S. (2009). The language planning situation in Sri Lanka. *Current Issues in Language Planning, 10*(1), 69–150. https://doi.org/10.1080/14664200902894660.

Cummins, J. (1997). Cultural and linguistic diversity in education: A mainstream issue? *Educational Review, 49*(2), 105–114. https://doi.org/10.1080/0013191970490202.

Cummins, J. (2007). Rethinking monolingual instructional strategies in multilingual classrooms. *Canadian Journal of Applied Linguistics/Revue canadienne de linguistique appliquée, 10*(2), 221–240.

Cummins, J. (2009). Fundamental psycholinguistic and sociological principles underlying educational successs for linguistic minority students. In T. Skutnabb-Kangas, R. Phillipson, A. Mohanty, & M. Panda (Eds.), *Social justice through multilingual education* (pp. 19–35). Clevedon, UK: Multilingual Matters.

Dafouz, E. (2018). English-medium instruction and teacher education programmes in higher education: Ideological forces and imagined identities at work. *International Journal of Bilingual Education and Bilingualism, 21*(5), 540–552. https://doi.org/10.1080/13670050.2018.1487926.

Dearden, J. (2014). *English as a medium of instruction: A growing global phenomenon*. London: British Council; Oxford University. Retrieved from https://ora.ox.ac.uk/objects/uuid:4f72cdf8-b2eb-4d41-a785-4a283bf6caaa.

Díaz, A. (2018). Challenging dominant epistemologies in higher education: The role of language in the geopolitics of knowledge (re)production. In I. Liyanage (Ed.), *Multilingual Education Yearbook 2018: Internationalization, stakeholders and multilingual education contexts* (pp. 21–36). Cham, Switzerland: Springer.

Dong, Y. (2015). Critical thinking education with Chinese characteristics. In M. Davies & R. Barnett (Eds.), *The Palgrave handbook of critical thinking in higher education* (pp. 351–368). New York: Palgrave Macmillan.

Ennew, C. T., & Fujia, Y. (2009). Foreign Universities in China: A case study. *European Journal of Education, 44*(1), 21–36. https://doi.org/10.1111/j.1465-3435.2008.01368.x.

Fang, F. (2018). Review of English as a medium of instruction in Chinese universities today: Current trends and future directions. *English Today, 34*(1), 32–37. https://doi.org/10.1017/S0266078417000360.

Fernando, S. (2011, October 26). From dethroning English to planning for a trilingual society: Keynote address by Sunimal Fernando at the 9th International Language and Development Conference on 'Language and Social Cohesion', Colombo, October 18, 2011 (Part 3). *Daily News*. Retrieved from http://www.dailynews.lk/2001/pix/PrintPage.asp?REF=/2011/10/25/fea0.

Filipi, A. (2019). Language alternation as an interactional practice in the foreign language classroom. In I. Liyanage & T. Walker (Eds.), *Multilingual education yearbook 2019: Media of instruction & multilingual settings* (pp. 25–42). New York: Springer.

Fillmore, N., & Handayani, W. (2018, March 28). Language matters: Language and learning in Bima, Indonesia. Retrieved from http://www.devpolicy.org/language-matters-language-and-learning-in-bima-indonesia-20180328/.

Forman, R. (2012). Six functions of bilingual EFL teacher talk: Animating, translating, explaining, creating, prompting and dialoguing. *RELC Journal, 43*(2), 239–253. https://doi.org/10.1177/0033688212449938.

García, O., & Kleyn, T. (2013). Teacher education for multilingual education. In C. A. Chapelle (Ed.), *The encyclopedia of applied linguistics* (pp. 1–6). Oxford: Blackwell. Retrieved from https://doi.org/10.1002/9781405198431.wbeal1145.

Graham, K. M., Choi, Y., Davoodi, A., Razmeh, S., & Dixon, L. Q. (2018). Language and content outcomes of CLIL and EMI: A systematic review. *Latin American Journal of Content and Language Integrated Learning, 11*(1), 19–37. https://doi.org/10.5294/laclil.2018.11.1.2.

Hashimoto, K., & Glasgow, G. P. (2019). CLIL for who? Commodification of English-medium courses in Japan's higher education. In I. Liyanage & T. Walker (Eds.), *Multilingual education yearbook 2019: Media of instruction & multilingual settings*. New York: Springer.

Heugh, K. (2011). Theory and practice: Language education models in Africa: Research, design, decision-making and outcomes. In A. Ouane & C. Glanz (Eds.), *Optimising learning, education and publishing in Africa: The language factor: A review and analysis of theory and practice in mother-tongue and bilingual education in sub-Saharan Africa* (pp. 105–156). Hamburg: UNESCO Institute for Lifelong Learning (UIL) & Development of Education in Africa (ADEA)/African Development Bank.

Hu, G., & Duan, Y. (2018). Questioning and responding in the classroom: A cross-disciplinary study of the effects of instructional mediums in academic subjects at a Chinese university. *International Journal of Bilingual Education and Bilingualism*, (Published online July 12, 2018). https://doi.org/10.1080/13670050.2018.1493084.

Huang, F. (2003). Policy and practice of the internationalization of higher education in China. *Journal of Studies in International Education, 7*(3), 225–240. https://doi.org/10.1177/1028315303254430.

Hughes, R. (2008). Internationalisation of higher education and language policy. *Higher Education Management and Policy, 20*(1), 111–128. https://doi.org/10.1787/17269822.

Hyland, K. (2016). Academic publishing and the myth of linguistic injustice. *Journal of Second Language Writing, 31*, 58–69. https://doi.org/10.1016/j.jslw.2016.01.005.

Irshad, M. (2018). Trilingualism, national integration, and social coexistence in postwar Sri Lanka. In I. Liyanage (Ed.), *Multilingual education yearbook 2018: Internationalization, stakeholders & multilingual education contexts* (pp. 107–124). New York: Springer.

Kirkpatrick, A. (2012). English in ASEAN: Implications for regional multilingualism. *Journal of Multilingual and Multicultural Development, 33*(4), 331–344. https://doi.org/10.1080/01434632.2012.661433.

Kosonen, K. (2017a). Language of instruction in Southeast Asia (Paper commissioned for the 2017/8 Global Education Monitoring Report, Accountability in education: Meeting our commitments). Retrieved from unesdoc.unesco.org/images/0025/002595/259576e.pdf.

Kosonen, K. (2017b). Language policy and education in Southeast Asia. In T. L. McCarty & S. May (Eds.), *Language policy and political issues in education* (pp. 477–490). Cham, Switzerland: Springer.

Lassegard, J. P. (2016). Educational diversification strategies: Japanese universities' efforts to attract international students. In C. C. Ng, R. Fox, & M. Nakano (Eds.), *Reforming learning and teaching in Asia-Pacific universities: Influences of globalised processes in Japan, Hong Kong and Australia* (pp. 47–75). Singapore: Springer.

Li, M., & Exley, B. (2019). Benefits of translanguaging and transculturation exchanges between international higher degree research students and English medium research supervisors. In I. Liyanage & T. Walker (Eds.), *Multilingual education yearbook 2019: Media of instruction & multilingual settings* (pp. 121–135). New York: Springer.

Li, X., & Roberts, J. (2012). A stages approach to the internationalization of higher education? The entry of UK universities into China. *The Service Industries Journal, 32*(7), 1011–1038. https://doi.org/10.1080/02642069.2012.662495.

Little, A. W. (2011). Education policy reform in Sri Lanka: The double-edged sword of political will. *Journal of Education Policy, 26*(4), 499–512. https://doi.org/10.1080/02680939.2011.555005.

Littlewood, W., & Yu, B. (2011). First language and target language in the foreign language classroom. *Language Teaching, 44*(1), 64–77. https://doi.org/10.1017/S0261444809990310.

Liu, W. (2016). Conceptualising multilingual capabilities in Anglophone higher degree research education: Challenges and possibilities for reconfiguring language practices and policies. *Education Sciences, 6*(4), 1–12. https://doi.org/10.3390/educsci6040039.

Liyanage, I. (2012). Critical pedagogy in ESL/EFL teaching in South-east Asia: Practices and challenges with examples from Sri Lanka. In K. Sung & R. Pederson (Eds.), *Critical ELT practices in Asia: Key issues, practices, and possibilities* (pp. 137–152). Rotterdam, The Netherlands: Sense Publishers.

Liyanage, I. (2018a). Internationalization of higher education, mobility, and multilingualism. In I. Liyanage (Ed.), *Multilingual education yearbook 2018: Internationalization, stakeholders & multilingual education contexts* (pp. 1–20). New York: Springer.

Liyanage, I. (2018b). Trilingualism and languages policy in education in Sri Lanka. In K. J. Kennedy & J. C.-K. Lee (Eds.), *Routledge international handbook on schools and schooling in Asia* (pp. 492–501). New York: Routledge.

Liyanage, I. (2019). Language Education Policy in Sri Lanka. In A. Kirkpatrick & A. L. Liddicoat (Eds.), *The Routledge international handbook of language education policy in Asia* (pp. 399–413). New York: Routledge.

Liyanage, I. (in-press). Bilingualism and multilingualism in secondary education in Australia. In I. Menter, T. Tatto, & L. Perry (Eds.), *Bloomsbury education and childhood studies: Secondary education (Australia, Web)*. London: Bloomsbury.

Luo, C. (2014, September 23). One-third of Chinese do not speak Putonghua, says Education Ministry. *South China Morning Post (International edition)*. Retrieved from http://www.scmp.com/news/china-insider/article/1598040/3-10-chinese-citizens-do-not-speak-putonghua-says-education.

Lyster, R., & Ballinger, S. (2011). Content-based language teaching: Convergent concerns across divergent contexts. *Language Teaching Research, 15*(3), 279–288. https://doi.org/10.1177/1362168811401150.

Ma, F. (2019). Trilingualism and medium of instruction models in minority schools in Qinghai Province, China. In I. Liyanage & T. Walker (Eds.), *Multilingual education yearbook 2019: Media of instruction & multilingual settings* (pp. 137–149). New York: Springer.

Macaro, E. (2009). Teacher use of codeswitching in the second language classroom: Exploring 'optimal' use. In M. Turnbull & J. Dailey-O'Cain (Eds.), *First language use in second and foreign language learning* (pp. 35–49). Bristol, UK: Multilingual Matters.

Macaro, E., Curle, S., Pun, J., An, J., & Dearden, J. (2018a). A systematic review of English medium instruction in higher education. *Language Teaching, 51*(1), 36–76. https://doi.org/10.1017/s0261444817000350.

Macaro, E., Tian, L., & Chu, L. (2018b). First and second language use in English medium instruction contexts. *Language Teaching Research*, (Published online July 16, 2018), 1–21. https://doi.org/10.1177/1362168818783231.

Mauranen, A., Hynninen, N., & Ranta, E. (2016). English as the academic lingua franca. In K. Hyland & P. Shaw (Eds.), *The Routledge handbook of English for academic purposes* (pp. 44–55). New York: Routledge.

Pennycook, A. (2007). The myth of English as an international language. In A. Pennycook & S. Makoni (Eds.), *Disinventing and reconstituting languages* (pp. 90–115). Clevedon, UK: Multilingual Matters.

Perera, M., & Kularatne, S. A. (2014). An attempt to develop bilingualism in Sri Lanka through content and language integrated learning (CLIL). *International Journal of Arts & Sciences, 7*(3), 107–116.

Preece, S. (2011). Universities in the Anglophone centre: Sites of multilingualism. *Applied Linguistics Review, 2*, 121–146. https://doi.org/10.1515/9783110239331.121.

Premarathna, A., Yogaraja, S. J., Medawattegedara, V., Senarathna, C. D., & Abdullah, M. R. M. (2016). *Study on medium of instruction, national and international languages in General Education in Sri Lanka*. Retrieved from http://nec.gov.lk/wp-content/uploads/2016/04/9-Final.pdf.

Rong, M. (2007). Bilingual education for China's ethnic minorities. *Chinese Education and Society, 40*(2), 9–25.
Shohamy, E. (2012). A critical perspective on the use of English as a medium of instruction at universities. In A. Doiz, D. Lasagabaster, & J. M. Sierra (Eds.), *English-medium instruction at universities: Global challenges* (pp. 196–213). London: Longman.
Simons, G. F., & Fennig, C. D. (2018a). *Ethnologue: Languages of the World: China*. Retrieved from https://www.ethnologue.com/country/CN.
Simons, G. F., & Fennig, C. D. (2018b). *Ethnologue: Languages of the World: Indonesia*. Retrieved from https://www.ethnologue.com/country/ID.
Simons, G. F., & Fennig, C. D. (2018c). *Ethnologue: Languages of the World: Sri Lanka*. Retrieved from https://www.ethnologue.com/country/LK.
Theobald, M., Busch, G., & Laraghy, M. (2019). Children's views and strategies for making friends in linguistically diverse English medium instruction settings In I. Liyanage & T. Walker (Eds.), *Multilingual education yearbook 2019: Media of instruction & multilingual settings* (pp. 151–174). New York: Springer.
Tochon, F. V. (2019). Educational globalization and the creation of split identities. In I. Liyanage & T. Walker (Eds.), *Multilingual education yearbook 2019: Media of instruction & multilingual settings* (pp. 63–80). New York: Springer.
Tran, L. T., & Nguyen, H. T. (2018). Internationalisation of Vietnamese universities through English medium instruction (EMI): Practices, tensions & implications for local language policies In I. Liyanage (Ed.), *Multilingual education yearbook 2018: Internationalization, stakeholders & multilingual education contexts* (pp. 91–106). New York: Springer.
Trudell, B. (2016). *The impact of language policy and practice on children's learning: Evidence from Eastern and Southern Africa*. Nairobi: United Nations International Children's Emergency Fund (UNICEF) Eastern and Southern Africa Regional Office. Retrieved from https://www.unicef.org/esaro/UNICEF(2016)LanguageandLearning-FullReport(SingleView).pdf.
Turner, M., & Cross, R. (2016). Making space for multilingualism in Australian schooling. *Language and Education, 30*(4), 289–297. https://doi.org/10.1080/09500782.2015.1114627.
Walker, T., Liyanage, I., Madya, S., & Hidayati, S. (2019). Media of instruction in Indonesia: Implications for bi/multilingual education. In I. Liyanage & T. Walker (Eds.), *Multilingual education yearbook 2019: Media of instruction & multilingual settings* (pp. 209–229). New York: Springer.
Walter, S. L., & Benson, C. (2012). Language policy and medium of instruction in formal education. In B. Spolsky (Ed.), *The Cambridge handbook of language policy* (pp. 278–300). Cambridge, UK: Cambridge University Press.
Wang, G. (2016). *Pains and gains of ethnic multilingual learners in China: An ethnographic case study*. Singapore: Springer.
Wang, A., Liyanage, I., & Walker, T. (2019). Scrutinising critical thinking (CT) in Chinese higher education: Perceptions of Chinese academics. In I. Liyanage & T. Walker (Eds.), *Multilingual education yearbook 2019: Media of instruction & multilingual settings* (pp. 189–208). New York: Springer.
Wickramasuriya, S. (2005). The present socio-economic-political culture & the myth of English as an access to social equality in post-colonial Sri Lanka. In *Proceedings of the 33rd Annual Conference on the Australian and New Zealand Comparative and International Education Society* (pp. 166–182). Armidale, NSW, Australia. Retrieved from http://ro.uow.edu.au/edupapers/1146/.
Widodo, H. P. (2016). Language policy in practice: Reframing the English language curriculum in the Indonesian secondary education sector. In R. Kirkpatrick (Ed.), *English language education policy in Asia* (pp. 127–151). Cham, Switzerland: Springer.
Wijesekera, H., & Alford, J. (2019). Bilingual Education classrooms in Sri Lankan schools: A social space for ethnolinguistic reconciliation. In I. Liyanage & T. Walker (Eds.), *Multilingual education yearbook 2019: Media of instruction & multilingual settings* (pp. 81–102). New York: Springer.
Wright, S. (2016). *Language policy and language planning: From nationalism to globalisation* (2nd ed.). London: Palgrave Macmillan.

Yi, Y., & Adamson, B. (2019). English in a Mongolian ethnic minority primary school. In I. Liyanage & T. Walker (Eds.), *Multilingual education yearbook 2019: Media of instruction & multilingual settings* (pp. 175–188). New York: Springer.

Yun, H. (2016). Reorienting Tibetan high school students' English language learning. In I. Liyanage & B. Nima (Eds.), *Multidisciplinary research perspectives in education* (pp. 27–36). Rotterdam, The Netherlands: Sense Publishers.

Zacharias, N. T. (2013). Navigating through the English-medium-of-instruction policy: Voices from the field. *Current Issues in Language Planning, 14*(1), 93–108. https://doi.org/10.1080/14664208.2013.782797.

Zamel, V. (1997). Toward a model of transculturation. *TESOL Quarterly, 31*(2), 341–352. https://doi.org/10.2307/3588050.

Zhang, Z., Wen, L., & Li, G. (2015). Trilingual education in China's Korean communities. In A. Feng & B. Adamson (Eds.), *Trilingualism in education in China: Models and challenges* (pp. 47–64). Dordrecht: Springer.

Indika Liyanage (Ph.D.) is Associate Professor in TESOL and Discipline Leader (TESOL/LOTE) at Deakin University, Australia. He is also an Honorary Professor at the Faculty of Education, Sichuan Normal University, and Researcher at the Research Centre for Multi-culture, Sichuan Province, People's Republic of China. He has been an English language teacher educator and doctoral supervisor for many years. He has published widely and worked as an international consultant on TESOL in the Pacific.

Tony Walker (Ph.D.) is a Research Fellow in TESOL and LOTE in the School of Education, Deakin University, Australia. He worked in Australia as an English teacher and language teacher educator for many years, and continues to publish in the field and to work with teacher educators in Asia as an international consultant on academic writing.

Language Alternation as an Interactional Practice in the Foreign Language Classroom

Anna Filipi

Abstract Language alternation (code- or language-switching) has been a long-standing focus of research in language classrooms and multilingual communities. We know about its functions, about the distribution and frequencies in speakers' use of their languages, about the cognitive impact of language alternation on learning, and about social and interactional accounts of language alternation that are concerned with indexing shifting identities and social inequalities, and with showing how they are deployed as interactional resources in languaging practices. This chapter presents an overview of recent research in the Conversation Analytic (CA) tradition which treats language alternation in the foreign language classroom as a social practice. It describes how the micro-analytic methods of CA have contributed to understanding language alternation through analysis of two samples from Australia: a secondary Italian foreign language classroom and a tertiary Japanese foreign language classroom. The focus of the analyses is on the language alternation practices between teacher and learners and between learner and learner. The chapter ends with a consideration of the implications of this research for language teacher education with reference to medium of classroom interaction.

Keywords Conversation analysis · Language alternation as a social and learning practice in the classroom · Medium of instruction · Medium of interaction

A. Filipi (✉)
Faculty of Education, Monash University, Melbourne, Australia
e-mail: anna.filipi@monash.edu

1 Introduction

There is now a substantial body of work on the study of language alternation[1] practices in the second or foreign language classroom. Much of this work has been centred on uncovering and reporting the functions, distribution, policies and frequency of language alternation, often through ethnographic instruments such as interviews, stimulated recall and observations (e.g., Butzkamm, 1998; Cook, 2001; Duff & Polio, 1990; Eldridge, 1996; Ferguson, 2003; Kim & Elder, 2005; Littlewood & Yu, 2011; Macaro, 2005, 2009; Scott & De La Fuente, 2008; Turnbull & Arnett, 2002; van der Meij & Zhao, 2010). However, as attention has turned to social accounts of language learning, analytical interest has shifted to investigations of the languaging competencies of bilinguals who alternate languages for a range of social purposes including for learning (e.g., Cenoz & Gorter, 2011; Turnbull & Arnett, 2002; Turnbull & Dailey-O'Cain, 2009), for indexing their bilingual identities (e.g., Bolton & Botha, 2019; Canagarajah, 2001; Kramsch, 2009) and for indexing social inequalities (e.g., Setati, Adler, Reed, & Bapoo, 2002).

In the last decade and a half, theoretical approaches such as those intrinsic to Conversation Analysis (henceforth CA) that enable analysis of interactions at a micro-level in order to uncover the social properties of interaction, have begun to emerge and gain momentum.[2] CA is particularly powerful because it offers the researcher/analyst a set of findings on the organization of interaction with respect to turn-taking, sequence organization and epistemics, as well as a set of methods for analyzing naturally-occurring interactions.

The aim of this chapter is to elucidate the contributions that CA has made and can make to the study of language alternation practices. I start by discussing how CA views language alternation as a practice which will include a brief review of studies conducted in the classroom. Next I provide a precis of the major findings in CA as well as an overview of the essential features of analysis that underpin its methods. This is followed by the analysis of two transcripts to demonstrate the ways in which a CA analysis can contribute to our understanding of language alternation. Finally, in the conclusion, I briefly discuss the possible applications of findings in teacher education and the language classroom.

---

[1] While the debates about terminology are robust and ongoing, the term "language alternation" based on Gafaranga's (2007, 2018) conceptualization of the practice will be used in this chapter. [See Lin (2013) for a recent discussion about terminology.]

[2] This was an Australian comedy aired on TV in 2006. It involved participants walking through a door and improvising a scene.

2 Background

2.1 *CA Perspectives on Language Alternation*

Research in CA is driven by the fundamental principles that talk is action, that it is orderly, that it emerges in situ, and that speakers orient to the order (Hutchby & Wooffitt, 2008; Sidnell & Stivers, 2013; ten Have, 2007) and to the progressivity of talk (Stivers & Robinson, 2006). CA researchers are therefore concerned with uncovering the orderliness of speakers' sense-making, everyday practices as they unfold turn-by-turn, and as they construct, and both account for and are accountable for their actions. It is this interactional and organizational perspective that drives CA perspectives on language alternation.

The two most influential contributors to our understanding of language alternation based on an interactional or organizational approach are Auer (e.g., 1984, 1998) and Gafaranga (e.g., 2007, 2018). Auer was among the first to conceptualize the practice of shuttling between languages or codes as a resource fundamental to meaning making which occurs in situ. Based on Gumperz's (1982) notion that it serves as a contextualization cue to index meaning, much like gesture or prosody, this reconceptualization of language alternation shifted the view of languages or codes as being neat, clearly defined and separate from each other to a view that positioned a speaker's languages as part of a repertoire, invoked and (re)negotiated in concert with others to achieve some interactional purpose. The purpose could include speakers indexing their identities as bi- or multilingual speakers or solving some complex task. (See Lin, 2013; Musk & Cromdal, 2018, for reviews of this research.)

The interactional work surrounding the alternation of languages is organized both sequentially, turn-by-turn in a local order (Auer, 1984) and with reference to an overall order through a larger set of sequences in an episode or activity (Gafaranga, 2018). This is best illustrated through an example in the classroom where the medium[3] (Gafaranga, 2007; Gafaranga & Torras, 2001) of classroom interaction might be the second language (L2) in line with a pedagogical policy. However, throughout the lesson, speakers may alternate to their first language (L1) thereby temporarily suspending the medium (Gafaranga & Torras, 2002) to deal with some matter best done through their L1. They then alternate back again to the L2. Of course, speakers may also continue in the L1 in which case it is considered to be a medium switch rather than medium repair (Gafaranga & Torras, 2002).

Another important concept in organizational approaches to language alternation relates to the distinction between discourse- and participant- or preference-related alternation (Auer, 1984, 1998; Liebscher & Dailey-O'Cain, 2005). The former works to mark boundaries between different actions or phases, while the latter is motivated by medium preferences, which in the L2 classroom may be determined by language proficiency (Kunitz, 2018).

---

[3] For discussions surrounding the terms medium versus language alternation, and how to determine a base language and normative language choice, see Gafaranga and Torras (2001).

Against this CA 'landscape', specific studies of language alternation practices in the L2 classroom have yielded particularly rich descriptions and findings both from the perspective of the teacher interacting with learners and learners interacting with other learners. Two recent studies in the primary school context, where the medium of instruction was English, are Stoewer (2018) (in a Mother Tongue Instruction (MTI) after school programme in Sweden) and aus der Wieschen and Sert (2018) (in an English Foreign Language (EFL) programme in Denmark). Notwithstanding the use of English as medium, the teachers drew on both languages shared with their learners to work on an aspect of language. In Stoewer's study this was done through translation requests and in aus der Wieschen & Sert's, through the creation of opportunities by the teacher for learners to use their Danish to establish understanding. How understanding is established (or assumed) in programmes where L2 use only is "a (self- or externally imposed) policy-prescribed medium of instruction" (Bonacina & Gafaranga, 2011, p. 331, comment added) is also a key focus of analysis in secondary and tertiary programmes (e.g., Cheng, 2013; Filipi, 2018a, 2018b; Hoang & Filipi, 2019; Morton, 2015; Üstünel, 2016; Üstünel & Seedhouse, 2005).

In the study by Filipi (2018a, 2018b), in a secondary Italian foreign language programme in Australia, the decision to adopt a policy of L2 use as medium of instruction (MOI) was made by the teacher at the local level. The analysis of the classroom data reveals the teacher's epistemic expectations about what she assumed students would or should know. This was evident through her allocation of turns to particular students, her adherence to her L2 use policy, and the multimodal packaging of her pursuits of student responses, all of which were actions that resisted switching to the learners' L1 which she did only as a last resort when these resources had been exhausted. Filipi (2018a) also reports that the learners oriented to a stance of being viewed as competent by using opportunities made available in the context to build their responses rather than admitting not knowing or not understanding.

In the tertiary context, similar patterns of formulating, supporting, and finally alternating to the L1 when the supportive actions were unsuccessful were reported in Üstünel's (2016) and Üstünel and Seedhouse's (2005) studies of EFL classes in Turkey. In Üstünel (2016), students were also shown to support each other through their L1 translations. In contrast to the above, in Hoang and Filipi's (2019) study, the novice teachers in an EFL tertiary programme, oriented to the L2 only policy by always commencing with an instruction in English, but then almost immediately switched to the L1 to repeat the instruction without waiting for displays of non-understanding. All three studies indicate that there was a different overall order with respect to medium choice for both teachers and students, and that the different practices around medium use had consequences for the ensuing learner actions, and ultimately for learning.

Turning to learners' alternation practices, which have attracted less research attention, what emerges is the important role of medium selection in conducting assigned learning tasks. Typically in these contexts, students are assigned a group task and may be free to choose their languages to achieve an outcome, usually a presentation or report back. Medium choice thus becomes a resource for achieving the task or sub-tasks within a larger task. Tran's (2018) study, located in an EFL Vietnamese university course, provides an example of how students resorted to the L1 to conduct word searches, and how these were collaboratively achieved. In Kunitz (2015, 2018), set in an Italian foreign language tertiary context, and Reichert and Liebscher (2018), set in a L2 German tertiary class, students were involved in planning, practice and rehearsal. The language alternation practices in these studies indexed a change in orientation to the other speakers, to the interaction itself, and to the different tasks implied in planning and rehearsal. In other words, learners alternated languages for both discourse purposes, as in differentiating between practice and rehearsal (Reichert & Liebscher, 2018) or product and process (Kunitz, 2018), and participant-related purposes, as in conducting word searches in their L1 in L2 discussion tasks (Tran, 2018) or producing assessments in the L1 in a predominantly L2 as medium of interaction in a Content and Language Integrated Learning (CLIL) class (Morton & Evnitskaya, 2018). According to Liebscher and Dailey-O'Cain (2005) such practices are akin to those of bilinguals observed outside the classroom. Furthermore, as Morton and Evnitskaya (2018, p. 80) maintain: "Even if there is an orientation to a norm of almost exclusive L2 use, it will be impossible for aspects of the learners' plurilingual repertoires not to emerge in interaction".

Taken together, the above brief summary indicates that language alternation is organized, achieved through collaboration and socially distributed for a wide-ranging set of purposes. These involve solving interactional problems that arise in the moment or doing the work of 'learning', including providing evidence of learning and understanding. Therefore, as a practice, alternating languages is not merely deployed for solving issues of 'language', be it for gaps in vocabulary or for points of grammar.

2.2 Systems in Conversation Analysis

As a research field in its own right that spans sociology, applied and interactional linguistics and discursive psychology, CA research has expanded exponentially since the pioneering work of Harvey Sacks, Emanuel Schegloff and Gail Jefferson in the 60s and early 70s, resulting in a very impressive set of findings about the organization of talk both in everyday, mundane interactions and in institutional interactions. Three important 'systems' in interaction that have been uncovered by this research are turn-taking, sequence organization, and epistemics, each of which is briefly explained below.

2.2.1 Turn-Taking

Given the preoccupation with uncovering the orderliness of talk, and showing how speakers are intent on progressing their talk, it is not surprising that research on turn-taking has found that turns are rule-governed. Sacks, Schegloff, and Jefferson (1974) first described a set of rules for the selection of next speaker. Since then there has been further work that has elucidated how a range of features in turn design are fundamentally involved in self- or other-speaker selection including embodiment (e.g., Goodwin, 1981), prosody and phonetic design (e.g., Wells & MacFarlane, 1998) and grammar (e.g., Ford & Thompson, 1996; Sorjonen, Raevaara, & Couper-Kuhlen, 2017). The rules that govern speaker selection ensure that speakers do not talk over each other, and that if they do, that one speaker will drop out; they also ensure that gaps between one speaker and the next are kept to a minimum one beat, measured as one tenth of a second; and finally, they ensure that if there is trouble in understanding, speakers will initiate repair and/or actually repair talk so that mutual understanding is established and/or restored. More recent work has also shown that speakers' orientation to order is achieved by monitoring the progression of a turn temporally and with reference to how it is tied to what has gone before. This is referred to as "next turn proof procedure" (Sidnell, 2013, p. 79) which offers a display of how a current speaker interprets the previous speaker's utterance, leading to a sequential turn-by-turn analysis.

2.2.2 Sequence Organisation

Turns are organized into pre-, base, post and insert sequences (Schegloff, 2007). The most basic unit is the base sequence often made up of adjacency pairs such as the pervasive Question and Answer pair. These paired utterances are fitted together such that a question, for example, makes a particular answer relevant as a response or answer. As the name suggests, pre-sequences, such as a summons to elicit a speaker's attention, go before a base sequence, while post sequences follow the base sequence. Insert sequences are usually repair sequences that temporarily suspend a base sequence in order to deal with a problem of misunderstanding or mishearing.

2.2.3 Epistemics

When speakers interact they work hard to establish mutual understanding. They have distinct territories of knowledge which they draw on, and in doing so, they design their talk based on what they expect their recipients will know (Sacks & Schegloff, 1979). This is referred to as epistemics (Heritage, 2012). Evidence for these assumptions or expectations are reflected in the particular design of a speaker's turn, in the episode of talk beyond the single turn, as well as in speakers' use of specific conversational resources such as the *do you remember* recognition check (Schegloff, 1988; Filipi, 2018b; Shaw & Kitzinger, 2007; You, 2015) and the *no-one knows* epistemic status check (Filipi, 2018b; Sert, 2013).

Displays of the ways in which speakers create these epistemic expectations as they monitor each other's turns in order to produce a fitting next action, emerge turn-by-turn and result in a turn-taking system that works efficiently and in an orderly manner. Such monitoring reveals how epistemic imbalances are constantly adjusted as participants work to establish mutual understanding and shared knowledge states (Heritage, 2012).

2.2.4 The Process of Analysis

Conversation Analysis provides an inductive approach to the analysis of interaction. It is data-driven and uses audio- and/or video-recorded, naturally occurring data as the focus for analysis. In transcribing the data, the analyst seeks to capture as many details as possible because nothing can be dismissed a priori as being of no value. S/he is concerned with capturing the minutiae of talk including the timing of the gaps both between speakers and within a speaker's turn, prosodic features such as pitch, rise, fall and continuing intonation, dysfluency through perturbations, and nonverbal features. Thus, not just what is said but also how something is said and reacted to by the next speaker is fundamental to the organization of interaction.

In analyzing the data, the analyst begins with what has been referred to as unmotivated looking (Hutchby & Wooffitt, 2008; Sidnell, 2013; ten Have, 2007); s/he then analyses the data with reference to the normative conduct of speakers in turn-taking, sequence organization and epistemics (described above). An important driver of the analyses is to understand why a speaker has designed his/her turn in a particular way ("why that now?", Schegloff & Sacks, 1973) or used a specific resource to accomplish the action.

2.2.5 Transcription Notations

As just stated, in working within a CA research framework, the analyst is concerned with capturing the minutiae of interaction. This is conveyed through transcription which becomes a record of the interaction itself. A set of notations originally developed by Jefferson (1984) (and which has subsequently been further expanded to include verbal and non-verbal features) is used. Below is a selection of the notations that are relevant to the two transcripts to be analyzed here. (The notations for gaze, gaze disengagement, pointing and gesture co-occurring with talk are from Filipi, 2001).

[	—overlapped talk (when speakers speak at the same time)
{	—gesture co-occurring with words
°	—talk that is softer than the surrounding talk
CAPS	—talk that is louder than the surrounding talk
:	—sound stretching
(0.0)	—pauses and gaps measured in tenths of a second
- - -	—gazing
,,,	—gaze disengagement
P→	—pointing
=	—a latched turn (i.e. no gap between one speaker and the next)
> <	—talk that is faster than the surrounding talk.

2.2.6 Bilingual Transcriptions

In transcribing bilingual data, Hepburn and Bolden (2013) provide a suggested format of a three-line transcription for bilingual interactions which will also be adopted in the analyses of the two transcripts. The first line conveys the original utterance in the relevant language. A "morpheme-by-morpheme English gloss" (Hepburn & Bolden, 2013, p. 69), or word-for-word translation and abbreviations of the original language utterance (that gloss grammatical features such as particles that cannot be translated easily or that have no direct equivalents in English (Sidnell, 2010)), is given in the second line. In the third line, the interactional meaning or pragmatic English translation of the original language utterance is provided. In this chapter, the original language line (Italian in excerpt 1) and the romanised script, romaji, for the Japanese excerpt 2, is presented in Courier New 10 font, while the translations are in Times New Roman 12 (italicised for the pragmatic meaning). Where the morpheme-by-morpheme or word-for-word translation equates with the interactional meaning, a two-line transcription is used.

3 Analyses

Having provided some background about both the findings and methods intrinsic to CA, and having explained how transcription is conducted, I now turn to two examples to illustrate what this process of analysis can reveal about language alternation practices and MOI in the classroom. The first example is taken from a teacher fronted Italian foreign language lesson in an Australian secondary school, while the second is from a group task in an advanced Japanese foreign language class in an Australian tertiary context.

3.1 Excerpts

In Excerpt 1, the class is made up of 26 mainly 13-year-old students in their first year of Italian at High School,[4] equivalent to A1 level in the Common European Framework Reference for languages (CEFR) (Council of Europe, 2001). In her teaching, the teacher adopts a policy of using Italian as her MOI. However, she has a different expectation for students whom she expects will use Italian for participation in drills and for responding to basic instructions but English (their L1) for everything else. (See Filipi, 2018a, 2018b, for further details and discussion of the teacher's differential language expectations using the same corpus.)

---

[4] Although it should be noted that a small number of students would have had exposure to Italian in primary school but in a limited capacity of 50 min/week.

Excerpt 1: Practising a drill: when is your birthday?

The excerpt starts with a switch to a new pattern in a drill that requires students to ask each other about their birthdays. This is tightly controlled as a whole class activity.

```
 1 T:      bene, bene. eh:: vediamo un po',
 2         ((T walks between tables, scanning the room.))
           good, good.   um let's just see
 3         {Emma, (0.7) Emma {domanda a:: Peter quando fa lui il compleanno.
           {((P→Emma))        {((P→Peter))
           Emma          Emma      ask       Peter   when    it's his   birthday.
 4          (1.5)
 5 Emma:  [(        )
 6 T:→   [you want to know when it's his birthday.
           ((----→Emma, shrugs her shoulders))
 7          (0.4)
 8         {come-  can you help Vera?
           how
           {((----→Vera. Vera----→at her book))
 9          (0.3)
10 Vera:  [quan-
           ((when))
11 T:      {[Peter's over there. ecco Peter.
                                 there's Peter.
           {((T: P----→ Peter then back at Vera. Vera----→at Peter and her notes.))
12 Vera:  qua- quando {(fa il) comple{anno.
           whe- when is his birthday.
13                      {((----→Peter))  {((----→T))
14 Peter: il- il mio compleanno (0.3) um …
           my   my    birthday
```

The teacher's *bene, bene* in line 1 marks both the end of the previous activity and the beginning of the next one. We note her embodied actions of walking around the class as she scans the room to nominate a student to participate in the drill. In choosing Emma, she waits for her to engage through gaze and then scans the room again to nominate Peter as Emma's co-speaker. The gap of 1.5 in line 3 is decidedly long even for the L2 classroom where the normal wait time has been reported to be one second (Smith & King, 2017). In lines 5 and 6, both Emma and the teacher take a turn in overlap, but Emma's utterance is not recoverable. The teacher's turn is a medium repair (Gafaranga, 2018) where she switches to English to explain what Emma needs to do. This action, which occurs in an insertion sequence and temporarily suspends the main question and answer sequence, indicates that the teacher is assuming that Emma did not understand the instruction in Italian. This is made more salient through the embodied shrugging of her shoulders. In line 7, another gap ensues (briefer this time) which provides enough time for Emma to be able to formulate a turn. Next, the medium of interaction is temporarily restored through what appears to be the beginning of another question (*come, how*). However, the teacher self-repairs and then asks another student, Vera, if she is able to help (Emma). The actions in this turn are interesting. First, the teacher has now assumed that the lack of comprehension was not in fact due to the choice of medium because the medium repair did not result in success either. She thus selects Vera to answer on Emma's behalf, indicated by her formulation of 'help' which casts Vera in a more 'knowing' position, and as someone who can assist. Indeed, this action results in eventual success as Vera's turn, in overlap initially and then in the clear after a further teacher instruction in both languages, achieves the expected outcome in the drill.

The excerpt illustrates several points. First, from the teacher's perspective, the L2 is her MOI. This is also reflected in the sequence organization through her directive which is located in the base or main sequence and through the insert sequence where the L1 is located. Second, she provides a long interactional space for Emma to be able to formulate a response. Third, her switches to English are produced to aid comprehension when other resources have failed or to progress the lesson (see Filipi, 2018a for a further discussion of lesson progressivity). Fourth, her epistemic assumptions through her turn allocation and her linguistic choices (i.e. *can you help*) that ascribe a 'knowing' state to one student over another, are clearly in evidence and emerge through (in)actions in the preceding turn. With respect to Emma, the long silence before formulating a response (in overlap) can be interpreted in two ways: either she does not wish to admit that she does not know or understand what is being asked of her, and is therefore orienting to a desire to be perceived as competent (see Waring, 2016, on the ways in which learners strive to be perceived as being competent), or that her silence masks a lack of interactional competence not just in the L2 (as described by Cheng, 2013, for learners of Mandarin) but also in her L1.

Excerpt 2 provides an example of the L2 as medium of classroom interaction, as a group of advanced learners of Japanese collaborate to complete a discussion task. The task required students to work in groups to discuss and describe a distinctive feature of Conte, Manzai (both comics in Japan), and Variety (a show). The lecturer has just asked them to summarise the discussion and to nominate a spokesperson who will present the results of their discussion to the class.

Excerpt 2: [Jack(J), Minsoo(M), Gabby(G) and Ichiro(I)].[5]

---

[5]I would like to thank Hyesun Ko who generously provided this previously unanalyzed transcript from her dataset, collected as part of her Ph.D. study.

```
1  I:    nante     kaiteta?
         what-QT   write-ASP-PT
         what did you write
2                 (0.4) ((G P→I's handout with index finger))
3  I:    sinario ga      kimatterutte        kaiteiru    kedo
         scenario-NOM    be fixed-ASP-QT     write-ASP   but
         I wrote that the scenario is fixed but,
4  G:    [( ? )]
5  M:    [watashimo.
         I-TOP
         me too.
6  G:    bamende     settei [sareteiru].
         scene-P     set up  PASS-ASP
         it's set up according to the scene
7  M:    °soone° ano,
         right-P FL
         that's right well
8        gekinoyoode sono  jo sono sutoriga
         drama likely the     the story-TOP
         it's like a skit where   the story
9        kimattete   sorega      nagarede tsuzuite   tsuzuite
         be set-ASP  that-TOP    stream-P continue-P continuously-P
         is fixed and that there is a story flow, so (the Conte) continues
10 J:    °a::h°
11       ((J & G nod and I write something on the handout))
12 G:    {kontotte are nanka sukuriputoga   kaitenai        hoodesho
         {((nods, ---J.))
         Conte-QT well something script-TOP wrtite-ASP-NEG side-TAG
         Conte is, well,   something like a script that is not written, isn't that right?
13 M:    {mochiron      kaitearujan
         {((M nods, M&G ---→ at each other))
         of course     write-ASP COP-N
         of course     (the script) is written
14 G:    kaitearuka?
         write-ASP-Q
         the script is written?
15 M:    {kaitearunjanai?
         {((---G))
         write-ASP-N-COP-NEG
         is the script written?
16 G:    { kai (.) te nain janaika.
         {((G & J ---→at each other))
         write -ASP-NEG-N- COP-NEG-Q
         the script is not written is it?
17 →     isn't it like ah- like ah:::
18 J:    {um
         {((nods ---G))
19 G:→   [nande ano:]
         why     well
20 J:    {[tabun] tabun    nantonaku kaite aru °to omoo°
         {((---G))
         maybe    maybe    somehow   write-ASP-QT-think
         maybe    maybe    I think somehow (the script) is written
```

```
21 G:      soo[ka?
           is that so?
22 J:         [tatoeba
              for example
23 G: →    {[ I thought it was like u:m=
           {((nods))
24 J:      =nandaroo?
           what?
25 G:      what was that (.) old Australian program?
26 M:      a:h
27 G: →    are nandatta?=
           that what-PT
           what was that?
28 J:      =which one (.) Saturday?
29 G: →    no=
30 M:      =no=
31 G:      =the one (    ) day:. they used to come in=
32 M:      =uh=
33 G:      =used to knock and come in and then it was [like what
34 I:                                                 [thank god you're here⁵.
35 G:      {yeah=
           {((G ---→I))
36 J:      =yeah, yeah, yeah [wow!
37 G: →                      [sonna   kanjide   sukuriputo
           kaitenaikedo
                             like that feeling-P script    write-ASP-NEG-but
                             it's like that, the script is not written but,
38         [bamenga] atte.
           scene-TOP exist-TE
           there is a scene.
 ...
43 J:      =ma sookamoshirenai
           well  it may be
           (3.1)
```

As can be seen, the students are clearly orienting to the L2 as the medium for their discussion. However, alternation to English occurs in line 17 in the context of a disagreement. Just prior to the switch, students have been trying to pin down a definition of Conte, a skit, for the oral report back to the class. As can be seen in lines 12 and 13, a disagreement emerges between two of the learners, Gabby and Minsoo about this definition, and whether it is written (scripted) or not (improvised). Initially, Gabby builds her turn with a tag-question in Japanese in line 12. Tag-questions have been characterized as polar questions and therefore make *yes* or *no* relevant as a next response (Raymond, 2003). Here, Gabby's question is strongly tilted towards eliciting a *yes* response and therefore an agreement with her definition that Conte is improvised or unscripted. However, Minsoo responds through a strong disagreement with this definition (*mochiron kaitearujan, of course it's written*). After several more turns to establish an agreed definition (lines 14, 15, 16), in line 17 Gabby finally switches to English to launch a word search (the name of an Australian show), which as an action has been shown to be a common practice among learners as they work on retrieving a lexical item while working on tasks in the L2 (see Markee & Kunitz, 2013; Tran, 2018). It is at this point that a third student, Jack, joins the discussion and continues in overlap with Minsoo to suggest that he agrees that the script is written, therefore tentatively (as indicated by *tabun maybe*) aligning with Minsoo. In line 23, Gabby recycles her word search, and this time all her group members participate, so that they are collectively able to retrieve the title of the show. This allows Gabby to complete her example by making connections between the Australian show and what she believes to be Conte (an improvised skit). The medium of interaction, the L2, is thus restored (line 37). However, her attempts to elicit an agreement from the others through this example do not result in a shift in position. Indeed, in line 41, Jack makes the comment *ma sookamoshirenai* (*well it may be*) which, while not openly disagreeing, is nonetheless noncommittal and could therefore be construed as not agreeing.

The language alternation observed in this transcript is an example of the deployment of the learners' L1 to conduct a word search. In this respect, it resembles the bilingual word search behaviour investigated by Markee and Kunitz (2013) and Tran (2018) where it provides a clear example of medium repair. It also offers a display of the collaborative nature of the word search as an activity as learners work together to solve a linguistic issue which temporarily stymies the progress of a task. However, while in both of those studies the searches were conducted for linguistic purposes (to retrieve a word or a more grammatically accurate structure), in the transcript just analyzed there are two important differences. First, the search is topic related, conducted to recall the name of a TV comedy show. It draws on a shared memory that invites collaboration through collective remembering based on a presupposition that all participants have equal access to the memory. In other words, it is making a claim to a shared epistemic territory (Heritage, 2012). Second, it occurs in the context of a disagreement, and is invoked as an example to elicit the agreement of the co-participants in the face of resistance to the definition being offered. It therefore offers a resolution to the problem in defining Conte. This needs to be resolved for the task to be completed.

4 Conclusion

In addressing the issue of MOI (and medium of interaction) and multilingualism, I have sought to provide a brief overview of the perspectives that the micro-analytic methods of CA can bring to our understanding of the practice of language alternation. CA is data-driven as an approach, seeking as it does to understand how speakers collaborate to establish common states of knowledge in order to achieve intersubjectivity by analyzing how speakers make sense of talk as it unfolds turn-by-turn. This allows a different set of understandings to emerge. As the brief literature review and the analyses of the two transcripts have shown, social order is oriented to by speakers and made visible through their language alternating practices. Principally, these are matters for interaction as speakers 'do' and 'practice' being multilingual. In the process, they collaboratively establish a medium of instruction and interaction, one that is not fixed but rather negotiated and renegotiated locally to address issues that emerge as they bring their language resources to bear on the work of learning, teaching and being social. As the above analyses have sought to show, ultimately, the classroom is a social space and the actions of the speakers in not being able to complete a response when called upon to do so, or in facing a disagreement that stymies task completion, are issues that the participants have to carefully manage in order to restore and maintain affiliation while at the same time being mindful of the need to progress the activity. Having recourse to more than one language provides opportunities to draw on them as additional resources not just for learning but also for 'doing' being social.

The findings have application for teacher education and pedagogy. CA is increasingly 'speaking' to a range of professions as findings are used for application and intervention (see for example, the collection in Antaki, 2011). Principal among these is for teachers and learners to develop a greater awareness of what interaction 'in the wild' looks like in both their L1 and in their L2. This can be done through staged pedagogies in general language courses that involve participants collecting data of both their L1 and L2 interactions for the classroom and then engaging in a series of steps from noticing/awareness-raising to guided analysis, to practice, to use and to reflection (as advocated for example by Barraja-Rohan, 2011; Cheng, 2016; Filipi and Barraja-Rohan, 2015), and to build into the steps ample opportunities for assessment for learning through quality feedback practices. In content based programmes such as CLIL, similar practices have been advocated by Morton (2015) in the context of vocabulary teaching. Morton proposes using video data together with a set of focus questions to stimulate teacher attention to the ways that languages are used in vocabulary teaching. Filipi and Markee (2018) provide an elaborated discussion and review of CA applications and approaches in teacher education and L2 pedagogy and highlight the need to give students adequate time to build their responses, and to allow for moments of reflection and discussion when understanding talk or instructions in the L2 breaks down. This is a practice that, when done well, can also contribute to the development of metacognitive skills achieved through interaction. Finally, we know that attention continues to shift away from the unattainable, and progressively irrelevant, native speaker norms as we work towards attaining bilingualism as the goal for student learning (Liebscher & Dailey-O'Cain, 2005). It therefore becomes important to create space in class for the principled use of students' languages as we increasingly appreciate how each contributes to the important work of understanding, and building knowledge and skill in the classroom.

References

Antaki, C. (2011). Six kinds of applied conversation analysis. In C. Antaki (Ed.), *Applied conversation analysis: Intervention and change in institutional talk* (pp. 1–14). Basingstoke, UK: Palgrave Macmillan. https://doi.org/10.1057/9780230316874.0006.

Auer, P. (1984). *Bilingual conversation*. Amsterdam: John Benjamins Publishing Company. https://doi.org/10.1075/pb.v.8.

Auer, P. (1998). Introduction: Bilingual conversation revisited. In P. Auer (Ed.), *Code-switching in conversation* (pp. 1–28). London: Routledge.

aus der Wieschen, M. V., & Sert, O. (2018). Divergent language choices and maintenance of intersubjectivity: The case of Danish EFL young learners. *International Journal of Bilingual Education and Bilingualism*. https://doi.org/10.1080/13670050.2018.1447544.

Barraja-Rohan, A.-M. (2011). Using conversation analysis in the second language classroom to teach interactional competence. *Language Teaching Research, 15*(4), 479–507. https://doi.org/10.1177/1362168811412878.

Bolton, K., & Botha, W. (2019). Multilingualism and language mixing among Singapore university students. In I. Liyanage & T. Walker (Eds.), *Multilingual education yearbook 2019: Media of instruction & multilingual settings* (pp. 43–61). New York: Springer.

Bonacina, F., & Gafaranga, J. (2011). 'Medium of instruction' vs. 'medium of classroom interaction': Language choice in a French complementary school classroom in Scotland. *International Journal of Bilingual Education and Bilingualism, 14*(3), 319–334. https://doi.org/10.1080/13670050.2010.502222.

Butzkamm, W. (1998). Code-switching in a bilingual history lesson: The mother tongue as a conversational lubricant. *International Journal of Bilingual Education and Bilingualism, 1*(2), 81–89. https://doi.org/10.1080/13670059808667676.

Canagarajah, S. (2001). Constructing hybrid postcolonial subjects: Codeswitching in Jaffna classrooms. In M. Heller & M. M. Jones (Eds.), *Voices of authority: Education and linguistic difference* (pp. 193–212). Westport, CT: Ablex.

Cenoz, J., & Gorter, D. (2011). Focus on multilinguals: A study of trilingual writing. *The Modern Language Journal, 95,* 356–369. https://doi.org/10.1111/j.1540-4781.2011.01206.x.

Cheng, T-P. (2013). Codeswitching and participant orientations in a Chinese as a foreign language classroom. *The Modern Language Journal, 97*(4), 869–886. https://doi.org/10.1111/j.1540-4781.2013.12046.x.

Cheng, T.-P. (2016). Authentic L2 interactions as material for a pragmatic awareness-raising activity. *Language Awareness, 25*(3), 159–178. https://doi.org/10.1080/09658416.2016.1154568.

Cook, V. (2001). Using the first language in the classroom. *The Canadian Modern Language Review, 57*(3), 402–423. https://doi.org/10.3138/cmlr.57.3.402.

Council of Europe. (2001). *The Common European Framework Reference for languages: Learning, teaching, assessment*. Cambridge, UK: Cambridge University Press.

Duff, P. A., & Polio, C. G. (1990). How much foreign language is there in the foreign language classroom? *The Modern Language Journal, 74*(2), 154–166. https://doi.org/10.1111/j.1540-4781.1990.tb02561.x.

Eldridge, J. (1996). Code switching in a Turkish secondary school. *ELT Journal, 50*(4), 303–311. https://doi.org/10.1093/elt/50.4.303.

Ferguson, G. (2003). Classroom code-switching in post-colonial contexts: Functions, attitudes and policies. *AILA Review, 16,* 38–51. https://doi.org/10.1075/aila.16.05fer.

Filipi, A. (2001). *The organisation of pointing sequences in parent-toddler interaction*. Doctoral thesis, Monash University.

Filipi, A. (2018a). Making teacher talk comprehensible through language alternation practices. In A. Filipi & N. Markee (Eds.), *Conversation analysis and language alternation: Capturing transitions in the classroom* (pp. 183–204). Philadelphia, The Netherlands: John Benjamins Publishing Company.

Filipi, A. (2018b). Using language alternation to establish epistemic status in an Italian as a second language lesson. In P. Seedhouse, O. Sert, & U. Balaman (Eds.), *Conversation analytic studies on teaching and learning practices: International perspectives*. Hacettepe University. *Journal of Education, 33*(Special issue), 36–53. https://doi.org/10.16986/huje.2018038795.

Filipi, A., & Barraja-Rohan, A.-M. (2015). An interaction-focused pedagogy based on conversation analysis for developing L2 pragmatic competence. In S. Gesuato, F. Bianchi, & W. Cheng (Eds.), *Teaching, learning and investigating about pragmatics: Principles, methods and practices* (pp. 231–252). UK: Cambridge Scholars Publishing.

Filipi, A., & Markee, N. (2018). From research in conversation analysis to applications: Exploring pedagogical practices that benefit language alternation. In A. Filipi & N. Markee (Eds.), *Conversation analysis and language alternation: Capturing transitions in the classroom* (pp. 205–224). Philadelphia, The Netherlands: John Benjamins Publishing Company.

Ford, C. E., & Thompson, S. A. (1996). Interactional units in conversation: Syntactic, intonational, and pragmatic resources for the management of turns. In E. Ochs, E. A. Schegloff, & S. A. Thompson (Eds.), *Interaction and grammar* (pp. 134–184). Cambridge: Cambridge University Press.

Gafaranga, J. (2007). *Talk in two languages*. New York: Palgrave Macmillan. https://doi.org/10.1057/9780230593282.

Gafaranga, J. (2018). Overall order versus local order in bilingual conversation: A conversation analytic perspective on language alternation. In A. Filipi & N. Markee (Eds.), *Conversation analysis and language alternation: Capturing transitions in the classroom* (pp. 35–60). Philadelphia, The Netherlands: John Benjamins Publishing Company.

Gafaranga, J., & Torras, M.-C. (2001). Language versus medium in the study of bilingual conversation. *The International Journal of Bilingualism, 5*(2), 195–219. https://doi.org/10.1177/13670069010050020401.

Gafaranga, J., & Torras, M.-C. (2002). Interactional otherness: Towards a redefinition of codeswitching. *International Journal of Bilingualism, 6*(1), 1–22. https://doi.org/10.1177/13670069020060010101.

Goodwin, C. (1981). *Conversational organization: Interaction between speakers and hearers*. London: Academic Press.

Gumperz, J. J. (1982). *Discourse strategies*. Cambridge, UK: Cambridge University Press. https://doi.org/10.1017/CBO9780511611834.

Hepburn, A., & Bolden, G. B. (2013). The conversation analytic approach to transcription. In J. Sidnell & T. Stivers (Eds.), *The handbook of conversation analysis* (pp. 57–76). West Sussex, UK: Wiley Blackwell.

Heritage, J. (2012). Epistemics in action: Action formation and territories of knowledge. *Research on Language and Social Interaction, 45*(1), 1–29. https://doi.org/10.1080/08351813.2012.646684.

Hoang, L., & Filipi, A. (2019). In pursuit of understanding: An analysis of language alternation practices in an EFL university context in Vietnam. *Language Learning Journal, 47*(1), 116–129. https://doi.org/10.1080/09571736.2016.1221439.

Hutchby, I., & Wooffitt, R. (2008). *Conversation analysis* (2nd ed.). Cambridge, UK: Polity Press.

Jefferson, G. (1984). Notes on a systematic deployment of the acknowledgement tokens "yeah"; and "mm hm". *Papers in Linguistics, 17*(2), 197–216. https://doi.org/10.1080/08351818409389201.

Kim, S.-H. O., & Elder, C. (2005). Language choices and pedagogic functions in the foreign language classroom: A cross-linguistic functional analysis of teacher talk. *Language Teaching Research, 9*(4), 355–380. https://doi.org/10.1191/1362168805lr173oa.

Kramsch, C. (2009). *The multilingual subject: What foreign language learners say about their experience and why it matters*. Oxford, UK: Oxford University Press.

Kunitz, S. (2015). Scriptlines as emergent artifacts in collaborative group planning. *Journal of Pragmatics, 76*, 135–149. https://doi.org/10.1016/j.pragma.2014.10.012.

Kunitz, S. (2018). L1/L2 alternation practices in students' task planning. In A. Filipi & N. Markee (Eds.), *Conversation analysis and language alternation: Capturing transitions in the classroom* (pp. 107–128). Philadelphia, The Netherlands: John Benjamins Publishing Company.

Liebscher, G., & Dailey-O'Cain, J. (2005). Learner code-switching in the content-based foreign language classroom. *The Modern Language Journal, 89*(2), 234–247. https://doi.org/10.1111/j.1540-4781.2005.00277.x.

Lin, A. Y. M. (2013). Classroom code-switching: Three decades of research. *Applied Linguistics Review, 4*(1), 195–218. https://doi.org/10.1515/applirev-2013-0009.

Littlewood, W., & Yu, B. (2011). First language and target language in the foreign language classroom. *Language Teaching, 44*(1), 64–77. https://doi.org/10.1017/S0261444809990310.

Macaro, E. (2005). Codeswitching in the L2 classroom: A communication and learning strategy. In E. Llurda (Ed.), *Non-native language teachers: Perceptions, challenges and contributions to the profession* (pp. 63–84). Boston, MA: Springer Science and Business Media. https://doi.org/10.1007/0-387-24565-0_5.

Macaro, E. (2009). Teacher use of codeswitching in the second language classroom: Exploring 'optimal' use. In M. Turnbull & J. Dailey-O'Cain (Eds.), *First language use in second and foreign language learning* (pp. 35–49). Bristol, UK: Multilingual Matters.

Markee, N., & Kunitz, K. (2013). Doing planning and task performance in second language acquisition: An ethnomethodological respecification. *Language Learning, 63*(4), 629–664. https://doi.org/10.1111/lang.12019.

Morton, T. (2015). Vocabulary explanations in CLIL classrooms: A conversation analysis perspective. *The Language Learning Journal, 43*(3), 256–270. https://doi.org/10.1080/09571736.2015.1053283.

Morton, T., & Evnitskaya, N. (2018). Language alternation in peer interaction in content and language integrated learning (CLIL). In A. Filipi & N. Markee (Eds.), *Conversation analysis and language alternation: Capturing transitions in the classroom* (pp. 61–82). Philadelphia, The Netherlands: John Benjamins Publishing Company.

Musk, N., & Cromdal, J. (2018). Analysing bilingual talk: Conversation analysis and language alternation. In A. Filipi & N. Markee (Eds.), *Conversation analysis and language alternation: Capturing transitions in the classroom* (pp. 15–34). Philadelphia, The Netherlands: John Benjamins Publishing Company.

Raymond, G. (2003). Grammar and social organization: Yes/no interrogatives and the structure of responding. *American Sociological Review, 68,* 939–967. https://doi.org/10.2307/1519752.

Reichert, T., & Liebscher, G. (2018). Transitions with "okay": Managing language alternation in role-play preparations. In A. Filipi & N. Markee (Eds.), *Conversation analysis and language alternation: Capturing transitions in the classroom* (pp. 129–148). Philadelphia, The Netherlands: John Benjamins Publishing Company.

Sacks, H., & Schegloff, E. A. (1979). Two preferences in the organization of reference to persons in conversation and their interaction. In G. Psathas (Ed.), *Everyday language: Studies in ethnomethodology* (pp. 15–21). New York: Irvington.

Sacks, H., Schegloff, E. A., & Jefferson, G. (1974). A simplest systematics for the organization of turn-taking for conversation. *Language, 50,* 696–735. https://doi.org/10.1353/lan.1974.0010.

Schegloff, E. A. (1988). Presequences and indirection. Applying speech act theory to ordinary conversation. *Journal of Pragmatics, 12,* 55–62. https://doi.org/10.1016/0378-2166(88)90019-7.

Schegloff, E. A. (2007). *Sequence organization in interaction. A primer in conversation analysis* (Vol. 1). Cambridge: Cambridge University Press.

Schegloff, E. A., & Sacks, H. (1973). Opening up closings. *Semiotica, 8,* 289–327. https://doi.org/10.1515/semi.1973.8.4.289.

Scott, V. M., & De La Fuente, M. J. (2008), What's the problem? L2 learners' use of the L1 during consciousness-raising, form-focused tasks. *The Modern Language Journal, 92,* 100–113. https://doi.org/10.1111/j.1540-4781.2008.00689.x.

Sert, O. (2013). 'Epistemic status check' as an interactional phenomenon in instructed learning settings. *Journal of Pragmatics, 45*(1), 13–28. https://doi.org/10.1016/j.pragma.2012.10.005.

Setati, M., Adler, J., Reed, Y., & Bapoo, A. (2002). Incomplete journeys: Code-switching and other language practices in mathematics, science and English Language classrooms in South Africa. *Language and Education, 16*(2), 128–149. https://doi.org/10.1080/09500780208666824.

Shaw, R., & Kitzinger, C. (2007). Memory in interaction: An analysis of repeat calls to a home birth helpline. *Research on Language & Social Interaction, 40*(1), 117–144. https://doi.org/10.1080/08351810701331307.

Sidnell, J. (2010). *Conversation analysis*. West Sussex, UK: Wiley Blackwell.

Sidnell, J. (2013). Basic conversation analytic methods. In J. Sidnell & T. Stivers (Eds.), *The handbook of conversation analysis* (pp. 77–99). West Sussex, UK: Wiley Blackwell.

Sidnell, J., & Stivers, T. (Eds.). (2013). *The handbook of conversation analysis*. West Sussex, UK: Wiley Blackwell.

Smith, L., & King, J. (2017). A dynamic systems approach to wait time in the second language classroom. *System, 68,* 1–14. https://doi.org/10.1016/j.system.2017.05.005.

Sorjonen, M.-L., Raevaara, L., & Couper-Kuhlen, E. (Eds.). (2017). *The design of directives in action*. Philadelphia, The Netherlands: John Benjamins Publishing Company.

Stivers, T., & Robinson, J. D. (2006). A preference for progressivity in talk. *Language in Society, 35*(3), 367–392. https://doi.org/10.1017/S0047404506060179.

Stoewer, K. (2018). What is it in Swedish? Translation requests as a resource for vocabulary explanation in English mother tongue instruction. In A. Filipi & N. Markee (Eds.), *Conversation analysis and language alternation: Capturing transitions in the classroom* (pp. 83–106). Philadelphia, The Netherlands: John Benjamins Publishing Company.

ten Have, P. (2007). *Doing conversation analysis* (2nd ed.). Los Angeles: SAGE.

Tran, H. Q. (2018). Language alternation during L2 classroom discussion tasks. In A. Filipi & N. Markee (Eds.), *Conversation analysis and language alternation: Capturing transitions in the classroom* (pp. 165–182). Philadelphia, The Netherlands: John Benjamins Publishing Company.

Turnbull, M., & Arnett, K. (2002). Teachers' uses of the target and first languages in second and foreign language classrooms. *Annual Review of Applied Linguistics, 22,* 204–218. https://doi.org/10.1017/S0267190502000119.

Turnbull, M., & Dailey-O'Cain, J. (2009). Introduction. In M. Turnbull & J. Dailey-O'Cain (Eds.), *First language use in second and foreign language learning* (pp. 1–14). Bristol, Buffalo, Toronto: Multilingual Matters.

Üstünel, E. (2016). *EFL classroom code-switching*. Basingstoke, UK: Palgrave Macmillan.

Üstünel, E., & Seedhouse, P. (2005). Why that, in that language, right now? Code-switching and pedagogical focus. *International Journal of Applied Linguistics, 15*(3), 302–325. https://doi.org/10.1111/j.1473-4192.2005.00093.x.

van der Meij, H., & Zhao, X. (2010). Codeswitching in English courses in Chinese universities. *The Modern Language Journal, 94*(3), 396–411. https://doi.org/10.1111/j.1540-4781.2010.01090.x.

Waring, H. Z. (2016). *Theorizing pedagogical interaction: Insights from conversation analysis*. New York: Taylor Francis.

Wells, B., & Macfarlane, S. (1998). Prosody as an interactional resource: Turn-projection and overlap. *Language and Speech, 41,* 265–294. https://doi.org/10.1177/002383099804100403.

You, H.-J. (2015). Reference to shared past events and memories. *Journal of Pragmatics, 87,* 238–250. https://doi.org/10.1016/j.pragma.2015.02.003.

Anna Filipi (Ph.D.) is a Senior Lecturer in the Faculty of Education at Monash University where she teaches in the post-graduate TESOL and Languages Education programmes. Her main area of research is Conversation Analysis which she has applied to the study of very young children's interactional development, to language alternation practices of teachers in the target language as medium of instruction, and to high stakes language testing. She is widely published and her most recent book (co-authored with Numa Markee) is titled *Conversation Analysis and language alternation: Capturing transitions in the classroom.*

Multilingualism and Language Mixing Among Singapore University Students

Kingsley Bolton and Werner Botha

Abstract This chapter discusses the dynamics of language mixing among Singaporean university students and how such mixing practices are an integral part of students' linguistic behaviour at university, both inside and outside formal classroom contexts. The study draws on a large-scale language survey of undergraduate students, as well as qualitative language data collected at one of Singapore's leading universities. The findings reveal how Singaporean students are able to shift between various languages inside and outside their classrooms, and may also have relevance for a range of other multilingual contexts, particularly in relation to language use in higher education.

Keywords English-medium education · EMI · Code-mixing · Code-switching · Language mixing · Multilingualism · Translanguaging · Globalization · Singapore

1 Introduction

There has been a great deal of linguistic research in Singapore over the past few decades, including various studies of language policies, multilingualism and varieties of English in Singapore. A number of these studies have highlighted the dichotomy between Standard Singapore English (SSE) and Colloquial Singapore English (CSE), other studies have adopted a features-based approach to SSE and CSE (frequently referred to as 'Singlish'), and yet others have investigated attitudinal issues in relation to identity (Bolton & Ng, 2014). Since the early 2000s, the government has sought to promote the use of 'correct' or 'standard' English through the national education system, as well through the initiative known as the Speak Good English Movement, which might be seen as much an ideological as a linguistic intervention (Wee 2014). According to Low's (2014) study of research from the 1970s to recent past,

K. Bolton (✉) · W. Botha
Nanyang Technological University, 48 Nanyang Avenue, Singapore 639818, Singapore
e-mail: KBolton@ntu.edu.sg

W. Botha
e-mail: WBotha@ntu.edu.sg

previous studies of Singapore English have prioritized such topics as "language in use" (including variation, pragmatics, language and literature, and culture and identity), "language education" (general education, writing, classroom discourse, using ICT, pronunciation, and so on), "linguistic features", "language policy/planning", "language acquisition", and "language pathology" (Low 2014, p. 448). Despite this relative abundance of research, however, one important gap in Singaporean linguistic research has been the description of the language practices of young people in Singapore today, especially in the context of higher education.

The obligatory use of English as a medium of instruction from primary school to university has been linked to the nation's success as an educational hub and as a global player in engineering, science and business (Bolton & Botha, 2017; Bolton, Botha & Bacon-Shone, 2017). In this context, perhaps, the use of English in higher education has appeared unproblematic and unremarkable, although the key argument we present in this study is that—despite official language policies—language practices are distinctly multilingual, and that students constantly switch between different languages and language varieties on their university campuses. These language practices may not at first be observable in the formal classrooms of these students, but become very evident if one studies the use of languages when students are socializing, or even when they are discussing their studies with each other.

In order to analyse the patterns of language use among university students, this study presents results of a research project conducted at a leading Singaporean university (henceforth identified as 'the University'). This study discusses the use of multiple languages within students' educational lives at the University. As mentioned earlier, while the Singaporean education system has been a documented success in its implementation of English as a medium of instruction, the one important and underexplored dimension has been the realities of language use in universities and how these compare with the aims and ideals of the official English-medium policy of the government and Singaporean higher education institutions. Broadly, for this study we sought to investigate the following research questions:

(1) What are the linguistic backgrounds of undergraduate students at the University?
(2) How do students use languages in their spoken communication within their formal classrooms?
(3) To what extent do students mix languages in their spoken communication in the University?
(4) How do students use languages in their academic context, outside the classroom?

In the next section, we present an overview of the sociolinguistic context of Singapore and of language use in Singapore's higher education system. We then discuss the research methods and research findings, including the prevalence of language mixing among students. Throughout the discussion of our research findings, we refer to various types of language alternation as 'language mixing', and, for various reasons, choose not to distinguish between 'code-mixing' and 'code-switching'.[1] In

---

[1] That being said, the notion of 'language mixing' in this article broadly follows the concept of Auer's (1990) 'code-alternation', as a cover term where different languages (or semiotic systems)

the closing sections of the article, we also comment on the relevance of our research results to current discussions of 'translanguaging' in such fields as applied linguistics, educational linguistics, and sociolinguistics.

2 The Sociolinguistic Context in Singapore

Singapore has four official languages: English, Mandarin, Malay and Tamil. English is used overwhelmingly as the working language of the government and is the official medium of teaching and learning in Singapore's education system. Mandarin, Malay, and Tamil are designated as 'mother tongues' and each ethnic group is assigned one of these and is taught their official mother tongue as a second language at school. Consequently, Chinese students typically learn Mandarin, Malays learn Malay, and Indians learn Tamil. Currently some 35% of the population reportedly speak Mandarin as a usual home language, while almost 37% reportedly use English, indicating that English and Mandarin are the predominant languages used in Singaporean society today. This is not surprising, given that in 2015 some 74% of the population were ethnically 'Chinese', some 13% were 'Malay', and some 9% were 'Indian' (SingStat, 2016).

3 Language Use in Singapore's Higher Education

There are six local universities currently in Singapore, providing degree courses to over 90,000 students. Besides these universities, there are five institutes in Singapore, known as polytechnics, providing three-year diploma programs to some 70,000 students (Singapore Ministry of Education 2015). A number of foreign universities have also established branch campuses in Singapore. The two largest comprehensive universities in Singapore are the National University of Singapore (or NUS) (with some 38,000 students), and Nanyang Technological University (or NTU) (32,000 students). These two universities have a relatively long history compared with the other institutions, and are the only local universities in Singapore that were founded before this century. NUS was established in 1980 and was followed by Nanyang Technological University in 1991, as well as four newer universities in the 2000s: Singapore Management University (2000), SIM University (2005), Singapore University of Technology and Design (2009) and Singapore Institute of Technology (2009). English is the medium of instruction at all of these institutions, which is also the case at all other levels of public education in Singapore (Bolton & Botha, 2017; Bolton et al., 2017).

---

are juxtaposed in ways that facilitate communication between interlocutors. One major reason for our use of the term 'language mixing' as a cover term is that differences between 'code-switching' and 'code-mixing' are often blurred in the vernacular speech of Singaporeans (see Botha 2019).

Two related studies on multilingualism in Singapore higher education, by Siemund, Schulz and Schweinberger (2014), Leimgruber, Siemund and Terassa (2018) have investigated the language backgrounds, language use, and language preferences of some 300 students in various types of institutions, including universities and polytechnics. The study concluded that English plays an important role in the lives of these students, that Colloquial Singapore English is an important identity marker for many of these students, and that most university students in their study were found to be either bilingual or trilingual. Another study by Chong and Seilhamer (2014) suggests that Singaporean Malay university students retain a strong sense of Malay identity, partly through the Malay language, even though English has become an integral part of their lives. Despite the fact that these studies have shed some light on the multilingual language practices of Singaporean university students, it still remains unclear how English-medium instruction (EMI) connects, or fails to connect, with the language backgrounds of these students, especially in the formal education context.

It is generally evident that English medium education in Singapore has been highly successful, to an extent unequalled by other nations in Asia, particularly in terms of promoting proficiency in English (Bolton, 2008; Bolton et al. 2017). Even so, we believe it is important to consider the wider multilingual ecology of Singaporean society, and the often complex multilingual worlds of Singaporean university students. At the University where this current study was conducted, for example, it is clearly evident that students often switch from more formal registers of English in the classroom to language mixing (routinely involving Singapore Colloquial English, Malay, Mandarin and Indian languages) in the corridors and cafeterias. It is in this context that we set out to investigate how the home languages of students, and how their personal language experiences intersect with their academic language needs at the University.

4 Methods

One aspect of the research presented in this article involved a large-scale sociolinguistic survey at a university in Singapore, while another aspect of the research involved ethnographic fieldwork that captured the sociolinguistic realities of language use of full time undergraduate students at the university. The response rate for the student survey was very high with some 8280 completed questionnaires, a number that represented 28.2% of the student population at the University. Of these students, 7575 were undergraduates and 705 were postgraduate students. The questionnaire was highly detailed, comprising 114 items, with sub-sections dealing with the personal characteristics of students, their linguistic and educational backgrounds, their reading practices, their writing skills, spoken communication, language mixing, presentation skills, online learning, self-assessment of language skills, and perceived areas of difficulty. The online surveys were carried out between October and December 2014, and the data were subsequently checked for consistency, and the undergraduate

Table 1 University undergraduate students and survey sample by residence status

Residence status	University	Survey
Singapore citizen	77.7%	71.5%
Singapore Permanent Resident	5.6%	4.9%
Non-Singapore citizen or Non-Permanent Resident	16.6%	21.0%
Missing	–	2.7%
	N = 23,155	N = 7717

Table 2 University postgraduate students and survey sample by residence status

Residence status	University	Sample
Singapore citizen	23.8%	14.3%
Singapore Permanent Resident	10.9%	4.7%
Non-Singapore citizen and Non-Permanent Resident	65.3%	74.3%
Missing	–	6.7%
	N = 6164	N = 705

results were weighted in order to correct for sampling bias.[2] At the undergraduate level, it was found that Engineering students were over-represented in the survey, and as a result, it was decided to weight the undergraduate survey results by College to match those of the general University population, and those results presented below reflect this weighting. It needs to be pointed out here that the focus in this article is on the results of undergraduate students, the vast majority of whom are either Singaporean citizens or Singaporean Permanent Residents (see Table 1), whereas the vast majority of postgraduates are international students (see Table 2), most notably from mainland China. This indicates that there are, in fact, two very different populations of students at the University, with very different language backgrounds. The issue of postgraduate students at the University has already been discussed in Bolton and Botha (2017), and the main concern in this article is on the multilingual language practices of the predominantly Singaporean undergraduate students.

In the second part of the study three undergraduate students (One Chinese, one Malay, and one Indian) from the University volunteered to participate in this part of the research, and each of these students agreed to act as the 'ego' (or main subject) of their respective social networks. All the members of these social networks were informed of the research and consent was obtained for gathering linguistic data for this project. It was explained to these students that some of their interviews and discussions with the main subject would at times be recorded, but that they would be aware of the situations when the recordings would be done. In order to protect the identities of the participants, these subjects were anonymised in the reporting of results related to this project. Once the final number of participants in the study was

---

[2] The statistical analysis was carried out with the generous assistance of Professor John Bacon-Shone from the Social Sciences Research Centre of The University of Hong Kong.

Table 3 Primary language of instruction in school

Primary language of instruction	Age (%)
English	88.1
Others	11.9
Total	100

confirmed, the main subject of each social network would meet members of their university social networks in social settings on the university campus (such as at a restaurant on campus or in their university dorm rooms) and record their discussions. The aims with these naturalistic recordings were to capture the patterns of language use between these students on the university campus, as well as to explore how these students use various languages and language varieties when discussing various aspects of their studies. After excerpts of the conversations between students were transcribed, a number of the students were invited to comment on their language use, and selections of their commentary are included in our discussions below.

5 Results

In this part of the chapter we present a description of various aspects of language use by undergraduate students in the domain of education. The results are discussed in terms of the research aims introduced above, where the first aim concerned the linguistic backgrounds of the students (Bolton et al. 2016). As can be seen from Table 3, undergraduate students overwhelmingly reported the use of English as a primary language of instruction in their schools, before coming to university, with almost 90% stating that English was used as the main language of teaching.

The home language acquisition background of these students is presented in Fig. 1, which indicates that a majority of students reported that their first language was Mandarin Chinese, or another language or language variety. Thus, although some 41% reported learning English, many more reported having learnt Chinese or another language as a first language. Nearly 60% of students also reported that they spoke Mandarin Chinese at home, compared with 50% who reported using English as a home language. It should be noted, however, that many students responded that they use more than one language or language variety at home (Fig. 2).

The multilingual home contexts of these students are visibly displayed in Fig. 3, which shows that nearly half of the students spoke more than one language variety at home with 12% of students reporting three or more languages as usual languages at home.

Another interesting finding concerned the students' self-reports of their 'most proficient language', with results indicating that the majority of undergraduate students felt most proficient in English, followed by some 30% who felt most proficient

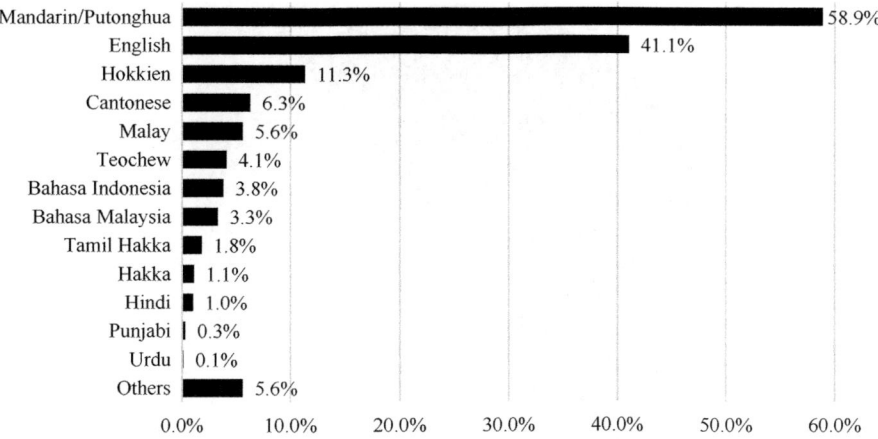

Fig. 1 First language learnt as a child

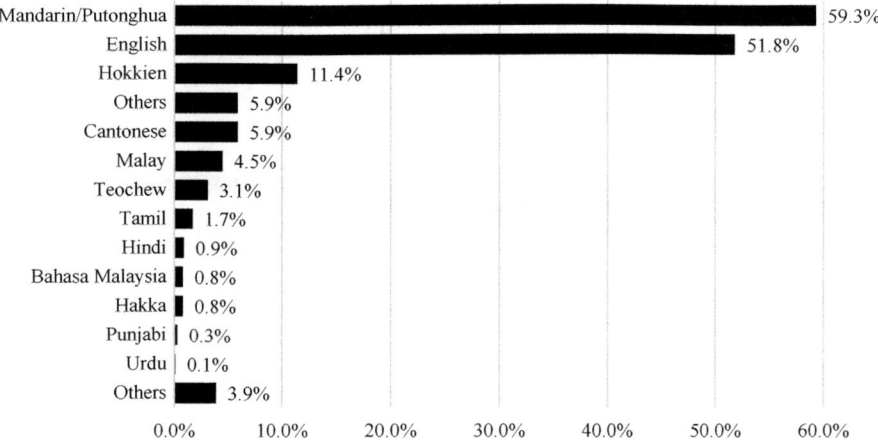

Fig. 2 Language(s) usually spoken at home

in Mandarin (see Fig. 4). Only 1.3 and 0.5% of the students stated that they felt most proficient in Malay and Tamil, respectively.

The results reported on in Fig. 4 are somewhat unsurprising, especially considering students frequent and prolonged exposure to English in their formal education, and the emphasis that is placed on English-medium education in Singapore (Bolton & Botha, 2017). Even at the University where this survey was carried out, it was found that English has a very strong presence in students' formal education, as can be seen in the results presented in Table 4. From these results it can be seen that, among other educational contexts, more than 95% of students reported that 'All/Almost all' of their lectures were conducted in English, strongly suggesting a clear and rigorous implementation of the EMI language policy in Singapore's higher education.

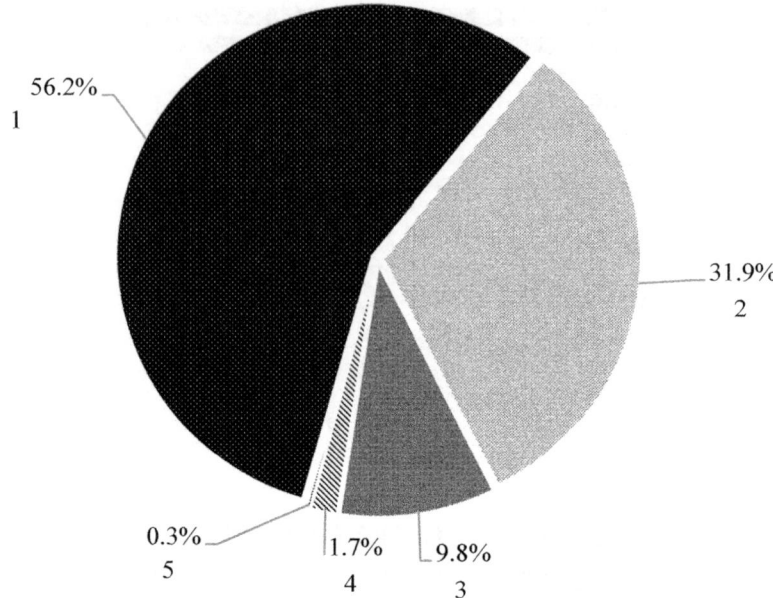

Fig. 3 Number of language(s) usually spoken at home

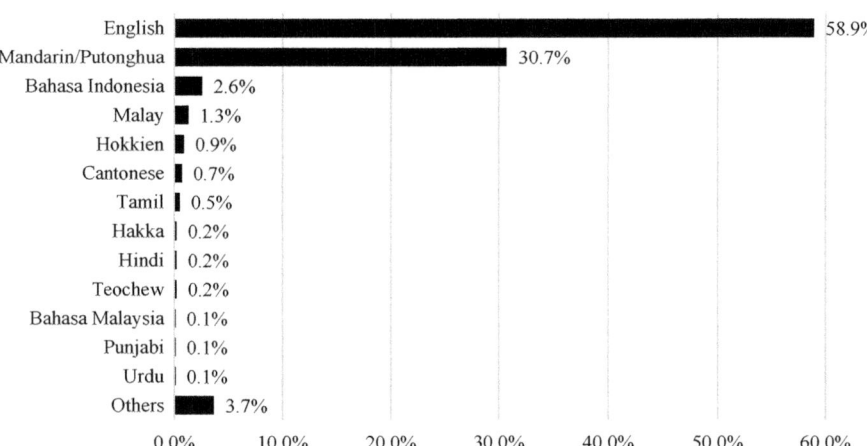

Fig. 4 Most proficient language

Multilingualism and Language Mixing Among Singapore University ... 51

Table 4 Use of English as a medium of instruction at NTU

	All (%)	Almost all (%)	About half (%)	Very few (%)	None (%)	Does not apply (%)
Lectures	90.2	5.3	1.3	1.7	1.0	0.4
Tutorials/seminars	90.4	6.1	1.1	1.9	0.4	0.2
Laboratory sessions/workshops	78.7	4.8	0.6	1.0	0.9	14.1

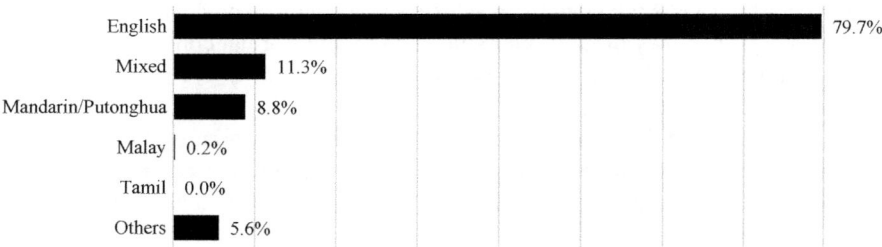

Fig. 5 Language used when discussing academic matters in the classroom

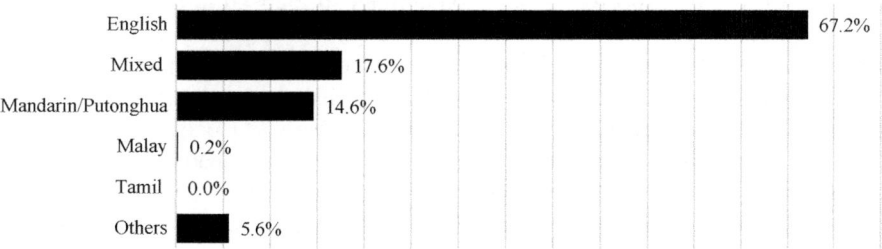

Fig. 6 Language used when socializing with classmates

These results are also confirmed by the reported use of languages when discussing academic matters in students' formal classroom contexts, where some 80% of the undergraduate students reported using only English. Nevertheless, one interesting finding here, however, is that just over 11% of these students reported mixing languages in the classroom, and nearly 9% indicated the use of Mandarin/Putonghua.

It is striking to note, as students leave their classrooms and begin socializing with their classmates—even while still in the academic context—their patterns of language use become more varied and their use of additional languages, language varieties and language mixing increases. The increasing use of additional languages is evident from students' self-reports on their use of languages (see Figs. 5 and 6), and the closer examination of the results concerning the mixing of languages add a further dimension of complexity to our analysis.

One of the questions in the survey asked students to report on the 'mixing of languages by other students', and nearly 50% of the respondents stated that other students mix languages when talking to fellow students inside the classroom. In a related question, undergraduates were also asked about their own language mixing practices, to which some 34% stated that they 'Always' or 'Very often' mixed languages with other students during classroom communication. Thus, the quantitative results from the survey indicate that language mixing practices are rather common among the undergraduate student population at the University. These results were confirmed by our qualitative research on this issue, which involved the recording and transcription of naturally-occurring conversations between students on campus. These recordings were intended to reveal the actual language practices of undergraduate students when they discuss their studies in more informal contexts on campus. The transcriptions in Extracts 1, 2 and 3, present data of direct relevance to the research issues set out in Sect. 1.

The first example, Extract 1, is taken from a conversation between three ethnic Chinese Singaporean students, who were in their second year of an Engineering program at the University. In this extract, they are talking about their homework and discussing Newtonian mechanics.

As can be seen from Extract 1, there evidently exists linguistic fluidity in the patterns of language use of the students concerned. The most striking feature presented in this extract is that specific subject content and specialized terms related to this topic of 'Coriolis derivative' are discussed in English, while the rest of the conversation is in Mandarin Chinese. The intersection between English and Mandarin in this exchange is also evident, and it is clear how English, as an educational language, connects with the language repertoires of these Chinese students, especially with regards to how topics related to specific content knowledge leads to a switch to a greater use of English among these students. One obvious explanation of this pattern of language mixing is the influence of EMI education on the linguistic repertoires of these students who are either bi- or multilingual.

A similar pattern of language behaviour was also observed among Malay students. In the second example, Extract 2, two Malay students from the Linguistics program are talking about question formats for one of their up-coming exams.

As can be seen from Extract 2, and similar to the Chinese students in Extract 1, the Malay students in this extract switch to English when discussing academic matters relating to their studies. In this extract, two students are discussing question formats in their exams, and switching was found to most frequently occur when specific reference is made to academic matters, such as when N switches more to English in line 129 to discuss question formatting (open-ended questions versus MCQ questions). Again, this patterning of language mixing is an obvious effect of EMI education on the linguistic repertoires of these students.

A different pattern of language use was observed among Indian students. In the third example below, Extract 3, two Indian students from the English Literature program are talking about one of their assignments.

In Extract 3 the two Indian students are talking about one of their assignments for one of their English Literature subjects. What is interesting in this exchange (and different from the Chinese and Malay students in Extracts 1 and 2) is that these students only use English when discussing their studies. In all of the recordings

Multilingualism and Language Mixing Among Singapore University ... 53

Extract 1 Conversation between three undergraduate Engineering students, discussing their homework

	JW:	Coriolis is sometimes *shi ni* spin *ni zhe ge* direction but Coriolis an opposite direction.. can be one.. when you walking into the circle. (Coriolis is sometimes *you* spin *your this* direction but Coriolis an opposite direction.. can be one.. when you walking into the circle.)
	T:	Orh=.
	JW:	<X X>@@ you say Coriolis *hen nan* visualize.. cannot *hen chao nan* visualize *de* it can go opposite of *ni de* spinning direction. (<X X>@@ you say Coriolis *very difficult to* visualize.. cannot *extremely difficult to* visualize [possessive] it can go opposite of *your* spinning direction.)
	J:	Okay.. *wo deng yi xia yao qu kan yi xia.* (Okay.. *I'll have a look later.*)
5	T:	Technically can just do the.. absolute time derivative shit.. like how they derive <X X>.
	J:	[<X X>.]
	T:	<X X> and absolute thing like your S right *bu shi..* let's say your distance *jiu shi* R VR right then you= differentiate it with respect to time then you come up with two terms.. R.. RER as in R.. to the power to the direction of ER *dui bu dui.* (<X X> and absolute thing like your S right *isn't it..* let's say your distance *it's just* R VR right then you= differentiate it with respect to time then you come up with two terms.. R.. RER as in R.. to the power to the direction of ER *is that right*)
	J:	Uh huh.
	T:	So you differentiate it.
10	JW:	But Coriolis *shi shen me ah?* R dot. (But *what is* Coriolis ah? R dot.)
	T:	No then *ni cong* velocity *zai chu lai.* (No then *from* velocity *it emerges.*)
	JW:	[R dot two dot] R dot theta dot.
	T:	So *ni kan* ah that term *jiu shi* uh= if you differentiate *bu shi bian cheng* R dot DR. (So *you see* ah that term *is* uh= if you differentiate *doesn't it become* R dot DR.)
	J:	Ah.
15	T:	Plus.
	JW:	*wei shen me ni nong dao jiang cheem.* (*Why do you have to make it so difficult.*)
	T:	[R theta] dot E theta.. @ that's why I read textbook.
	J:	[*ren jia kan* textbook *de*=.] ([*others refer to* the textbook [possessive]=.])
	T:	[*hui jia hai yao*] *kan* textbook. ([*go home and still have to*] *refer to the* textbook.)
20	J:	*kan* textbook *de*=. (*refer to the* textbook [possessive]=.)
	T:	I see how they derive the thing.
	JW:	[*suo yi shi*] R dot theta dot.. *shi ma?* ([*so it is*] R dot theta dot.. *is that right?*)
	T:	Ah.
	JW:	Coriolis.. okay okay then *wo ying gai dong le shi* R *suo yi shi* R cross theta *hai shi* theta cross R? (Coriolis.. okay okay then *I think I understand it now* R *so it's* R cross theta *or* theta cross R?)
25	T:	*mei you* cross. (*doesn't* cross.)
	J:	They still cross.. *you* cross. (They still cross.. *it does* cross.)
	JW:	Confirm cross.. coriolis confirm *shi* cross *de.* (Confirm cross.. coriolis confirm *it does* cross [possessive].)
	J:	Ah.
	JW:	*zhe ge zhe ge wo yong wo yong yuan hui ji de zhe ge* ^cross because theta you theta cross R give you opposite direction from cross. (*I will always remember that this will* ^cross because theta you theta cross R give you opposite direction from cross.)
30	T:	[Cross outward.]

Extract 2 Conversation between two undergraduate Linguistics students, discussing question types for their course exams

	S:	This sem..
	N:	Oh *kenape tak ambik* year 1? Year 1 was easier *sia*.. A lot of stuffs were easier in year 1 *sia* apparently. Astro=
		(Oh, *why didn't you take it in* year 1? Year 1 was easier *sia*.. A lot of stuffs were easier in year 1 *sia* apparently. Astro=)
	S:	No because I wanted to clear Gerpe this sem= so I don't have to..
	N:	Gamelan oh my God.. this year *aku dengar* Gamelan is *rabak gile*..
		(Gamelan oh my God.. this year *I heard* Gamelan is *quite bad*..)
	S:	*Tak= Aku* stress for previous sem also.. Stress *gile*..
		(*No= I was* stress for previous sem also.. Stress *crazy*..)
	S:	*Tapi dier dapat* A.
		(But, they got an A.)
	H:	Ya *Alhamdulillah*..
		(Ya, praise be to God..)
	N:	Yours *ade macam* open-ended question eh?
		(*Does* yours *have* open-ended question eh?)
130	S:	*Ade*.. Eh *takde*..
		(*Have*.. Eh *don't have*..)
	H:	*Kitorang kene* label *aje* like for=
		(*We just need to* label *just* like for=)
	N:	Label then MCQ *kan*?
		(Label then MCQ *isn't it*?)
	S:	Eh *taka de jugak yang kite kene* name some *kan*?
		(Eh *no, there are also those that we need to* name some *isn't it*?)
	N:	Ya like open-ended <X X>
	H:	Eh= oh ya=
	N:	Theirs is different *tau* apparently.. Theirs is no MCQ at all.. First part is the open-ended whatever one word one word.. Ah= answer..
		(Theirs is different *you know* apparently.. Theirs is no MCQ at all.. First part is the open-ended whatever one word one word.. Ah= answer..)
	H:	[Ah..]
	N:	Then the last part is explain what like *macam* essay-based ah.. Sort of like short answer questions..
		(Then the last part is explain what like *like* essay-based ah.. Sort of like short answer questions..)

between these Indian students only English was used. This can be explained in the context of language shift among the Indian community in Singapore, where, over the last few decades, this community has increasingly used English as a home language, instead of Tamil or other Indian language varieties, echoing Leimgruber's (2013, p. 7) claim that Tamil's "fate seems sealed" in Singapore, with now only around 3% of the population speaking Tamil as a home language (with around 9% of the population being Indian). Perhaps also compounding this shift is the high number of people in the Indian community who now have university degrees, the highest number of all the ethnicities in Singapore, with some 35% of Indians having obtained a university degree according to the 2010 census data, compared to some 22% of Chinese and 5.1% of Malays.

Extract 3 Conversation between two undergraduate English Literature students, discussing an assignment

25	S:	How's your essay coming?
	J:	Told you right, I haven't started
	S:	Huh= what were you doing all this while?
	J:	I was..reading up about the presentation thing..and also on..some of the essays <X X>
	S:	What you doing on ah..your presentation?
30	J:	Ah= we doing poetry..erm= Williams, Wallace Stevens and.. William Carlos William, the one we did in year one ah..the red wheelbarrow and everything
	S:	How come you all choose that one..its so done..to death
	J:	Huh?
	S:	Its so done to death
	J:	Ah= it doesn't matter lah=
35	S:	Yes it does
	S:	Oh just now Doctor Yong right..hmm= she was saying how we measure originality of thesis is not like ooh its been overdone…blah blah, what kind, what, what, need something new I can possibly say, she say maybe the orginity, originality can come from ah= how you engage with the= text and the secondary text cos it can be like oh these few authors talk about this but there is a= lap, lasse, lapse in the..I dunno why I cannot breathe right now @
	J:	@ I knew you had breathing problems

6 Discussion

In this section of the article, we discuss our findings concerning language mixing by undergraduates, in relation to both quantitative and qualitative data, before moving on to consider students' own explanations of language choice and language use at university. In addition, we also consider recent research on translanguaging, and question its applicability and utility in the Singapore context.

6.1 Language Mixing by Undergraduates

From the quantitative and qualitative results presented above, a number of interesting trends can be observed, which we will discuss below. After discussing the multilingual backgrounds of students in our survey sample, we consider the gap between the self-reported language practices of students in the formal classroom situations and their multilingual language practices outside their classes, but which relate to their language use in the educational context. After that we consider the bi- and multilingual language practices of Singaporean university students more broadly in the educational context.

From our survey, it is evident that Singaporean university students are typically from homes where more than one language or language variety is spoken at home, very often not English. This is also highlighted in Figs. 1 and 2 above which indicate that these students' first language learnt' is typically not English, but rather Mandarin Chinese or another language or language variety. The survey results shown in Fig. 2 indicate that only some 51% of the students reported speaking English usually at home. These results indicate that bilingualism and multilingualism is certainly the norm for most of these students, even for those students who regularly use English as a home language, but who are in regular contact with other languages and language varieties in the home context. One important finding mentioned above is that many of these students do not speak either only English or only Mandarin, or some other language variety as a home language, but rather use more than one language or language variety at home. However, what is evident here is that the use of English as an educational lingua franca in these students' school education certainly has an impact on their views about their proficiency in English, with nearly 60% indicating that they are most proficient in English, with only some 30% choosing Mandarin Chinese, just over 1% Malay, and only 0.5% Tamil.

Considering the language policy of Singapore higher education, it is perhaps unsurprising to find that English has such a strong presence in students' formal education, such as in their lectures, tutorials and seminars, laboratory sessions and workshops (as illustrated by Table 4). This indicates a clear and rigorous implementation of the EMI language policy in Singapore's higher education. However, once students start discussing academic matters with one another inside and outside their classrooms, there appears to be a noticeable increase in the use of other languages, with some 34% of undergraduates stating that they 'Always' or 'Very often' mixed languages inside their classroom discussions.

In this context, it appears that the Chinese and Malay students seem confident in language mixing practices when discussing aspects of their studies with one another. One factor here is that English seems to be typically used when students are directly referring to aspects of their studies, and has a clearly dominant presence in such interchanges, while other languages (such as Mandarin Chinese or Malay) are less salient in these interchanges. This would suggest that there is a strong impact of English as medium of instruction on the bi- and multilingual language repertoires of these students, where switches to academic terms and phrases are used more frequently as opposed to the more general language use of students. It needs to be pointed out that in this context, however, it appears that this type of language mixing typically only occurs in intra-ethnic communicative situations and where students know one another. In inter-ethnic communicative situations, or when students do not know one another well, English is typically used, most often in a variant of 'Singapore English'.

6.2 Explaining Language Mixing

As part of the qualitative research for this study, we also asked the students themselves to comment on and explain their own language mixing practices at the University. In the case of the Chinese students, one of the interlocutors, Michael, commented that one determinant of language choice was the home language background of the students concerned. In his own case, English was the main language of his family, and for that reason, he claimed not to mix languages very often, but noted that his classmates from Chinese-using homes preferred to use Mandarin, and he accommodated to them.

> I don't think I mix languages as much [...] but for people who are used to speaking Chinese at home, then they're more used to thinking in Chinese. So when we discuss like coursework, with friends who usually speak more Chinese right, I will try to use more [Chinese] and mix languages more to try and empathize a bit more with my friends. [...] Uh I really think it depends on who's talking to who lah, so if I were to speak to more English-speaking friends I would talk mostly in Singlish and English. (Michael, male, Singaporean Chinese undergraduate, Year 4 Engineering)

However, Michael also noted that the ethnicity of his interlocutors was also an important factor, because 'if I were to speaking to Malay friends I wouldn't use as much Chinese, but I would probably still use like a lot of English'.

Ethnicity was also an important factor in the case of the Malay students, although this was also influenced by friendship and the closeness of social networks, as one of the female undergraduates, Aisha, explained thus:

> Um, I think for us because we are Malay Singaporeans, so we use Malay in our language uh when we speak to each other because it kinda makes us very comfortable with each other and also um part of course because we know the Malay language. So it makes it um like there's a sense of solidarity I guess and to establish the fact that we are friends. Also, I will speak English more if I speak to someone who is a Malay but uh someone that I'm not close to. Um but for interacting with [my friends], we tend to use a lot of code-mixing uh in our conversations. (Aisha, female, Singaporean Malay undergraduate, Year 4, Linguistics)

In the third case, that of the Indian students, it was interesting to note that Rajesh reported that Indian students rarely, if ever, used Tamil (their official 'mother tongue'), and that this was just a language they learnt at school rather than using it in their everyday lives.

> On a personal basis it's been quite a number of years since I've formally uh like used Tamil in terms of relating to education. [...] Many Singaporean Indians also feel that the Tamil language is something that is used in school and in formal settings so to get your 'O' level grades. (Rajesh, male, Singaporean Indian undergraduate, Year 4, English literature)

Rajesh then went on to explain that when talking to other Indian students, the usual language of choice was 'Singlish', which was used for a range of different reasons, including the self-identification of these students as 'Singaporean' rather than 'Indian':

> I think it is more of a of my identity as being a Singaporean, not as an Indian um because [...] when two people if you are talking about like a business thing uh and you immediately um bond or click over Singlish, it becomes like a very natural conversation as opposed to having it uh in a proper English or proper formal kinda thing. (Rajesh)

As these extracts from the students' own explanations of their language behaviour and language mixing indicate, a range of different reasons may influence their language choice in their educational contexts, including home background, shared ethnicity, social distance, and claimed identity, all of which may be explained with close reference to the sociolinguistic history and contemporary dynamics of Singapore society. Our belief is that research of this kind has a great potential to expand our knowledge of language contact and language use in multilingual contexts, including higher education. Whether such behaviour is best described as 'language mixing', 'code-switching', 'code-mixing', or even the now-fashionable term 'translanguaging' is a question of debate.

6.3 'Translanguaging' or 'Language Mixing'

Over the last twenty years, but particularly during the last decade, the term 'translanguaging', as a synonymous or even replacement term for code-mixing, code-switching, or other terms related to language mixing has become extraordinarily popular in applied linguistic and sociolinguistic research. The first uses of the word, as is well known, can be traced back to the study of language use in Welsh schools in the 1990s (Williams 1996), and later popularized by a number of influential volumes on bilingual education, including Baker (2001), Canagarajah (2013), Garcia and Li (2014), so much so that what was originally a somewhat obscure term "is now a household name in international conferences, symposia and summer schools and the central topic of highly cited publications" (Jaspers, 2018, p. 1). Although this term has gained greatly in popularity, particularly with reference to elementary education in the US and community language schools in the UK, relatively few studies of translanguaging have been carried out in higher education. Research articles that have focused on university students have included Li's (2011) study which looked in detail at the 'flexible bilingualism' of three young Chinese students in London; Gu (2014) which investigated the negotiation of translanguaging practices (including code-switching and translation) by mainland Chinese students in the context of a Hong Kong university; a study by Hafner, Li, and Miller (2015) who mentioned translanguaging along with 'plurilingual practices' with reference to students' multi-modal group work at another university in Hong Kong; and a book chapter by Heugh, Li, and Song (2017) which studied the language practices of Chinese students at an Australian university. In the case of the latter study, it is ironically notable that although the authors valorize the term 'translanguaging' as an alternative to 'code-switching', when it comes to the methodological issue of coding their data, they plump for the descriptive labels of "code-mixing" and "code-switching" (Heugh et al., 2017, p. 273). The volume by Mazak and Carroll (2017) contains case studies on translanguaging in higher education from a wide range of societies, including Denmark, Hong Kong, India, Puerto Rico, South Africa, the Basque Country, the Ukraine, and the United Arab Emirates, although what exactly constitutes translanguaging in such societies varies considerably, and is perhaps more defined by activist ideology and rhetoric rather than detailed sociolinguistic description, as this quotation from Carroll bears witness:

> First and foremost, it is a language ideology or a bilingual lens through which citizens view the world. In taking bilingualism as the norm, this ideology runs counter to monolingual language ideologies that have dominated the rhetoric around nation building and institutions of higher education […] it is a lived theory of how authentic language actually plays out in

the lives of those who use more than one language. This lived theory exists in both formal and informal education in contexts worldwide [...where] educators can take a pedagogical stance to allow, advocate and implement translanguaging in their own classrooms. (Carroll, 2017, p. 181)

At another level, many accounts of translanguaging argue that the boundaries between languages are increasingly liquid given today's multilingual contact environments of super-diversity in an era of globalization, and that it is theoretically necessary to deconstruct the "idealized boundaries between languages and language varieties" (Li, 2018, p. 19). Whether or not this framework is applicable or indeed useful to the Singapore context, however, is a matter of debate and perspective at the very least. One riposte to the notion of linguistic fluidity in the Singapore context might highlight the salience of linguistic boundaries in the community as result of highly focused language policies which have, if anything, emphasized the borders between the four official languages (English, Mandarin, Malay and Tamil) rather than reducing or blurring them (Bolton and Ng 2014). Future studies on the language repertoires and language mixing practices of Singapore university students in various educational contexts may need to consider the applicability and relevance of a translanguaging framework in such contexts, an issue we aim to consider in greater detail in our own future research on the language practices of students in multilingual education in Singapore and across the Asian region.

7 Conclusion

It would certainly appear that even though the educational linguistic environment at the University where this study was conducted is dominated by English, multilingual language use is common and clearly evident among students on the campus, especially when they are discussing their studies, and where they have access to a range of languages and varieties. The use of English as the medium of education in Singapore is a complex issue, involving a number of important considerations. The first of these is the official language policy of the nation, where Singapore has been very successful in implementing its policy of English as the medium of teaching and learning at all levels of education. However, from a sociolinguistic perspective, another consideration involves the actual language practices of university students themselves, where 'English' in various forms may give way to language mixing, and related forms of language choice, as noted in a recent article on the language habits of Singapore students by Siemund et al., who assert that:

language use is no either/or-matter, but the product of a complicated mesh of factors comprising speaker competencies, preferences, attitudes and motivations, parameters of the communicative situation, and the topic of conversation. Singaporeans do not speak English *or* Singlish, Mandarin *or* Cantonese, Malay *or* Mandarin, or Mandarin *or* English. They typically command several codes. [...] Multilingualism may be regarded as a process not a state. (Siemund et al. 2014, p. 341, italics in original)

In the current study, we have expanded the scope of description by showing how the language practices of these students vary according to various situational conditions. In the teaching context, English is used almost exclusively as the medium of instruction, but as soon as students start communicating with one another, even in classroom discussions, there is an increased use of multiple languages and language varieties, including Colloquial Singapore English (or 'Singlish'). In this context of language mixing, we believe that an important consideration is the ethnicity of students, where students of the same ethnicity, and who know one another, skillfully and smoothly deploy language mixing as a key linguistic resource. Such types of language practices are most evident with ethnic Chinese and Malay students, and also in somewhat less visible but more subtle fashion with ethnic Indian students, who choose to use different varieties of Singapore English for different purposes. The results of this study are part of an ongoing research project investigating the use of languages in Singapore higher education. Relatively few studies of this kind have been previously carried out, particularly with reference to the sociolinguistic realities of students' actual language practices. It is hoped that this current study will pave the way for further research based on the rigorous analysis of sociolinguistic data, at both the macro- and micro-levels of investigation.

References

Auer, P. (1990). A discussion paper on code alternation. In European Science Foundation (Ed.), *Network on code-switching and language contact* (pp. 69–89). Papers for the Workshop on Concepts, Methodology and Data, Basel, January 12–13, 1990.

Baker, C. (2001). *Foundations of bilingual education and bilingualism*. Clevedon: Multilingual Matters.

Bolton, K. (2008). English in Asia, Asian Englishes, and the issue of proficiency. *English Today, 24*(2), 3–12.

Bolton, K., Bacon-Shone, J., Botha, W., Heah, C., Kathpalia, S. S., Li, S. Y., et al. (2016). *The communication needs of students at Nanyang Technological University. Survey report*. Singapore: Language and Communication Centre, NTU.

Bolton, K., & Botha, W. (2017). English as a medium of instruction in Singapore higher education. In B. Fenton-Smith, P. Humphreys, & I. Walkinshaw (Eds.), *English medium instruction in higher education in Asia-Pacific: From policy to pedagogy* (pp. 133–152). Cham: Springer.

Bolton, K., Botha, W., & Bacon-Shone, J. (2017). English-medium instruction in Singapore higher education: Policy, realities and challenges. *Journal of Multilingual and Multicultural Development, 38*(10), 913–930.

Bolton, K., & Ng, B. C. (2014). The dynamics of multilingualism in contemporary Singapore. *World Englishes, 33*(3), 307–318.

Botha, W. (2019). The functions of language mixing in the social networks of Singapore university students. *International Journal of the Sociology of Language*. In press.

Canagarajah, S. (2013). *Translingual practice: Global Englishes and cosmopolitan relations*. New York and Abingdon: Routledge.

Carroll, K. S. (2017). Concluding remarks: Prestige planning and translanguaging in higher education. In C. M. Mazak & K. S. Carroll (Eds.), *Translanguaging in higher education: Beyond monolingual ideologies* (pp. 177–185). Bristol: Multilingual Matters.

Chong, E. L. J., & Seilhamer, M. F. (2014). Young people, Malay and English in multilingual Singapore. *World Englishes, 33*(3), 363–377.
Garcia, O., & Li, W. (2014). *Translanguaging: Language, bilingualism and education*. Hampshire: Palgrave Macmillan.
Gu, M. (2014). From opposition to transcendence: The language practices and ideologies of students in a multilingual university. *International Journal of Bilingual Education and Bilingualism, 17*(3), 310–329.
Hafner, C. A., Li, D. C. S., & Miller, L. (2015). Language choice among peers in project-based learning: A Hong Kong case study of English language learners' plurilingual practices in out-of-class computer-mediated communication. *The Canadian Modern Language Review, 71*(4), 441–470.
Heugh, K., Li, X., & Song, Y. (2017). Multilingualism and translanguaging in the teaching of and through English: Rethinking linguistic boundaries in an Australian University. In B. Fenton-Smith, P. Humphreys, & I. Walkinshaw (Eds.), *English medium instruction in higher education in Asia-Pacific: From policy to pedagogy* (pp. 259–279). Cham: Springer.
Jaspers, J. (2018). The transformative limits of translanguaging. *Language & Communication, 58*, 1–10.
Leimgruber, J. R. E. (2013). *Singapore English: Structure, variation, and usage*. Cambridge: Cambridge University Press.
Leimgruber, J. R. E., Siemund, P., & Terassa, L. (2018). Singaporean students' language repertoires and attitudes revisited. *World Englishes, 37*(2), 282–306.
Li, W. (2011). Moment analysis and translanguage space: Discursive construction of identities by multilingual Chinese youth in Britain. *Journal of Pragmatics, 43*, 1222–1235.
Li, W. (2018). Translanguaging as a practical theory of language. *Applied Linguistics, 39*(1), 9–30.
Low, E.-L. (2014). Research on English in Singapore. *World Englishes, 33*(4), 439–457.
Mazak, C. M., & Carroll, K. S. (Eds.). (2017). *Translanguaging in higher education: Beyond monolingual ideologies*. Bristol: Multilingual Matters.
Siemund, P., Schulz, M. E., & Schweinberger, S. (2014). Studying the linguistic ecology of Singapore: A comparison of college and university students. *World Englishes, 33*(3), 340–362.
Singapore Ministry of Education. (2015). Higher education division. Retrieved from http://www.moe.gov.sg/about/org-structure/hed/.
SingStat. (2016). *General household survey 2015*. Singapore: Department of Statistics, Ministry of Trade & Industry. Retrieved from http://www.singstat.gov.sg/publications/publications-and-papers/GHS/ghs2015.
Wee, L. (2014). Linguistic chutzpah and the Speak Good Singlish movement. *World Englishes, 33*(1), 85–99.
Williams, C. (1996). Secondary education: Teaching in the bilingual situation. In C. Williams, G. Lewis, & C. Baker (Eds.), *The language policy: Taking stock* (pp. 39–78). Llangefni, UK: CAI.

Kingsley Bolton is Professor of English Linguistics at Nanyang Technological University, Singapore. He has published widely on English in the Asian region, language and globalization, sociolinguistics, and world Englishes. He is Co-editor of the journal World Englishes, and Series Editor of the new Routledge book series, Multilingual Asia.

Werner Botha is Assistant Professor at Nanyang Technological University in Singapore. His academic interests include the use of English in Asian higher education, educational linguistics, multilingualism, and language variation, with particular reference to the Asian region. Recent publications include research articles on the spread and use of English in China's higher education, sociolinguistic variation in Cantonese and language variation in Singapore.

Educational Globalization and the Creation of Split Identities

François Victor Tochon

> *What happens when, by virtue of being newly immersed in another culture and another language, we realize that we are being viewed in light of a set of presuppositions that make different beings of us? (Tochon, The Foreign Self)*

Abstract Media of instruction may value the other culture to the detriment of the local culture and develop identification processes that have consequences on various stakeholders in terms of cultural and identity capital. This comparative and international Education study focuses on three cases that illustrate how multilingual settings impacted the sense of identity of language teachers in Asian contexts. It also explores how phenomena such as cultural inclusion, immersion, and the transcultural are enmeshed in the creation of global identities. They may create a split between the first language and culture and global culture. Internationalization has a deep effect on people of the upper middle class who tend to situate their sense of belonging in an imaginary that projects their future outside their country. The emphasis on English as the world dominant language tends even to modify local identities and places the source of economic attraction, pride and the sense of worth outside the Nation-State. The exception may be in bilingual settings where both linguacultures are welcome and respected, taught, and integrated.

Keywords Case studies · Chinese · Culture · English · Foreign self · Globalization · Identity · Media of instruction · Symbolic capital

---

F. V. Tochon (✉)
University of Wisconsin-Madison, Madison, USA
e-mail: ftochon@education.wisc.edu

1 Language Education on Slippery Ideological Slope

While Transnational Education is now regularly crossing 'the West' and 'the East,' English under the disguise of the internationalization of Higher Education increases academic monolingualism with the growing number of English-only packages, and changes academic values in Asia to the point of changing identities. Le-Ha (2017) demonstrates that Asia chooses to go with Western ideals; its universities are seeking an affiliation with the West in the context of regional growth, global trends, and commercialization of education. As notes De Costa (2018, online), "both the host institution and host country become stepping stones as these students aspire to eventually move on to the West."

In this Yearbook chapter, I focus on three cases unveiling how much global reforms internationalizing education impacted the sense of identity of language teachers in Asian contexts. Indeed, internationalization and study abroad have an effect on the teachers, most of whom are of the upper middle class and tend to situate the sense of who they are in an imaginary that projects their future outside their country. The sense of being out-of-place in one's own country suggests that a colonization of the mind is happening, in which cultural capital from abroad creates new bonds that may undermine the sense of local belonging and re-shaping the social contract outside the nation-state. Subtle (and less subtle) incentives to assimilate to 'the West,' are present in medias of instruction and instructional experiences, whether produced locally or not. They tend to undermine local values while giving primacy to the other culture to the point of scaffolding what Tochon (2003) defined as the foreign self. The foreign self is the result of the accumulation of foreign cultural capital that creates a hybrid, transnational and potentially transplanted self through imaginary futures of prospective migration.

1.1 Instructional Resources and Experiences in the Game of Valuing and Devaluing

Instructional designers and study abroad planners are most often aware of the overt goals of the curriculum policies they contribute to create but may not be alerted to the impacts and the covert implications of policy enactment, and the implicit side-effects of their educational policies might have. "Overt Language Policies refer to those language policies that are explicit, formalized … and manifest. Covert Language Policies… refer to language policies that are implicit, informal, unstated, de facto, grass-roots and latent" (Shohamy, 2006, p. 50). Most research focuses on the rationales for overt policies and their use for progress and reforms, yet a large scope of impacts is understudied, affecting the derivation process from centralized policy making to decentralized regulatory procedures and public information, which may have adverse effects on the very goals of the policies being proposed. As well, the way overt policies are implemented by local regulators may pursue covert goals that are implicit or that might have covert implications that create side effects in certain populations. The way policy change is announced and implemented, may impact the reception of the change in the target populations.

Today, most policies and their regulations are systemic in the sense that they aim at maintaining order through a bureaucratic system rather than protecting human, civil and social rights and promoting humane values. A policy values certain actions and, in the same stroke, it devalues other functions. It disempowers as much as it may empower. Instructional media as well as globalization policies enter the same binary logic of *do*s and *don't*s imposed to people whatever their context. Language education policies enacted in study abroad and instructional media may divide and split populations. For example, a Scholarship Council may sponsor study abroad for younger teachers rather than older ones. The category of younger and older teachers splits two populations of teachers as those having value for the future and those who have none. Inclusion, as a category of meaning, creates, in its own definition, a form of exclusion. Popkewitz, Diaz, & Kirchgasler (2017) study how the systems of reason underlying schooling processes embody historically generated standards about what is to be expressed, enminded, and acted upon. Educational worldviews create issues of power, as well as political, and social exclusion. The transnational perspectives interrelate with curricula and how education orders and divides what is thinkable and doable. The authors argue that taken-for-granted conceptions of educational reform produce differences which, at the same time, include and exclude. Thus policies that aim to prevent splits *create splits* by the mere fact that they impose a form of definition across groups of people. Naming implies making differences. For example, creating a law against dividing people may create the division it is naming.

Media of instruction are the tools of broader and sometimes covert policies. They are part of the curriculum game of valuing and devaluing certain contents, certain attitudes, and certain people. For instance, defining language competency entails specifying who is incompetent. The criteria being used may not relate to proficiency. This is a crucial side effect of any defining process, as the definitions are imposed in the form of regulations and policies and are then formatted into textbooks, evaluations, and instructional experiences. As Shohamy (2006, p. 93) demonstrated, language tests associated with instructional media are "a set of mechanisms which are used in subtle ways to manipulate language and create de facto language policies." They are "imposed by groups in power to affect language priorities, language practices and criteria of correctness often leading to inclusion and exclusions and to perpetuate ideologies" (ibid). Instructional media are powerful as they manipulate language behaviors: What languages should be valued? What content and methods of teaching should be used? How to select a corpus of study? Authorities manipulate languages through instructional media in (a) determining the prestige and status of languages; (b) standardizing and perpetuating the language of correctness; and (c) suppressing language diversity.

Examples are numerous and may go from testing College admission in Hebrew with Arab populations, forcing Turkish teachers of English to use British textbooks promoting neoliberal ideologies that are contrary to their belief system, using French textbooks in Elementary school in the French West Indies to eradicate Creole. The language of correctness imposes dominant values and encourages uniformity. As Shohamy suggests (ibid, p. 93), instructional mediation lends "apparent objectivity to judgments based on prescriptive ideologies." School textbooks have their own genre based on simplification (Tochon, 2000), they may "sciencify" discrimination and convey values veiled as facts and evidence. In a similar way, when knowledge of a foreign language is a condition for accessing higher education, the policies are de facto de-legitimizing people because of their not knowing of the language and raises the foreign language to the rank of national value, bringing colonialism in the classroom. Some provinces like Zhejiang province in China (Hong, 2018) are trying to modify this trend in training English majors to learn about Chinese culture in the English language, which in turn may be used as a tool to bring Chinese cultural capital to the Anglo world.

1.2 The Divided Self

Our concepts of normality rest on implied norms that derive from our surrounding culture. Curricula are not exempt from this normative power. Curricula create cultural norms, and "normalize" behavior. Learned knowledge as well as life experiences amalgamate as storied complexes accessible for retrieval (Holland, Holyoak, Nisbett, & Thagard, 1994). They become constitutive of identities.

Identity (what one views as oneself) depends heavily on cultural settings; development depends on stimulation from the environment. The self depends on its interrelation with its setting for its structuring. Freud (2010) had provided a fully developed theory of the genesis of identity, which is very close to the social-interactionist principles of Vygotsky (1978). He characterized the sense of self as a layer of memory produced through social interaction. One can view the ego as an organ that represents the reality it has internalized following on numerous interactions with the world. Sandwiched between the requirements of the world and the requirements of its own drives, it seeks to reconcile them, organize them, and make them compatible in a productive fashion. Since it represents reality (the influence of the surrounding world), the role of the ego is to influence the outside world to govern the id and its tendencies.

Jung (1960) proposed the notion of the complex as foundational in personality theory. Complexes are normal constituents of the psyche. Experience leaves mental and emotional marks. These ideational-affective kernels are emotionally charged phenomena acquired over the course of personal experience. They are the kernels of rational, affective, or symbolic representations of a situation. Jung's theory of complexes explains the existence of multiple "egos" and the fragmentation of identity associated with experiential adjustment and acculturation. It explains "personality code switching," when an individual has the impression of changing personalities along with languages or cultures. It explains the feeling, during certain periods of one's life, that one may have become foreign to oneself. Complexes are the product of experience. Thus a delicate process of attaining a balance occurs when you assimilate the elements of another culture: To the extent that these are poorly assimilated, they can form autonomous complexes and become antagonistic to the central identity. Complexes emerge from social experience and constitute, in a sense, life lessons that need to be digested.

The issue of the self as stranger and truth telling as a form of identity research was central in Laing's (1960) quest. This anti-psychiatrist taught the importance of group and community influence in identity formation. Laing (1967) melded phenomenology and psychiatry in order to free humans from the straitjacket of social conformity. He redefined normality by suggesting that the self's experience contradicts the normalness of socially accepted experiences. True normality is found at the end of an inner voyage, a descent into oneself to be freed from the pressure of society. It is a process that reverses the false values one has adopted through conformity. For Laing, the deepening of experience unveils the self.

Thus both Jung and Laing bring interesting perspectives on the divided self that may be used in the understanding of translingual and transcultural phenomena in search for a new Self. The uniqueness of such experiences is present in all three cases analyzed in this chapter.

1.3 Curriculum and Instruction and Immersion as Socialization

It is important to evaluate the impact of new practices on the sense people make of themselves, as in particular crosscultural practices may change "one's position relative to socially identified others" and thus develop what Holland, Lachicotte, Skinner, and Cain (1998, p. 125) have defined as positional identities: the "imaginings of self in worlds of action." Media of instruction as well as situated experiences of immersion are powerful instruments of socialization, and they play a role in creating identities. Identity is a complicated concept that is shaped and reshaped by the narratives of experience that people tell about themselves and hear from others about themselves (Connelly and Clandinin, 1999). It constitutes the way one defines, recognizes, and differentiates oneself from others: "personal identity deals with questions that arise about ourselves by virtue of our being people" (Olson, 2010, p. 1). Thus, socialization is key in identity development (Bourdieu, 2008). Wenger (2008) considered identity as situated practice in a social context, constantly re-negotiated as a part of community formation. Access to another language and culture develops new imaginaries.

"Language learning can be a way to retain one's identity or a threat to one's identity" (Yen, 2000, p. 33, in Chuang, 2017). Instruction provides information on what is correct to believe in. Textbooks operate a selection of contents that are highlighted as exemplary or particularly valuable. Medias of instruction create truths, and provide the rightful way to speak about things and consider people (Gay, 2003). Most often than not, English medias of instruction exhibit cultural contents that are "narrowly confined to White middle-class cultures in Western English-speaking countries" (Yim, 2007, p. 43). Chuang (2017, p. 63) notes that very few Blacks and Hispanics are represented in the textbooks she analyzed. Furthermore, such media convey implicit or explicit neoliberal ideologies. Thus Anglicization may appear as a tool for economic ideologies that are present in watershed in its medias of instruction.

To sum up, through learning experiences in the target linguaculture, identities are reshaped by the contacts with other worldviews through instructional experiences. In a similar way, guided instruction may preformat and reshape values that become foundational in identity change. For instance, Chinese teachers who migrate may soon perceive that their identity is changing in relation to their new environments once they have passed the initial phase of culture shock (Wang, Liyanage, & Walker, 2019; Zhu, 2015).

1.4 Culture Clash and Symbolic Capital

Learning a language is more than learning language forms. It entails a form of experiential apprenticeship of linguaculture (Blyth, 2015; Tochon, 2014) while accessing its symbolic capital. Language, culture, knowledge, and immersive spaces are intertwined (Skutnabb-Kangas, Maffi, & Harmon, 2003). Each linguaculture offers its own perspective and experiences. Language is connected to life, communities, and life as a whole (Harrison, 2018).

Symbolic capital, a term coined by Bourdieu (1984), refers to the resources available to a person or accumulated through the fulfillment of social obligations valued in the culture, which confer to that person honor, prestige or recognition. As a particular case of symbolic capital, the social assets of a person (her education, intellectual achievements, style of speech and dress, etc.) express her cultural capital. Cultural capital promotes social mobility. In terms of social and cultural capital, the covert implications of policies for mobility may be far reaching. De Costa (2018, online) notes that:

> Students are generally viewed as customers in this financially lucrative enterprise where English is often the medium of instruction. As a consequence, English becomes a commodity, a means toward realising an end that can potentially have negative social implications. One major implication is the reification of the (white) Western native English instructor whose variety of English and race are valued over the local variety of English used by local instructors. Put simply, a negative outcome of Transnational Education is that it can promote institutional racism through the adoption of 'rent-a-foreigner' hiring practices. More often than not, these foreign instructors are also paid more than their local counterparts to do the same job.

Medias of instruction may be understood as technologies that use institutionalized binaries, such as new/old, traditional/modern and normal/deviant that tend to separate the superior and the inferior. Such binaries associated with institutional categories act as power tools and impact identity formation; they determine and generate social stratifications. The connection of certain attributes, conceptual categories or qualities to certain features, events, objects or people have a historical background in which the categories of truth-production manifest fields of power relations. The reiteration of such institutional patterns of truth-statements is involved in the process of truth-production that characterizes medias of instruction. This is how cultural capital is related to economic capital.

1.5 Identity Implications of Language Instruction Experiences

Speaking multiple languages equips a person with communicative flexibility, that is, the "ability to adapt strategies to the audience and to see the signs, both direct and indirect, so that the participants are able to monitor and understand at least some of each other's meaning" (Gumperz, 1982, p. 14). *Identity capital* is an extension of Bourdieu's framework (Moje & Luke, 2009). For example, Beynon and Dossa (2003) found that teachers of Chinese and Punjabi ancestries 'market' their language abilities differently, focusing on resources such as learning grammatical rules and norms at school, or communication at home and in the community. Language as identity capital is further complicated by the individual's degree of fluency and mastery.

Curriculum policy decisions regarding language experiences and instructional media create priorities that impact identities. For example, two decades after the Kuomintang (Chinese Nationalist Party) came to Taiwan, the National Institute for Compilation and Translation was established to regulate and standardize national textbooks. The educational goals were part of the 1976 national curriculum:

> To help students understand the origin of Chinese civilization; to discuss Chinese geography, history, and the cultural diversity in China; to study how the Three Principle of the People by Dr. Sun Yat-Sen—nationalism, democracy, and livelihood—were fulfilled in Taiwan; to define Taiwan as a revival base for the KMT government to reunify China in the future; and to develop loyalty to Chinese nationalism. (Su, 2006, p. 43)

Nowadays, Taiwan is taking different curriculum decisions. Chuang (2017) overviews this history: Taiwan's status has yet to be fully recognized in the international arena. Young people in Taiwan have long been taught to learn the history of China rather than Taiwan. Minorities learned about themselves through the majority's instructional media. "When taught to learn about one's own culture in such a way, people tend to become confused about their identities, unsure of whether they should consider themselves Taiwanese, Chinese, both, or something else" (ibid, p. 18). Curriculum, as enacted through instructional medias, becomes the "culture's medium of social identity construction" (Mao, 2008, p. 585). Because media of instruction offer a split of identity between the East and the West (metaphorically speaking), Taiwanese have developed a sense of double identity, which is alluded to in several studies (Sung and Yang, 2009).

In her dissertation on "Imbalanced Cultural Representations of Learners' Experiences and Identities in Locally-Grown English Textbooks," Chuang (2017) analyzed and evaluated five textbooks used in Taiwan high schools to teach English; all five complete sets of textbooks were published locally. She explored qualitatively and quantitatively the way cultural features are "highlighted, hidden, revered, or devalued." How culture and textbook are enmeshed in implicit arguments of the value of each culture support her analysis of what has been neglected in creating and selecting instructional materials. Faint grain analysis indicated how symbolic meanings were conveyed through images and the choices of colors. The results for the analyses revealed a staggering imbalance between what and how items of the West and of the East are included in Taiwanese textbooks. Similarly, surveys demonstrated a preference for objects, people and features from the Anglo world.

Here are some patterns that were uncovered in Chuang's study (pp. 86–87, excerpts):

- "presenting Western items more extensively and more frequently while presenting Eastern items as trivial, supplemental accessories;
- associating lighter colored skin or hair with positive traits and positive actions while associating darker colored skin or hair with negative traits and negative actions;
- cloaking a seemingly negative past in a positive outcome when it involved Western items, but smearing a negative outcome over a seemingly positive past for Eastern items;
- portraying Westerners as the ones that others sought after for permission and advice while portraying Easterners as the ones that sought for such permission and advice;
- providing misleading information about Eastern items… and maybe even develop beliefs, about the respective cultures; and
- allowing Eastern characters to put up with belittlement and degradation coming from others without much, if any, rebuttals and refutation."

As a reminder, the study focused on textbooks created locally by five major textbook companies in Taiwan. What is surprising is the pattern "of portraying Westerners as the ones from which others requested recognition, permission, acceptance, and advice while portraying Easterners as the seekers of such tokens of value" (p. 99), which was analyzed in terms of "symbolic annihilation," a concept coined by Gerbner and Gross (1976) for visual media. Symbolic annihilation may be an extreme interpretation. Shifting identities may fluctuate, undecided between two cultures and the nascent attempt at re-defining their own. Such redefining phase may entail a period of interrogation on the cultural self and its choices, rather than annihilation. It may, as in the case of Korea, lead to new form of cultural assertiveness.

The situations I will examine in this chapter stem for a sense of in-between-ness induced by situations of hegemony and dominance in cultural capital, instructional media, and immersion experiences abroad. Education values rooted in Confucianism have motivated Asian people to pursue "learning which is traditionally believed to be the best way to attain virtue and wisdom and accomplish political and financial success" (Jahng, 2013, p. 73). However, learning practice may change identities that are reshaped by the contacts with the Western world through English communication. These contacts are all about enactments and experiences. Indeed Liyanage, Walker and Weinmann (2016) note that teacher beliefs and attitudes vis-à-vis other linguacultures may be shaped by policy discourses as experienced in enactments rather than implementations of intercultural policy. For example, regarding English teaching, Taiwanese schools prefer hiring foreign teachers over Taiwanese teachers of English. The tendency has been for a long time to value cultural features that are not from Taiwan. This situation has long term effects on identity processes. This chapter provides examples of this phenomenon. How do language teachers and educators perceive this impact of internationalization, multilingualism and multiculturalism in their own lives and profession? This is a central question in this study.

2 Research Methods

This study explores the perceived impacts of multilingual experiences in the personal and professional lives of language teachers, and how they construct meaning of the situation they live considering the trends of globalization and the impact of foreign languages in their country. Language education experiences associated with globalization have personal and professional impacts on various educational stakeholders (language teachers and teacher educators) who make sense of the current reforms and conceptualize phenomena such as inclusion, migration, multilingualism and the transcultural in terms of their personal and professional identities.

This researcher is regularly giving lectures in various States and countries, which provides opportunities to meet with language educators. During such stays, there are opportunities to casually meet with language teachers and teacher educators who have unique information on the curricula and reforms in their locations as well as globally. They agreed to share their perceptions of the current changes and the standardization of language education. 175 language teachers and educators of 12 countries shared their perceptions of the current changes and the standardization of language education. The study was exempted from Institutional Review Board approval, as the data collection was unobtrusive, anonymized, and not related to specific institutions.

To benefit from these face to face contacts for the purpose of research, open thematic interviews were the pretext of case studies with a focus on narratives of experience, lived anecdotes and critical incidents. Typically, the researcher met language educators for an in-depth and meaningful conversation (Feldman, 1999; Walsh, 1997). The questions dealt with past and present experiences with globalization, language education experiences, and how the changes impacted the personal and professional lives of the participants.

With the interviewees' oral assent, the anonymous conversations were audio recorded or detailed notes of the conversation were taken and transcribed. Then the narratives of experience were organized in a way to increase their cohesion to become standalone narrative cases. The sections that follow present three cases that provide examples of some impacts of globalization and education experiences on Asian teachers of English. The participants' fake names are:

Case 1: Bai-Ju, an English instructor and teacher educator in a University of mainland China;
Case 2: Luo, a male English instructor who lives in Yanbian, a region of China that is bilingual Korean and Chinese; and
Case 3: Anita, a Bilingual Education, English Elementary and Middle School teacher in Taiwan.

The cases were selected for the multilingual experiences of the participants and idiosyncratic positions due to their cultural substrates, life experiences, and locations, as expressed in our conversations.

3 Three Case Studies

I shall present here three cases that provide examples of some impacts of globalization and changes related to curriculum and immersion experiences abroad on the personal and professional identities of Asian teachers of English.

3.1 CASE 1 Bai-Ju, English instructor and educator in China

The first case with Bai, English instructor in a major Chinese university, suggests deep changes in her sense of identity as a person and as a language instructor, asking new questions about relationships in her own culture, social spaces and privacy, peace of mind as a single Chinese mother and family choices, the submissive role imposed by institutions, and the sense of feeling off-track, having become an outsider to her own culture.

> English changed my life totally: what I am and how I am dating. It is part of me, English defines me. It is part of me, it is a carrier of values and cultural values.
>
> I am still yellow inside, but I see things differently. I also had the experience of living abroad, one year in Florida, and I had a hard time to re-adjusting here, for example to the traffic, how to cross the road. It is completely different. We have less space, the space is crowded. We have much less privacy.
>
> I sometimes feel like an outsider. Like… some traditional values, you do not identify with them anymore. Like: a woman needs to get married before 30 years old. You want more equality rather than being submissive. We argue with men a bit more, it makes our life a bit harder.
>
> I still feel more Chinese. I can bear this situation, because I am 10 years older. I can survive with a decent life, keeping things at peace. Maybe one day I will breakdown. I cannot bear the burden of work as a working mother, the burden of family, of multitasking and keeping smiling. Oh! Each aspect of globalization defines me. It is my way of making a living, to see more, enlarge my vision, and to be more friendly, hospitable. I learned to put up with more. I have become the iron lady.
>
> English has made me an outsider. It made it impossible for me to find a husband: in the dating market, Chinese want a virtuous woman, I am off track. It is difficult to find someone

with whom I can discuss. I have dated a (foreign) boy and a (foreign) guy, at the end you still see the cultural gap: who should pay the bill, or your relationship with your parents-in-law. Now when someone asks me: "Should I date a foreigner?" I'd say think twice. But Chinese guys find me too autonomous. I need someone who is more open, and willing to learn new values, and tolerant to difference. I developed a cosmopolitan identity that is nowhere.

3.2 CASE 2 Luo, lives in a bilingual region of China

The second case is a case of bicultural integration, after mother-tongue Korean education in a bilingual prefecture of China, Luo developed Chinese as his second language and then English, while exploring later Japanese and Russian. Multilingualism helped him being flexible with textbooks and instructional media, skipping chapters or changing their order and adding online resources. As a College English teacher, Luo is competing with mobile phones that bring more knowledge fast. Luo's sense of identity is well grounded in his first language and culture which he uses daily, as well as Chinese which is part of his integrated culture. A sense of wholeness is expressed in his reflections. No conflict is perceived in his sense of being two in one, as a Korean Chinese citizen. This is an example of successful integration of the UNESCO rule requiring mother tongue education for minorities until 4th grade.

> I am Korean Chinese and my first language is Korean. Chinese is my second language, English is my first foreign language. At the University I learned Japanese for one year and I also did one year of Russian. I learned English for 20 years from 2d grade and middle school to now. All my basic education was in Korean schools. I studied in Korean. In this Autonomous region some parents want their children to go to Chinese school but I do not like that because I am Korean. My son goes in a Korean school.
>
> I was taught Chinese as a subject-matter from 2d grade, not through an immersion school. But Korean children play on the playground with Han (Chinese) children, they watch TV and thus learn Chinese outside their home and school. Here it is our home. There is no feeling of antagonism vis-à-vis Han people: we are integrated.
>
> Our identity is linked to our mother tongue, but our nation is China. When we watch a Korean team and a Chinese play soccer together, we support the Chinese soccer team, not the Korean team. The English textbooks are chosen by the teachers. We first think: what type of students do we have? They need to be prepared for the test. So we choose the textbook according to the level of the students.
>
> I can also change textbook during the semester, I can manage that because they are non-English majors. I go across all chapters. Sometimes I give homework with online resources, asking a composition about the favorite foods or activities or they may write a Power Point that they can show to the class. We teach to test because of the examinations. The online homework is for their normal grade. At the end of the semester, there is a final exam. I do it myself and I show it to other teachers to see if they feel that it is OK, before giving it to the class. I feel the students of the 1990s and those of today did not change much. Many are not motivated. The young generations of non-English majors are less motivated than English majors, but it depends upon the teacher's dynamics: if the teacher is well prepared and likes the discipline taught, it makes a difference. They get everything today on their smart phones.

3.3 CASE 3 Anita, Elementary and Middle School Bilingual Education teacher in Taiwan

The third case focuses on a K-8 Taiwanese teacher of English. Anita acknowledges the impacts of global changes on Education and Taiwanese culture across generations. Anita had the opportunity to do her Bachelor degree in Australia. When she came back to Taiwan, Anita worked in a private English-speaking kindergarten. Having been exposed to two cultures, Anita reflected on Taiwanese education. She did many comparisons as teacher, as a mother, and she observed her son grow in both cultures (Taiwanese and Australian), and then in a third culture in his American school.

> Taiwanese families are more than ever willing to learn other languages, because of the current unstable politics. Maybe 60 to 70% of the Taiwanese families perceive Taiwan as a distinct country while a minority of perhaps 30 to 40% perceive Taiwan as part of mainland China. Many Taiwanese want to be able to move abroad if things change in a direction that does not favor economic stability. Taiwanese people want to visit and move to other countries. Being pressured across cultures, first Japanese, then Chinese, then American created a situation in which the Taiwanese may have lost pride in their own culture. They do not know anymore who they are.
>
> …Taiwanese culture knows a decrease, it is not felt as good as before, it is waning. Our youth has less creativity. Our education has trained our kids to stop being creative. Grades and points matter more and they only count when the responses match precisely the preconceived answers. Students are penalized if they are unique, different and creative. They do not get the grade. Standardized testing has a role in this. My boy does not have the opportunity to discover and create who he is: we need to push him to be excellent in the imposed curriculum. He cannot realize his own aspirations and wishes.
>
> … We push students, our children, to be A+ . I see couples in Taiwan, if they can afford it, they will do everything to send their kid out of this country to be educated abroad. It is good when the kid goes with the mother, otherwise he or she comes back with another culture. Many children leave the family when they are early adolescents, around 13, and they will stay for 10 years outside Taiwan. These years as a teenager are so important in terms of preferences, belonging, sense of identity … they won't want to come back. Then they see things from a different point of view, and there is a conflict.
>
> My son went to bilingual kindergarten and started in English when he was 3 years old. The reason is in private school teachers are more open, more freedom is given to kids to do what they want, but you need the funding. We choose Chinese at home, unless he wants to code switch. I took him out of private school in Grade 4: he changed from the American to the Chinese school system. In Grade 4, he has to do all the subjects in English at school.
>
> It changes your eye, the way you act, for example about rights and responsibilities. He came home saying "I have my rights and won't do what my mom is asking." In Taiwan, you obey your mom. The private school is under U.S. values. I was very shocked with that, and the way he started to say things, such as: "So what?" So what – you do not see so many kids in Taiwan saying that to their parents. The good side of this is that he knows what he wants and is not afraid to fight for what he wants. It is totally different from what I learned when I grew up: I need to learn to be his friend, not his mom. It is so difficult… It is totally different from the Taiwanese old culture.
>
> It brings changes to society. In this generation young kids in Taiwan are kind of lost. They follow what is famous but do not know who they are and what is their position. They want to become others, while being more assertive on what they want. There is a political issue

Educational Globalization and the Creation of Split Identities

here: what is our future? There is uncertainty for the country. Uncertainty brings people to have no idea of what future is going to be. Everything is so uncertain.

4 Discussion

4.1 Complicated Transcultural Storylines

Multilingual life stories are often complicated and involve layers of intricate attributions and identifications that evolve over time, with numerous adjustments to a changing society in which global trends are volatile. They are highly sensitive, highly emotional, complex and evolving. Their uniqueness makes it difficult to make any generalization.

Bai-Ju, the mainland teacher may find the love of her life with a Chinese person having a different storyline of adjusted encounters with the foreign Self, creating a synergy between the postmodern and the past.

> Bai-Ju: I feel differently. Culture is another thing: they (Americans) may accept you but deep down they may not accept you as one of their own. It is an emotion, my roots are here, I find it more comfortable... After having lived abroad you feel more and more like a universal citizen, but my core is being Chinese.

Luo is a well-integrated man and key player in his community, does not feel that English changed much his identity but for the willingness to learn new international languages and a perception of being more cosmopolitan, which supports his interpreter role with visitors. Yet Luo, the peaceful example of the well-integrated Yanbian teacher may go through a shift with the possible opening of a unified Korea.

The Taiwanese teacher may find in the geopolitical reshaping of Asia a way to reconcile her aspirations to be Western (her inner white "banana," as she explains) and her assertiveness for Asian difference (the outer yellow "banana"), as ASEAN identity will grow and strengthen.

> Anita: Taiwanese people want to resemble people from other countries, their heroes are elsewhere, and there is a sense that we are losing our identity. Yet the trend is changing. Ten years ago the youth had British or American singers for idols; now their stars are Korean. In the past, they were looking for Western food and a steak house, now it's hotpots and Korean food.

At the present time, English is (still) the language of the wealthy...

> Bai-Ju: Chinese youth have less morality because of the influence of Western culture, a narrow part of Western culture: money is their god. Money regardless of everything. They think in terms of their own benefits. They are getting more and more selfish. The world is getting so small, they are thinking about themselves. Maybe the planet as a home is not a consideration for the youth. They place personal gains at the first place. They are not thinking at the country, nature, the world a a whole. Traditionally Chinese folks tend to sacrifice themselves to good causes, but now who would do it? That passed as a result of globalization.

Anita: She saw her kid change, and also as a teacher she noticed how children changed across generations in the middle and in the upper classes. She does not think this change really affects the low salary levels of Taiwanese society. English creates a two-tier society.

…Yet this situation may change if Han China becomes the largest cosmopolitan country in the world and an open and tolerant society, and if its teaching methods focused less on form and more on meaning and proficiency. Wealth in Asia may soon equate or surpass Western wealth. The Manchu and Thai-Korean-Japanese blocks of power tend to create new fashions and new trends, and could generate much creativity if their school systems got rid of outcomes-based education and standardized testing.

In the three cases analyzed, I provided anecdotal data suggesting that educational globalization has an impact on language educators. Furthermore, globalization tends to create—the teacher narratives suggest—split identities in which educators feel divided not only between two worlds but also two ways of being, two models of society, and two modes of feeling about their identity. Given the scenario that China and its historically extended territories is the largest English learning geographic space that fuels the desire of merging the best of both worlds in a yin-yang synergy, it may create new identities and imaginaries, no longer associated with the outside but propelled within the nation-state. The purpose of such imaginaries and synergy may be to propose a model of peaceful coexistence that may take generations to come to fruition. In the process, educational actors may observe the tempting cleavage but still feel divided with conflicting aspirations.

5 Conclusion

5.1 Language Education Policy and Identity Capital

Identity is a capital when it is firmly anchored in values that are interiorized and sedimented from reflected experiences and learned knowledge, not values that are exterior to the self (Bourdieu, 2008). Language education experiences, instructional medias and study abroad may support identity capital or devalue it.

5.2 The Policy Impact: Towards Multilingual Experiences and Open Curricula

Potentially (self-)destructive policies may emerge from doctrinal coercion to accepted and socialized forms of behavior in the name of a pre-formatted and imposed conception of harmony: mass education is based on standard outcomes that are the same for everyone. Educational normative systems imply forms of alienation and exclusion of people who deviate from the standards of behavior. Imposed school genres dictate how to think and how to express oneself. A situation in which everyone thinks the same way does not produce in the population the creativity required to solve the problems of the present and the future.

Potentially supportive policies may resemble the pluralist perspective lived in the Yanbian Prefecture, as an example of bilingual policy with fair regulation processes. Curricula that support initiative and decision making, such as open forms of project-based learning, are grounded in the results of motivation research that highlight the role of self-determination, self-regulation, and freedom of choice to promote learning autonomy. It has been demonstrated that learner autonomy leads to better, more meaningful and deeper learning (Little, 2007; Jiménez Raya, Lamb & Vieria, 2007; Jiménez Raya, & Vieira, 2011). Open plurilingualism is becoming a driving force behind many influential language education initiatives internationally. Learners' shared autonomy and learning choice may become a powerful policy for creative change in Education. Supporting creative and autonomous identities may require abundant instructional resources for plurilingual literacies (Tochon, 2014). A major issue in multilingual settings is indeed the creation of appropriate instructional media with a potential for positive and reflective cultural integration. If freedom to learn may predetermine successful creative learning and language proficiency, the plurality of pathways towards language apprenticeship may be the key unlocking the energies of intrinsic motivation. This builds up a case in favor of open instructional experiences. The main result in transnational education could be an open and multicompetent plurilingual multiliteracy model rather than English-only MOI. The core purpose of the chapter and the study focused on globalization of education and split identities, however it suggested ways out of the binaries. Indeed, hyper-medias of instruction could be multilingual and adapted to specific populations, such as language learners, heritage learners, and minorities. The advent of this new form of instructional media could support integrative identity capital in providing learning choices, as is proposed in the Deep Approach (Tochon, 2014). It would help re-conceptualizing democratic education: not targeting the same outcomes for all but allowing each student to develop their own dreams and reach their specific and customized outcomes.

Acknowledgements & Disclosure This study was sponsored by the School of Education of the University of Wisconsin-Madison through a sabbatical study leave of absence. Professor Tochon is President of Deep University International, a Section 509(a)(2) Charity and Chairman of the Deep Institute, Wisconsin.

References

Beynon, J., & Dossa, P. (2003). Mapping inclusive and equitable pedagogy: Narratives of university educators. *Teaching Education, 14*(3), 249–264.
Blyth, C. S. (2015). Exploring the complex nature of language and culture through intercultural dialogue. *Dialogue in Multilingual and Multimodal Communities, 10,* 139–165.
Bourdieu, P. (1984). *Distinction: A social critique of the judgement of taste.* Cambridge, MA: Harvard University Press.

Bourdieu, P. (2008). *Sketch for a self-analysis* (R. Nice, Trans.). Chicago: University of Chicago Press.

Chuang, Y.-J. (2017, April). *Can't You be more like them? Imbalanced cultural representations of learners' experiences and identities in locally-grown english textbooks*. Unpublished doctoral dissertation, Second Language Acquisition Program, University of Wisconsin-Madison.

Connelly, F. M., & Clandinin, D. J. (1999). *Shaping a professional identity: Stories of education practice*. London, ON: Althouse.

De Costa, P. (2018). A better way forward for transnational higher education. *University World News, 512*, July. Retrieved from http://www.universityworldnews.com/article.php?story=20180626103409378.

Feldman, A. (1999). *Conversation as methodology in collaborative action research*. Amherst, MA: School of Education, University of Massachusetts. http://people.umass.edu/~afeldman/ActionResearchPapers/Feldman1999.PDF.

Freud, S. (2010). *The Ego and the ID*. New York: CreateSpace.

Gay, G. (2003). Deracialization in social studies teacher education textbooks. In G. Ladson-Billings (Ed.), *Critical race theory perspectives on social studies: The profession, policies, and curriculum* (pp. 123–147). Greenwich, CT: Information Age.

Gerbner, G., & Gross, L. (1976). Living with television: The violence profile. *Journal of Communication, 26*(2), 172–199.

Gumperz, J. J. (1982). *Language and social identity*. Cambridge: Cambridge University Press.

Harrison, K. M. (2018). Plurilingual practices and storytelling pedagogy in schools of a thousand languages: Listening to displaced languages. In K. M. Harrison, M. Sadiku, & F. V. Tochon (Eds.), *Displacement planet earth. Plurilingual language education policy for 21st century schools* (pp. 293–311). Blue Mounds, WI: Deep Education Press.

Holland, J. H., Holyoak, K. J., Nisbett, R. E., & Thagard, P. R. (1994). *Induction—Processes of inference, learning, and discovery* (2nd ed.). Cambridge, MA: MIT Press.

Holland, D., Lachicotte, W. J., Skinner, D., & Cain, C. (1998). *Identity and agency in cultural worlds*. Cambridge, MA: Harvard University Press.

Hong, M. (2018). A study of english curriculum policies in Universities of Zhejiang Province, China. In M. Djuraeva & F. V. Tochon (Eds.), *Language policy or the politics of language: Reimagining the role of language in a Neoliberal Society* (pp. 155–170). Blue Mounds, WI: Deep University Press.

Jahng, K. E. (2013, December). *Troubling identities of Korean American children: Foucaultian genealogy of the construction of the childhood of Korean Americans in California and Hawaii*. Unpublished dissertation. University of Wisconsin-Madison, School of Education, Department of Curriculum & Instruction.

Jiménez Raya, M., Lamb, T., & Vieria, F. (2007). *Pedagogy for autonomy in language education in Europe: A framework for learner and teacher development*. Dublin: Authentik.

Jiménez Raya, M., & Vieira, F. (2011). *Understanding and exploring pedagogy for autonomy in language education—A case-based approach*. Dublin: Authentik.

Jung, C. G. (1960). *The structure and dynamics of the psyche. Collected works. 8*. Princeton, NJ: Princeton University Press.

Laing, R. D. (1960). *The divided self*. London: Tavistock.

Laing, R. D. (1967). *The politics of experience*. NewYork: Pantheon.

Le-Ha, P. (2017). *Transnational education crossing 'Asia' and 'the West.' Adjusted desire, transformative mediocrity and neo-colonial disguise*. London: Routledge.

Little, D. (2007). Language learner autonomy: Some fundamental considerations revisited. *Innovation in Language Learning and Teaching, 1*(1), 14–29.

Liyanage, I., Walker, T., & Weinmann, M. (2016). English as an additional language teachers, policy enactments and intercultural understanding. *TESOL in Context, 25*(2), 4–19.

Mao, C. (2008). Fashioning curriculum reform as identity politics—Taiwan's dilemma of curriculum reform in new millennium. *International Journal of Educational Development, 28*, 585–595.

Moje, E. B., & Luke, A. (2009). Literacy and identity: Examining the metaphors in history and contemporary research. *Reading Research Quaterly, 44*(4), 415–437.
Olson, E. T. (2010). Personal identity. In *Stanford encyclopedia of philosophy*. Retrieved from http://plato.stanford.edu/archives/win2010/entries/identity-personal.
Popkewitz, T. A., Diaz, J., & Kirchgasler, C. (2017). *A political sociology of educational knowledge: Studies of exclusions and difference*. New York: Routledge.
Shohamy, E. (2006). Language tests. In E. Shohamy (Ed.), *Language policy: Hidden agendas and new approaches* (pp. 93–109). New York: Routledge.
Skutnabb-Kangas, T., Maffi, L., & and Harmon, D. (2003). *Sharing a world of difference. The earth's linguistic, cultural, and biological diversity*. Paris, France: UNESCO Publishing. UNESCO, Terralingua, and World Wide Fund for Nature.
Su, Y. C. (2006). Political ideology and Taiwanese school curricula. *Asia Pacific Education Review, 7*(1), 41–50.
Sung, P., & Yang, M. (2009). National identity and its relationship with teachers' historical knowledge and pedagogy: The case of Taiwan. *Asia Pacific Journal of Education, 29*(2), 179–194.
Tochon, F. V. (2000). When authentic experiences are "Enminded" into disciplinary genres: Crossing biographic and situated knowledge. *Learning and Instruction, 10*, 331–359.
Tochon, F. V. (2003). *The foreign self: Truth telling as education research*. Madison, WI: Atwood.
Tochon, F. V. (2014). *Help them learn a language deeply—Francois Victor Tochon's deep approach to world languages and cultures*. Blue Mounds, WI: Deep University Press.
Tochon, F. V. (2019). Decolonizing world language education: Toward multilingualism. In D. Macedo (Ed.), *Decolonizing foreign language education: The misteaching of english and other colonial languages* (pp. 360–372). London: Routledge.
Vygotsky, L. S. (1978). *Mind in society. The development of higher psychological processes* (M. Cole, V. John-Steiner, S. Scribner, & E. Souberman, Eds.). Cambridge, MA: Harvard University Press.
Walsh, D. J. (1997). Éducateurs et parents: un point de vue personnel (Educators and parents: Un personal viewpoint). In F. V. Tochon (Ed.), *Éduquer avant l'école: l'intervention préscolaire en milieu défavorisés et pluriethniques (Educating before school: Preschool intervention in low-income and multiethnic settings)* (pp. 151–166). Montreal, QC: University of Montreal Press.
Wang, A., Liyanage, I., & Walker, T. (2019). Scrutinising critical thinking (CT) in Chinese higher education: Perceptions of Chinese academics. In I. Liyanage & T. Walker (Eds.), *Multilingual education yearbook 2019: Media of instruction & multilingual settings* (pp. 189–208). New York: Springer.
Wenger, E. (2008). Identity in practice. In K. Hall, P. Murphy, & J. Soler (Eds.), *Pedagogy and practice: Culture and identities* (pp. 105–114). Thousand Oaks, CA: Sage.
Yen, Y. (2000). *Identity issues in EFL and ESL textbooks: A sociocultural perspective*. Unpublished doctoral dissertation. ProQuest Dissertations & Theses database, UMI #9971668.
Yim, S. (2007). Globalization and language policy in South Korea. In A. B. M. Tsui & J. W. Tollefson (Eds.), *Language policy, culture, and identity in Asian contexts* (pp. 37–53). Mahwah, NJ: Lawrence Erlbaum.
Zhu, Y. (2015, August). *Exploring an immigrant teacher's practical knowledge and re-construction of identities—An autoethnography study*. Master Thesis Graduate School of the University of Wisconsin-Madison, School of Education, Department of Curriculum & Instruction.

François Victor Tochon heading World Language Education in the Department of Curriculum & Instruction at the University of Wisconsin-Madison, has a Ph.D. in Applied Linguistics, a Ph.D. in Educational Psychology, and six Honorary Doctorates and Professorships from universities in Argentina, China, and Peru and an Asia-Pacific association. With 45 books and 280 articles and book chapters to his credit, he has been Visiting Professor in 20 countries, and is published in 14 languages. He received the 2010 Award of Best Review of Research from the American Educational Research Association. As President of the International Network for Language Education Policy Studies, he received the 2012 Award of International Research Excellence from the University of Granada, Spain. Prof. Tochon received the 2015 Excellence in Diversity Award from the University of Wisconsin-Madison, the 2015 International Scholar Award of Shanghai Normal University, and 2015 Eminent Scholar Award from the University of Southern Queensland in Australia.

Bilingual Education Classrooms in Sri Lankan Schools: A Social Space for Ethnolinguistic Reconciliation

Harsha Dulari Wijesekera and Jennifer Alford

Abstract Decades of a school system ethnolinguistically segregated along Mother Tongue Instruction (MTI), compounded by a 30-year-long ethnic conflict, has had significant consequences for ethnic relations among the diverse population of Sri Lanka. The recently introduced Bilingual Education (BE)—English and Sinhala/Tamil—has enabled some core subjects to be taught using English Medium Instruction (EMI), bringing together students of different ethnicities in multiethnic, bi-media schools. This has created a new social space and, thereby, new possibilities for changing social relations. In this chapter, we explore BE students' ethnic identity orientations through analysis of their expressed feelings and perceptions towards ethnically diverse 'others', before and after joining multiethnic BE classrooms. Using the Bourdieusian conceptual triad of *habitus, capital* and *field*, we present analysis of data collected in two, multiethnic schools in Sri Lanka. The findings show that during early socialization in ethnically-exclusive institutions, such as family and monoethnic classrooms, students acquire insular, ethnocentric dispositions that undergo reorientation towards more supraethnic, inclusive dispositions when students get to know each other and study together in multiethnic BE classes. Learning through English as a common language, and cross-linguistic flexibility, made possible a growing positive inclination towards people of different ethnolinguistic backgrounds, and recognition, respect, and increased acceptance of diversity and heterogeneity. The findings are highly relevant to post-conflict, ethnolinguistically heterogeneous societies, especially in terms of how language in education could be utilized in promoting interethnic relations and thereby national solidarity.

Keywords Bilingual education · Bourdieu · English Medium Instruction · Ethnolinguistic identity · Social cohesion · Sri Lanka

---

H. D. Wijesekera (✉)
Postgraduate Institute of English, Open University of Sri Lanka, Colombo, Sri Lanka
e-mail: hdwij@ou.ac.lk

J. Alford
Queensland University of Technology, Brisbane, Australia
e-mail: jh.alford@qut.edu.au

1 Introduction

As a post-conflict country, Sri Lanka's most vital national concern is reconciliation and social cohesion. One way to achieve this is to inculcate solidarity among diverse groups through the education system which can provide shared lived experiences to diverse groups. This chapter presents evidence of how ethnically diverse bilingual education (BE) classrooms—English and Sinhala/Tamil, with some core subjects taught using English Medium Instruction (EMI)—can serve this national purpose, in contrast to classrooms ethnically polarized along Mother Tongue Instruction (MTI) in Sri Lanka. We present a snapshot here of a larger case study of multiethnic, BE classrooms in Sri Lanka that investigated students' ethnolinguistic identity reorientations, and conditions that triggered such transformations. In particular, this chapter presents how ethnic exclusivity begins to weaken and ethnic identity reorients towards more supraethnic or less ethnocentric inclusive identities given certain conditions. In this chapter, we consider identity orientations as a continuum—at one end, exclusive ethnocentrism, and at the other, a supraethnic inclusive identity.

This chapter is organised as follows: We first elucidate the complex contextual background to the research problem within Sri Lanka, and the nature of bilingual education in Sri Lanka. This is followed by theorizing the study's foci, using Bourdieusian theoretical perspectives, and the methodology. We then present interview, focus group, and observation data analysis simultaneously with interpretations. Finally, we offer conclusions, implications and suggestions.

1.1 The Complex Multiethnic, Multilingual Context of Sri Lanka

Sri Lanka is a multiethnic, multi-religious and multilingual island nation whose distribution of population is depicted in Table 1 (Census & Statistics, 2012).

Generally, Sinhala is the mother tongue of the Sinhalese (Sinhala-speaking people) whereas Tamil is the language of Tamil people. Most Muslims consider their mother tongue as Tamil while some Muslims use Sinhala as their home language or mother tongue. There is also a growing population, especially in urban areas,

Table 1 Distribution of Sri Lankan population—three major ethnic groups

Ethnicity	Population as %	Language	Religion
Sinhalese	74.9	Sinhala	Buddhism (main), Christianity
Sri Lankan Tamils	11.2	Tamil	Hindu (main), Christianity
Indian Tamils	4.1	Tamil	Hindu (main), Christianity
Sri Lankan Moors (Muslim)	9.3	Tamil	Islam

that use English as their home language irrespective of ethnicity. The Sri Lankan Constitution, by Articles 18 and 19 in Chapter IV, designates Sinhala and Tamil as National Languages, and English a link language between these two speech communities and the world outside. In the same Chapter, under Article 21, it sets rules for Medium of Instruction (MOI) in education: "(1) [a] person shall be entitled to be educated through the medium of either of the National Languages." In addition, the government recently introduced the concept of 'Trilingual Sri Lanka' as a part of the post-conflict reconciliation process, where learning of Tamil for Sinhalese and of Sinhala for Tamils is promoted.

2 MTI and Ethnically Polarized Schools

Even before independence from the British in 1948, the Sri Lankan education system adopted MTI—Sinhala or Tamil—starting from 1946, and subsequent to this EMI was renounced year by year. Sri Lanka's three-tiered school system that existed under the British, that is, English medium, bilingual and vernacular, led to intense socio-economic stratification (Bickmore, 2008; Kandiah, 1984). In 1889, the British Governor stressed that they did not want to have "a generation of half-educated idlers who deem that a little pigeon-English places them above honest work" (cited in Brutt-Griffler, 2002, p. 214). Access to EMI was therefore limited to a few, restricting social mobility for the masses so as to maintain the labour market required to serve British mercantile interests. This social disparity provoked the nationalist movements' demand for MTI, which they ultimately won. Unlike the earlier British MOI policy, MTI opened education for the masses after 1946. It expedited upward social mobility of the less privileged, irrespective of ethnicity, and brought greater social justice. Consequently, Sri Lanka reported the highest literacy rate in South Asia at the time.

However, in another sense, the introduction of MTI was counterproductive (Buckland, 2005; Coleman, 2007; Davis, 2015; Wijesekera, 2011, 2018; Wijesekera, Alford, & Mu, 2018), and polarized public schools along ethnicity lines. This polarization precluded the education system's potential to bring diverse ethnicities together to nurture mutual understanding among them through shared lived experiences. Instead, it created alienation and suspicion between communities (Wickrema & Colenso, 2003; Wijesekera, 2018), and contributed to a "narrow formulation of identity" (Cohen, 2007, p. 172) based on ethnolingualism in contrast to supraethnic 'Sri Lankan national identity' that goes beyond ethnically exclusive identities as Sinhalese, Tamils and Muslims. As Nadesan (1957) stressed, when the younger generation of two different ethnicities "study in different schools in their respective languages […], ignorant of one another's culture, language and achievements […] conflicts are bound to arise." The country endured a 30-year-long conflict which was officially ended in 2009 by military powers. Yet, reconciliation and national integration still seem far from reality as evident in disharmony and suspicion reflected among diverse groups in day-to-day experiences in the country. Even though language is not the only grievance, it is a major area of concern in the reconciliation process, as it was in the conflict. For instance, to promote interethnic cohesion, teaching of the Second National Language (2NL), that is Tamil to Sinhalese and Sinhalese to Tamils, has been introduced in the national curriculum to support the reconciliation process. However, research reports that learning of 2NLs has not generated much interest, especially among the majority Sinhalese population (Davis, 2015; Liyanage & Canagarajah, 2014), except in BE classrooms in multiethnic schools where students have reported inclination towards one another's languages (Wijesekera, 2018).

The Constitution of Sri Lanka (Parliament Secretariat, 2015) guarantees the strengthening of

> national unity by promoting co-operation and mutual confidence among all sections of the People of Sri Lanka, including the racial, religious, linguistic and other groups, and shall take effective steps in the fields of teaching, education and information in order to eliminate discrimination and prejudice. (Chapter VI - Article 5, p. 18)

Nevertheless, the Sri Lankan public school system acts in contrast to above legitimate national aspirations, and also against its own mandate outlined in the National Goals of Education: to facilitate learning to live together, and inculcate a socially cohesive nation (Wijesekera, 2018). Even today, almost all schools (10,049 out of 10,162 as depicted in the Table 2) are ethnically insular. They offer either Sinhala or Tamil medium, some with English medium as well, and keep young children of diverse ethnicities from having authentic lived experiences with each other, except for 113 bi-media schools (66 using Sinhala and Tamil mediums, and 47 using Sinhala, Tamil and English mediums or BE).

Even in these 113 bi-media schools, in 66 bi-media schools where Sinhala and Tamil mediums are available, Tamil-speaking and Sinhala-speaking students study separately in Sinhala medium and Tamil medium classrooms, alienated and excluded from each other (Wijesekera, 2011, 2018; Wijesekera, Alford, & Mu, 2018). The contrast, as depicted in Table 2, is in 47 bi-media schools where BE is available from Grade 6 in addition to MTI (Sinhala and Tamil mediums). To explain more, in the Sri Lankan BE programme, some subjects are taught through English while other subjects are taught in the respective mother-tongue of the child. Consequently, the Tamil-speaking and Sinhala-speaking students are now able to work together in

Table 2 Government schools by medium of instruction (Ministry of Education, 2016a)

School by available medium	No of schools
Sinhala only	6338
Tamil only	2989
Sinhala and Tamil	66
Sinhala and English	554
Tamil and English	168
Sinhala, Tamil and English	47
Total	10,162

one classroom when they learn some subjects through English. Basically, the BE classrooms in these 47 schools are the only state-operated social/education space where children of all ethnicities can meet, talk, work together and learn about each other. The focus of this chapter is this social space, and how this social space can help shape the ethnic identity dispositions of students towards reconciliation.

3 Ethnolinguistic Identity, Language and Conflict

In exploring bilingual learners' ethnic identity dispositions, we draw on theories of identity that take account of the crucial role of language in establishing, maintaining and negotiating identities. Language is "fundamental to collective and personal identity" (McCarty, Skutnabb-Kangas, & Magga, 2008, p. 299), and inseparable from one's self. Baker and Wright (2017, p. 349) claim that "language is one of the strongest symbols and boundary markers in having a group, regional, cultural or national identity". Similarly, ethnolinguistic identity is the "systematic distinctions between insiders and outsiders; between us and them" (Eriksen, 2010, p. 23) that are based on language. Ethnolinguistic identity, as a frame, leads to the ethnicized construction of otherness (Gabriel, 2014), a social group identity that takes ethnicity and language as the criteria for inclusion or exclusion of the ethnic us and other (Harwood & Vincez, 2012; Noels, Kil, & Fang, 2014). This has been the case for Sinhalese and Tamil groups in Sri Lanka (Chandra, 2006). In fact, language being one of the primary demarcations of two major ethnic groups, the civil conflict in Sri Lanka has also been defined as an ethno-linguistic conflict (Saunders, 2007). Linguistic differences "provided a powerful symbolic rallying cry" (Laitin, 2000, p. 557) in Sri Lanka, especially in cadre mobilizing (Buckland, 2005; Saunders, 2007), in addition to socio-economic disparities common to all ethnicities.

Bormann, Cederman and Vogt (2017) argue that language is the most conflict-fuelling and the most salient cause of civil conflicts. They claim this using data collected through Ethnic Power Relations-Ethnic Dimension (EPR-ED) that addressed multiple ethnic segments on the linguistic and religious dimensions. Their study obtained data from more than 700 politically relevant ethnic groups in 130 states across the world, and they conclude that "intrastate conflict is more likely within linguistic dyads than among religious ones" (p. 744). In Sri Lanka too, languages and the politicization of languages contributed to interethnic conflict where the MOI in schools played a crucial role (Nadesan, 1957; Wickrama & Colenso, 2003).

However, the process of identity work is not a simple one. Tajfel (1974, p. 67) argues that individuals constantly engage in a "continuing process of self-definition" to accomplish a self-fulfilling image of his/her own identity, and this results in in-group and out-group processing, which may depend on contextual circumstances. Thus, identity is a fusion of many, continually restyling intersections with social constructs such as languages, and hence creating multiplicity, fluidity and hybridity of one's identity (Canagarajah, 2007). For instance, Sri Lankan Tamils, while having an overarching national identity as Sri Lankans, may maintain their unique ethnic identity as Tamils. The process does not stop there as Tamils distinguish among themselves as Hindus, Catholics, Christians, Jaffna Tamils, Baticaloa Tamils and Indian Tamils. So, the identification process depends on various criteria—an endless continuing process of self-definition (Tajfel, 1978). These identity positionings may have inclinations and disinclinations towards certain identities dialogical to social circumstances. As such, exclusionary ethnic categorizations can also be unlearned through lived experiences with 'others' if the circumstances or logic of practice (Bourdieu, 1990) in the social space they occupy rejects exclusion or is at odds with ethnocentric mental categorizations (Cross & Naidoo, 2012). This we will explain more under theoretical discussion. This chapter reports that in multiethnic BE classrooms such unlearning is possible, given certain conditions.

4 Identity in Multilingual Spaces

As opposed to monolingual spaces with rigid language boundaries that exclude 'other' language speakers, multilingual spaces with flexible language boundaries may harness inclusive identities (Wijesekera, 2018). As in other social spaces, in the multilingual BE classroom also, the values assigned to different languages as linguistic capitals are "relative and 'open' to renegotiation" (Grenfell, 1998, p. 74) given the sociolinguistic conditions that emerge therein. For instance, the MOI policy in the BE classroom at practical level, or students' inclinations towards languages, or their ability to use those languages, may confer different values for languages and create "new forms of social relations in classrooms and schools" (Tollefson, 2015, p. 183). If a heteroglossic space where all languages are considered as one single system of symbols (Creese & Blackledge, 2015; Garcia, 2009) prevails in the classroom and confers equal value for all languages, then linguistic systems become unbounded. As such, fixed language identities which are inextricably linked to linguistic identity (Spolsky & Hult, 2008) may become blurred (Garcia & Wei, 2014; Tochon, 2019). Particularly, if the BE classroom considers "multilingualism at the center of language education policy" (Wiley & Garcia, 2016, p. 58) and allows students to freely navigate among their entire language repertoire creatively, then ethnolinguistic identities which were previously characterised and bounded by single languages may potentially transform towards more open-ended (Kramsch, 2008), or 'desirable identities' (Norton & Toohey, 2011), desirable to the given context—in the present case desirable identities in multiethnic multilingual BE classrooms. Theoretically, as we will discuss below, the dispositions or habitus of individuals may undergo changes according to the immanent rules of the game in the field (BE classrooms) that they occupy (Bourdieu, 1990). Such flexible language policies may nurture "a multilingual population with knowledge and respect for other languages and cultures" (Spolsky, 2011, p. 5), which Sri Lanka is in dire need of, at a time of reconciliation.

5 Current Sri Lankan Bilingual Education Programme—A Brief Overview

The Sri Lankan BE programme, which starts from Grade 6, and is available in a limited number of public, semi-government and private schools, does not have a legitimized policy per se that can be called "the BE policy" (Wijesekera, 2018). The BE Teacher Training Manual of the National Institute of Education (NIE, 2009) mentions that there is neither clarity nor policy on the BE. Hinkel (2005, p. 6) defines Sri Lanka's BE as "...*dual language* education (that) conforms to local curriculum standards, but the curriculum is delivered through two languages (English and mother tongue, either Sinhala or Tamil), with special attention to second language (English) development and content learning through a second language" (our additions).

Wijesekera (2011, 2018) found that Sri Lankan students of diverse ethnicities are unable to have lived experiences of acceptance of pluralism and tolerance towards 'others' that they learn through core subjects in the curriculum such as Social Studies and English, due to ethnically polarized Sinhala medium and Tamil medium classrooms. In contrast, the present BE programme in multiethnic (bi-media) schools brings different ethnicities together when students learn some subjects through English. This integration of two language groups may contribute "to the development of positive intergroup relationships between language minority students and language majority students" (De Jong & Howard, 2009, p. 85) in addition to language learning paybacks. This would have been more successful if the two-way immersion model of BE was implemented in Sri Lanka. That is, some subjects are taught in Sinhala whereas other subjects are in Tamil. As Liyanage and Canagarajah (2014) argue, had such a programme been implemented, interethnic 'connectedness' in Sri Lanka would have been promoted as it was in pre-colonial times. However, the exogenous, socio-economic values inherent in the English language have outweighed the value of such a two-way programme in two national languages.

The objectives of the Sri Lankan BE programme (Ministry of Education, 2016b) can be synthesized into two main legitimized aims. One is to fulfil the demand for English proficiency in the local and global job markets, and in higher education. The other is to create connectedness between the Tamil-speaking and Sinhala-speaking groups through English as a link language, in addition to connecting to the world outside.

6 Socially Situated Conditions for Transformation: The Theoretical Lens

This study draws on Bourdieu's (1977) Theory of Practice and its theoretical triad: habitus, field and capital. According to Bourdieu, the whole universe of social spaces is made of relatively autonomous social microcosms or fields which have specific internal "socially situated conditions" (Bourdieu, 1990, p. 55) of their own. The socially situated conditions in a field, in turn, are shaped by the capitals or resources at stake therein, which are also shaped by the outside markets of these capitals such as economic, cultural, social, linguistic capitals. These capitals also carry symbolic capitals because different values of capitals and amounts of them may confer varying powers. Similarly, the multiethnic BE class may have "socially situated conditions" specific to it where specific capital/s would be at stake. Among the linguistic capitals at stake in BE classes, English linguistic capital could be the most valued, for English as MOI is officially legitimised to deliver content. This is different from the MTI classes where mother tongue gains much capital value.

In Bourdieu's lens, ethnic distinctions are "socially legitimized and consecrated by social institutions such as family", schools, media, state, and are "conferred upon individuals" (Kramsch, 2010, p. 41) Accordingly, we conceptualised ethnic identity as *ethnic habitus*: "*a way of being habituated state ... a predisposition, tendency, propensity or inclination*" (Bourdieu & Passeron, 1977, p. 214, original emphasis) towards one's own ethnic group while having disinclination towards the ethnic 'others'. It is this process that confers legitimate membership of a particular ethnic group, as Sinhalese, Tamils or Muslims, for example.

Though habitus, including ethnic habitus, is historically acquired and embodied, it has "an infinite capacity for generating [... whose] limits are set by the *historically and socially situated conditions* of its production" (Bourdieu, 1990, p. 55, our emphasis). Analogously, BE students' ethnic habitus as "a product of history, that is of social experiences and education [...] may be changed by *history*, that is by new experiences, education and training" (Bourdieu, 2005, p. 45, original emphasis). As such, the overarching argument that sustained this study is that the BE classroom in multiethnic schools might create a new social space with specific "socially situated conditions"—conditions of metanoia where "a transformation of one's whole vision of the social world [habitus]" (Cross & Naidoo, 2012, p. 228, our addition) may occur.

However, we do not talk of a total transformation from exclusionary ethnocentric identity to inclusive supraethnic identity, or vice versa. Rather, we consider identity positioning as a continuum—at one end highly ethnocentric identity position, and at the other end a supraethnic inclusive identity position. It is these perspectives that are used in this analysis to interpret the findings.

7 Methodology

The overarching research questions of the study were: What ethnic group re/orientations take place among ethnically diverse students when they study together in multiethnic BE classrooms in Sri Lanka; and how does this occur? To answer these questions this chapter explores two sub-questions:

1. What feelings, perceptions and dispositions towards ethnically diverse "others" do students have before and after joining multiethnic BE classrooms?
2. How do languages in multiethnic BE pedagogy shape ethnic identity orientations of students?

In appropriating these questions, an ethnographically-informed qualitative approach was taken, and analysis was conducted through Bourdieu's epistemological stance—structural constructivism or constructive structuralism (Grenfell & Lebaron, 2014, p. 2). This means that the research explored the dialectic relations of the objective structures of the BE pedagogic field and the subjective structures of the BE students (their habitus) that are both structured and continuously structuring (Bourdieu & Wacquant, 1992). This was explored from different perspectives of the students, teachers, and other stakeholders.

8 The Schools

In this chapter, we use data from two multiethnic schools in Sri Lanka: pseudonymously, South College, in remote Sri Lanka, and Raveendranath College, in the commercial capital. South College starts at Grade 6 and the students who join the College at Grade 6 come from ethnically insular schools using either Sinhala medium or Tamil medium. Raveendranath College has classes from Grade 1, but the students of different ethnicities study separate from each other in MTI classes from Grade 1 to 5.

9 Data Collection

The first author audio-recorded and observed classrooms twice a week over 5–6 weeks in each school during regular teaching, as agreed to by teachers. Focus group discussions (FGDs) were conducted with BE students (6–8 in each group) representing Sinhala, Tamil and Muslim communities in each school. This was followed by semi-structured interviews with BE teachers and parents, conducted by the first author. This triangulation helped bring both emic and etic perspectives to the study, adding to the credibility of findings.

The data collection process was also framed through a Bourdieusian lens. The research questions had two levels—empirical and theoretical. For example, one question asked at the focus group discussions to explore transformations in students' inclinations towards group members is depicted in Table 3 (see Wijesekera, 2018 for more details). Table 3 shows the relationship between the empirical questions and the theoretical level of inquiry.

Questions included in the interviews, FGDs, and the observation protocols were also guided by Bourdieusian perspectives. These instruments were semi-structured

Table 3 Empirical and theoretical questioning of the focus group discussions—An example

Empirical level	Theoretical level
Overall classroom environment, Group formation and Interaction	
1. What are your (students') opinions and experiences about having students of all ethnicities in one class and working together with them? 2. Whom do you (students) prefer to work with in groups? Why?	a. How do the agents and groups of different ethnolinguistic habitus accrete social capital (mutual acquaintance and recognition) b. What systems of dispositions with regard to ethnic others (ethnolinguistic habitus) are sensed and practised by students: do they lean towards ethnocentrism or cosmopolitanism?

and therefore allowed new themes to arise. Data were analysed inductively using Bourdieu's theory of practice and conceptual tools—habitus, field and capital—as a lens to explain the themes that emerged, as discussed below.

10 Analysis of Data and Interpretation

In the following, we provide data analysis and interpretation to support our finding that students developed a more positive inclination towards people of different ethnolinguistic backgrounds, and recognition, respect, and increased acceptance of diversity and heterogeneity.

10.1 From Ethnocentric Habitus Towards Supraethnic Habitus

In general, the analysis of students' responses to the question, *what feelings towards ethnically diverse 'others' did you have before joining the multiethnic BE classrooms, and what feelings do you have now*? clearly illustrated ethnocentric dispositions students had before joining the multiethnic BE class have transformed in the BE classroom. The analysis shows that they had acquired highly ethnocentric dispositions during early socialization in ethnically exclusive social spaces such as family, schools and MTI classrooms. In contrast, in the ethnically inclusive BE classroom where they could meet, talk and interact with each other, these ethnocentric dispositions have moved towards supraethnic dispositions. This transformation was similar in both schools among all three student groups—Sinhala, Tamil and Muslim. To exemplify this transformation, we present data from the focus-group discussions, first at South College.

Tamil Student (3):   Before we were in other schools, we didn't see them [Sinhalese] like this. The problem was war.

Tamil student (6): When we watched news we thought Sinhala people were not good, [...] But it was only when we came to this school (BE class) we understood that they are as good as this much, they are very good.

Sinhala Student (5): [we] saw them [Muslim people] bit different from us, a bit bad way (before). Earlier we thought that they humiliate and disrespect our religion.

Sinhala student (4): When during the war we were scared of Tamils. After coming to bilingual class we got friendly with them we feel they are good.

Muslim student (3): We didn't meet them, so I didn't know about them. I thought they were bad. But now it's different, I know them and we are friends.

Muslim student (5): In my previous school there were only Muslim girls. I didn't know about Tamil and Sinhala students. But here, we all are here. Now I know they are also like us. [Earlier] we didn't have chances to acquaint with them.

It is evident that these South College students of all ethnicities did not have any previous opportunity to meet 'ethnic others' because their former schools were ethnically homogeneous. Their responses also show negative stereotypical conceptions about ethnic others, which were similar among individuals of the same ethnic group. For instance, all Tamil students perceived all Sinhalese as homogeneously bad, while Sinhala students perceived all Tamils as homogeneously bad, which is a characteristic of out-grouping of the 'other' (Tajfel, 1978).

The data from Raveendranath College illustrate that even in ethnically diverse bi-media schools, when students are ethnically segregated in separate classrooms due to MTI until they come to BE classes in Grade 6, this situation creates alienation and animosity among the students of diverse ethnicities.

Tamil Student (3): When we were in Grade 4 and 5 when we saw Sinhala people [students] we said, aha... they are coming we shall hit them, like that. From the little age we do [feel] like that.

Muslim Student (2) [who was in Tamil medium classes from Grade 1–5]: They are better than we thought. [...] we didn't know Sinhala medium students so we thought all of them were bad. [...] After we came to BE class a lot of Sinhala students were very good. They give a lot of help...

Sinhala Student (3): We didn't have any knowledge or understanding about them earlier... We thought that Tamils are bad... Now we realized that they are really cooperative, because now we are friends. In Grade 1–5 we were in two separate mediums, so there were separate classes for us and for them.

Sinhala Student (1): Muslim students have been with us since primary. So I didn't have any animosity with them.

Students' responses at Raveendranath College were more revealing and show that though the students had studied in the same school from Grade 1–5, they had lived developing negative dispositions towards each other, until they started studying together in the BE classroom. The responses of the Muslim student further illustrate that if students did not have any opportunity to know each other by studying in the same class, then their ethnocentric dispositions or out-grouping of ethnic others are perpetuated. In contrast, when they are together in one class they develop 'no animosity' towards each other as the Sinhala Student 1 expressed above (Muslim students in Sri Lanka may choose either Sinhala or Tamil as medium of instruction).

11 Theoretical Interpretation

In the student responses in both schools, it was evident that students of the same ethnic group homogeneously had negative and stereotypical dispositions towards the ethnic other. This can be delineated using a Bourdieusian lens:

> *it is certain that each member of the same class* [or same ethnic group] *is more likely than any member of another class* [another ethnic group] to have been confronted with the situations most frequent for members of that class [ethnicity] (Bourdieu, 1977, p. 85, our additions and emphasis),

Tamil students acquired dispositions/habitus, for instance, have been shaped by the "definitions that their elders offer them" (Bourdieu, 1984, p. 47): by Tamil families, Tamil TV channels, and Tamil medium schools. In other words, students that come from generally similar cultural practices acquire relatively homogeneous dispositions or *'taste'* that "functions below the level of consciousness" [… and] manifests itself in our most practical activities, such as the way we eat, walk, talk" (Bourdieu 1984, p. 466), which Jansen (2009, p. 51) defined as "inherited" "knowledge in the blood". This group distinctiveness makes inclusion and exclusion happen at a pre-conscious level and leads to the emergence of different groups based on, for example, ethnicity or language. What is evident in the above data is that when students are exposed to only monoethnic, monolingual social spaces such as family, monoethnic schools and monoethnic media they acquire ethnocentric dispositions and continue to live with "bitter knowledge" (Jansen, 2009, p. 114) about each other in the absence of shared lived experience with 'others'.

In contrast, as also evident in the above excerpts, the ethnocentric dispositions that these students bring to BE classroom from ethnically insular social spaces begin to reduce when they study together in multiethnic BE classrooms. As expressed in above excerpts, all students, irrespective of ethnicity, later realized when they come to know each other that the negative conceptions they previously held towards the ethnic others were misconceptions. This transformation towards less ethnocentric dispositions or supraethnic habitus takes place in relation to social conditions in multiethnic BE classrooms, which are different from those of monoethnic social spaces. This illustrates that it is possible that "one undergoes a process of *personal transformation* by sheer dint of being embedded within the field" (Shammas & Sandberg, 2016, p. 196, original emphasis). Habitus, though durable, has "an infinite capacity for generating products—thoughts, perceptions, expressions and actions; ... [yet its] limits are set by the historically and socially situated conditions of its production" (Bourdieu, 1990. p. 55). Agents who enter a new *field* feel a preconscious 'practical sense' of "what is appropriate in the circumstances and what is not" (Bourdieu & Thompson, 1991, p. 13). These conditions are evident in the following responses by the Math BE teacher at South College.

> ...in BE class the relationship between children is high. [...] everyone gets together and should continue education, [...] all together should go forward with own education. [...] there is no difference. In these (BE) classes, together they try to achieve own educational aim, they go together.

"What is appropriate" in the multiethnic BE classrooms is all students work together, reciprocate and cooperate to achieve common educational aims as a learning community. This togetherness is extended even to co-curricular activities. For instance, a Muslim student at South College expressed:

> We all get together and do our lessons and teamwork is there, when Sinhala students observe sill [Buddhist religious activity] we help them

Briefly, the analysis shows the importance of shared lived experiences in ethnically diverse social spaces to unlearn ethnocentric dispositions and acquire inclusive supraethnic dispositions. The findings also show that Sri Lanka has hitherto failed to use the formal education system as a social space to achieve this task due to ethnically polarized schools and classrooms along MTI, except in multiethnic BE classrooms in bi-media schools.

11.1 English: "It's like a Common Medium, so Everybody Is Equal"

Another finding is the contribution of English language as an "unmarked code" (Canagarajah, 2000, p. 126), a neutralizing force between the two contesting groups—Sinhala-speaking and Tamil-speaking. For instance, all student groups expressed that the feeling they previously had of segregation and alienation started to diminish with English coming to forefront in the BE classrooms. We draw from FGDs with Tamil students at Raveendranath College to exemplify this phenomenon.

Tamil Student 1: Because they speak in Sinhala, [and] we also couldn't handle Sinhala we couldn't understand. So they get just jealous (protective) [...] but with English medium people we can speak to them in English. So there were no fights in grades.

Tamil Student 6: Everyone should respect each other's' ethnicity and they shouldn't think that only their language is the best. That's where English comes in. That's why English should be there. So everyone will be interconnected.

Tamil Student 3:   It's like a common medium so everybody is equal...
Students: Yeah.
Tamil Student 3:   If you put Sinhala higher then Tamil language will be affected and it will affect Tamil people.
Tamil Student 2:   If you put Tamil language higher then it will affect Sinhala people.
Tamil Student 1:   So the solution is English.

According to these two groups of students, the lack of positive intergroup contact and presence of animosity was due to the lack of a common language of communication. Further evident is when English replaces Sinhala and Tamil as medium of communication; the contesting speech communities begin to feel comfortable because everybody becomes equal.

However, we argue that the lack of communication when students were in MTI classes in the primary grades does not necessarily mean that they were unable to speak English at that time. It may mean that English was not explicitly legitimized as a common language during this period. Instead, the legitimized MOI and hence language of communication was their mother tongues since they were studying through the medium of MTI. Unlike when they were in MTI classes, English has now become a legitimated language of communication through the BE programme. This explicit legitimatising of English may have shaped their linguistic habitus and persuaded communication in English, or might have made them regard their mother tongues less highly, diminishing the ascribed capital values for the respective mother-tongues. It is also visible in students' responses that the competition between the two forms of linguistic capital—of Sinhala and Tamil—is neutralized through the use of English. In other words, an equal leverage is created when English is the common communication medium, so that no more power is given to either group over the other. Equality is therefore created and discrimination is reduced. Also, 'oneness' may have been felt when they all become an English-speaking community or "a single linguistic community" (May, 2010, p. 153). To support this, we draw from the response of a BE student at Ravindranath College:

> When people are speaking in English the personality is different. I have seen it a couple of times, when Sinhala or Tamil speaking students speaking in completely English they feel that there wasn't a difference, and the way that the person is acting different.

What is apparent in the above views is that the ethnic habitus or language-based division in ethnicity is in some way eclipsed by English. For instance, when English is used as a common language which may also behave as an 'unmarked code', the feeling of '*a difference*' is replaced by commonality. It appears that English works as a 'neutralizing mediator', removing or reducing a power imbalance that would otherwise have been present when Sinhala and/or Tamil language was in use. It may have brought "value for people whose local languages and identities suffer from discriminatory markings of caste, *ethnicity*, and gender" (Canagarajah, 2005, p. 428, our emphasis). This effect is more obvious and boosted given the symbolic power of English linguistic capital. Though we interpret English as a 'neutralising' tool we do not disregard the overarching dominance of English given its high symbolic power that pervades every domain of global communication whether economic, educational, technological, or scientific. In fact, we argue that this high symbolic power may have over-powered Sinhala and Tamil or depreciated the capital values conferred to them. We suggest, though, that English as a powerful linguistic instrument plays an important role in redefining the logic of practice in multiethnic BE classrooms in Sri Lanka. It overcomes linguistic differences which otherwise would have been in existence if Sinhala or Tamil were the legitimised language of instruction.

12 Growing Respect for Each Other's Language and Culture

Another important phenomenon we observed in these BE classes was cross-linguistic flexibility where student navigated among all three languages. This was the case especially in South College, and to a certain extent in Raveendranath College. A Tamil student at South College elaborated cross-linguistic practices in the Citizenship Education classroom as below:

> It's like studying in all three languages. According to textbook the lesson is in English but when he [teacher] is explaining in Sinhala we can get the idea. And when we do group work in all three languages like writing definitions in all three languages, we can get the idea of that lesson in our mother tongue also.

This heteroglossic linguistic environment may have contributed to blurring ethnicities which were bounded by languages (Creese & Blackledge, 2015; Garcia, 2009; Garcia & Wei, 2014; Sayer, 2013; Wiley & Garcia, 2016), and may also have contributed largely towards creating an ethnic inclusivity (Theobald, Busch, & Laraghy, 2019). Though we do not embark on detailed analysis of cross-linguistic flexibility per se in this chapter we discuss the resulting impact of such heteroglossia below.

The data show students' growing recognition and respect towards each other's language and culture. Tamil students show greater motivation to learn Sinhala, which we discuss later. What is more important is the growing tolerance and even interest among Sinhala students towards Tamil language, which is in contrast to Sinhala students in Sinhala medium classes who lack willingness to learn Tamil, the 2NL (Davis, 2015). As reflected in the Sinhala students' responses at Raveendranath College below, it appears that when their Tamil friends converse in Tamil, the Sinhala students develop an openness towards learning the Tamil language.

Student (4): *When we were young we only associate with Sinhala students and Sinhalese. When I came here and heard Tamil I got scared instantly. [...]*
Student (3): *When we heard them talking in their language I initially thought I won't be able to talk with them. We didn't know if they scolded us or what they must be talking about us. But after we got to know each other and now we know them we don't feel much difference even when they talk in Tamil now and we cannot understand.*

Student (1): Some students in the class talk only in English, some in Sinhala and some in Tamil. When we overhear these we can have some knowledge about these languages. There our knowledge will improve so it is good.

It is evident that Sinhala students were initially scared and suspicious when they heard Tamil, but when they got to know about each other in the BE class these negative attitudes reduced. Now, as depicted in the last response, they see Tamil as a capital to accrue *'knowledge'*, together with motivation and an appreciation towards Tamil: *'When we overhear these we can have some knowledge about these languages.'* Being in the BE class, bitterness towards Tamil appears to have gone. In some instances, they even jumped into Tamil students' conversations as depicted below from a Sinhala BE student's response.

> After sometime when we listen to them, they also knew Sinhala and then they talked to us. And we also jump into their conversations and started to ask what they talked. Then our fears disappear and friendship developed.

Tamil students' responses demonstrated much higher motivation to learn Sinhala. The following excerpts exemplify the urge that the Tamil students have developed to learn Sinhala it being an important linguistic capital in the linguistic market of Sri Lanka.

(i) South College

Student (3): Because according to the condition of Sri Lanka most people speak Sinhala, so most important is to learn Sinhala. So we learn [in chorus].

Student (1): In the BE class we can learn so many things in Sinhala, and we can study the second (2NL) language also, for our O/level exam.

(ii) Raveendranath College

Student (1): And Sinhala friends help improve our Sinhala knowledge. And, in Sri Lanka the important language is Sinhala. If we don't know Sinhala it is not useful for us to live in Sri Lanka. Because Sri Lanka is our motherland and mostly Sinhala people live in Sri Lanka so it is good for us to know Sinhala language very well.

Student (2) (Sinhala speaking Muslim): And I wanted to talk to them [Tamil students] in Tamil since I wanted to improve my Tamil and in turn they would talk to us in Sinhala to improve their Sinhala.

The Tamil BE students were of the opinion that Sinhala is the most important language since it is spoken by majority so that they should learn it. It is evident that they learn Sinhala easily in the BE class and BE class is an investment in Sinhala linguistic capital which they need in future. In fact, as reported above, some Tamil BE students have chosen to offer Sinhala language—their 2NL—as a main subject in the public examination of General Certificate of Education (Ordinary level). This was further expressed by Tamil parents, as exemplified with one excerpt below.

Tamil parent (South College):   *My daughter and son both studied in bilingual classes, first when they were in Grade 6 they could speak a little bit English and Tamil thoroughly. Now they can speak all three languages, English Sinhala and Tamil. So I think my problems are over that they can face any challenge. This is (any) parents' wish and it is easily achieved in the English medium class.*

This Tamil parent held the same dispositions as their children regarding Sinhala language. Apart from more value given to English, the Tamil parents see Sinhala, the language of the 'other', as a valuable form of capital. They appreciate the opportunities offered in the BE programme to acquire it. All these comments illustrate those positive inclinations and dispositions towards the language of the other which are a mark of mutual respect, reciprocity and appreciation. In such a context, students' previously-held exclusionary, ethnocentric habitus can become less exclusionary, less bounded. Therefore, it can be suggested that being in the multilingual classroom where they overhear each other's languages may have contributed to developing mutual regard towards each other's languages.

The above circumstances illustrate that even though the students come to BE with a monolingual habitus this habitus is transformed in multiethnic BE classes. Though the legitimate logic of practice of the BE pedagogy is that of bilingualism—English and the students' mother tongue—it is evident in the findings that the implicit logic of practice at the practical level becomes trilingual—English, Sinhala and Tamil in the multiethnic BE classroom. It can be suggested that it is a strategy that students transpose their monolingual habitus to bilingual or even trilingual habitus, homologous to multiethnic multilingual BE pedagogy, so as to feel like a 'fish in water'. In such contexts, ethnic group separations defined by language become absorbent, and the "co-construction of positive bilingual identities" (Garcia-Mateus & Palmer, 2017, p. 247) becomes the norm in dialectic relation to the multiethnic and multilingual 'rules of the game' in the BE pedagogy.

13 Conclusion

The analysis highlights the importance of the education system in providing opportunity for ethnically diverse students to have authentic lived experience with ethnic 'others' to know each other and build reciprocity and mutual understanding. The study also demonstrates that the education system to date has been ethnically insular and has failed to provide for such endeavours in Sri Lanka. If steps are not taken, the children of Sri Lanka will continue to live with 'bitter knowledge' of each other. The findings also affirm that the transforming of ethnocentric habitus towards supraethnic inclusivity takes place in the multiethnic BE classroom because socially situated conditions in these classrooms require Sinhala, Tamil and Muslim students to work together in achieving their academic goals. Theoretically, the capital at stake in these classrooms is ethnic inclusivity not exclusivity. It is immanent with these objective structures of the BE field that the students' ethnic habitus begins to transform towards inclusivity.

Moreover, English being the linguistic capital with the highest value seems to be acting as a neutralizing medium between the other two linguistic capitals—Sinhala and Tamil. It appeared that English could create a "single linguistic community" (May, 2010, p. 153) or 'collective linguistic habitus' in the BE classroom that integrates the two segregated Sinhala and Tamil speech communities. (However, the larger study, on which this chapter draws, also provides evidence to the contrary; English, while bringing multiethnic BE students together, also creates segregation between English-knowing BE students and MTI students.) The study also demonstrates that the multiethnic BE pedagogy is a booster that motivates the learning of an ethnic other's language which is a characteristic of growing reciprocity, mutual recognition and interdependences between once hated groups (see Wijesekera, 2018), to which the flexibility of cross-linguistic navigation in the BE class may have contributed.

To conclude, this chapter explored ethnic group re/orientations that took place among ethnically diverse students when they studied together in multiethnic BE classrooms in Sri Lanka. This chapter shows how ethnically and linguistically segregated social spaces, including classrooms, can promote ethnocentric dispositions in the young people's minds. In contrast, BE classrooms in multiethnic schools can bring different groups together to promote mutual understanding and reciprocity, triggering transformation of ethnocentric dispositions towards inclusive dispositions within "socially situated conditions." As Shammas and Sandberg (2016, p. 196, original emphasis) posit, "one undergoes a process of *personal transformation* by sheer dint of being embedded within the field." As illustrated, the necessary conditions for this transformation from ethnocentrism to inclusivity are being and studying together, and having shared lived experiences enhanced by English as a common 'unmarked' code, together with cross-linguistic flexibility. These findings are highly relevant to MOI policy-making, especially in post-conflict countries such as Sri Lanka, for inculcating solidarity among diverse ethnic groups that is needed for sustainable reconciliation.

References

Baker, C., & Wright, W. E. (2017). *Foundation of bilingual education and bilingualism* (6th ed.). Bristol, England: Multilingial Matters.
Bickmore, K. (2008). Education for conflict resolution and peacebuilding in plural societies: Approaches from around the world. In K. Mandy, K. Bickmore, R. Heyhoe, M. Madison, & K. Mujidi (Eds.), *Comparative and International Education. Issues for Teachers* (pp. 249–272). Toronto, Canada: Canadian Scholars Press.

Bormann, N., Cederman, L., & Vogt, M. (2017). Language, religion, and ethnic civil war. *Journal of Conflict Resolution, 61*(4), 744–771. https://doi.org/10.1177/0022002715600755.

Bourdieu, P. (1977). *Outline of a theory of practice* (R. Nice, Trans.). New York, NY: Cambridge University Press.

Bourdieu, P. (1984). *Distinction: A social critique of the judgement of taste*. London, England: Routledge.

Bourdieu, P. (1990). *The logic of practice*. Stanford, USA: Stanford University Press.

Bourdieu, P., & Thompson, J. B. (1991). *Language and symbolic power*. (G. Raymond & M. Adamson, Trans). Harvard, USA: Harvard University Press.

Bourdieu, P. (2005). *The social structures of the economy*. Oxford, England: Polity Press.

Bourdieu, P., & Passeron, J. (1977). *Reproduction in education, society and culture*. London, England: Sage Publications.

Bourdieu, P., & Wacquant, L. J. D. (1992). *An invitation to reflexive sociology*. Cambridge, England: Polity Press.

Brutt-Griffler, J. (2002). Class, ethnicity, and language rights: An analysis of British colonial policy in Lesotho and Sri Lanka and some implications for language policy. *Journal of Language, Identity & Education, 1*(3), 207–234. https://doi.org/10.1207/S15327701JLIE0103_3.

Buckland, P. (2005). *Reshaping the future: Education and post conflict reconstruction*. Washington, D.C.: World Bank.

Canagarajah, A. S. (2000). Negotiating ideologies through English: Strategies from the periphery. In Thomas Ricento (Ed.), *Ideology, politics, and language policies: Focus on English* (pp. 121–132). Amesterdam, Philadelphia: John Benjamins Publishing.

Canagarajah, A. S. (2005). Dilemmas in planning English/vernacular relations in post-colonial communities. *Journal of Sociolinguistics, 9*(3), 418–447. https://doi.org/10.1111/j.1360-6441.2005.00299.x.

Canagarajah, A. S. (2007). Lingua franca English, multilingual communities, and language acquisition. *The Modern Language Journal, 91*, 923–939.

Census and Statistics Department. (2012). *Census of population and housing [Data file]*. Retrieved from http://www.statistics.gov.lk/PopHouSat/CPH2011/Pages/Activities/Reports/FinalReport/FinalReportE.pdf.

Chandra, K. (2006). What is ethnic identity and does it matter? *Annual Review of Political Science, 9*, 397–424. https://doi.org/10.1146/annurev.polisci.9.062404.170715.

Cohen, P. E. G. (2007). Mother tongue and other tongue in primary education: Can equity be achieved with the use of different languages. In H. Coleman (Ed.), *Language and development: Africa and beyond* (pp. 62–75). Ethiopia: British Council.

Coleman, H. (2007). Introduction: Language and the silent observers of development. In H. Coleman (Ed.), *Language and development: Africa and beyond* (pp. 1–10). Ethiopia: British Council.

Creese, A., & Blackledge, A. (2015). Translanguaging and identity in educational settings. *Annual Review of Applied Linguistics, 35*, 20–35. https://doi.org/10.1017/S0267190514000233.

Cross, M., & Naidoo, D. (2012). Race, diversity pedagogy: Mediated learning experience for transforming racist habitus and predispositions. *Review of Education, Pedagogy, and Cultural Studies, 34*(5), 227–244. https://doi.org/10.1080/10714413.2012.735558.

Davis, C. P. (2015). Speaking conflict: Ideological barriers to bilingual policy implementation in Civil War Sri Lanka. *Anthropology & Education Quarterly, 46*(2), 95–112. https://doi.org/10.1111/aeq.12093.

De Jong, E. J., & Howard, E. (2009). Integration in two-way immersion education: Equalising linguistic benefits for all students. *International Journal of Bilingual Education and Bilingualism, 12*(1), 81–99. https://doi.org/10.1080/13670050802149531.

Eriksen, T. H. (2010). *Ethnicity and nationalism: Anthropological perspectives*. London, England: Pluto Press.

Gabriel, S. P. (2014). 'After the break': Re-conceptualizing ethnicity, national identity and 'Malaysian-Chinese' identities. *Ethnic and Racial Studies, 37*(7), 1211–1224. https://doi.org/10.1080/01419870.2014.859286.

Garcia, O. (2009). Education, multilingualism, and translanguaging in the 21st Century. In T. Skutnabb-Kangas, R. Phillipson, A. K. Mohanty, & M. Panda (Eds.), *Social justice through multilingual education* (pp. 140–158). Bristol, England: Multilingual Matters.

Garcia, O., & Wei, L. (2014). *Translanguaging: Language, bilingualism and education*. New York, NY: Palgrave Macmillan.

García-Mateus, S., & Palmer, D. (2017). Translanguaging pedagogies for positive identities in two-way dual language bilingual education. *Journal of Language, Identity & Education, 16*(4), 245–255. https://doi.org/10.1080/15348458.2017.1329016.

Grenfell, M. (1998). Language and the classroom. In M. Grenfell & D. James (Eds.), *Bourdieu and education: Acts of practical theory* (pp. 72–88). London: Falmer Press.

Grenfell, M. J., & Lebaron, F. (Eds.). (2014). *Bourdieu and data analysis: Methodological principles and practice*. Oxford, GBR: Peter Lang AG.

Harwood, J., & Vincze, L. (2012). Ethnolinguistic identity and television use in a minority language setting. *Journal of Media Psychology, 24*(4), 135–142. https://doi.org/10.1027/1864-1105/a000071.

Hinkel, E. (2005). *Handbook of research in second language teaching and learning* (Vol. 1). NJ, USA: Lawrence Erlbaum Associates Inc.

Jansen, J. (2009). *Knowledge in the blood*. Stanford, CA: Stanford University Press.

Kandiah, T. (1984). Kaduva: Power and the english language weapon in Sri Lanka. In P. Colin-Tome & A. Halpe (Eds.), *Honouring EFC Ludowyk* (pp. 117–154). Colombo, Sri Lanka: Tisara Prakasakayo.

Kramsch, C. (2008). Ecological perspectives on foreign language education. *Language Teaching, 41*(3), 389–408.

Kramsch, C. (2010). Pierre Bourdieu: A biographical memoir. In A. A. J. Luke, (Ed.), *Pierre Bourdieu and literacy education*. Taylor and Francis.

Laitin, D. D. (2000). Language conflict and violence: The straw that strengthens the camel's back. In P. C. Stern & D. Druckman (Eds.), *International conflict resolution, after the Cold War* (pp. 531–568). Washington, D.C.: National Academy Press.

Liyanage, I., & Canagarajah, S. (2014). The teaching of local languages and interethnic understanding in Sri Lanka. In V. Zenotz, J. Cenoz, & D. Gorter (Eds.), *Minority languages and multilingual education* (pp. 119–135). Netherlands: Springer.

McCarty, T. L., Skutnabb-Kangas, T., & Magga, O. H. (2008). Education for speakers of endangered languages. In B. Spolsky & F. M. Hult (Eds.), *Handbook of educational linguistics* (pp. 297–312). Oxford, UK: Blackwell Publishing.

May, S. (2010). Language policy. In M. Grenfell (Ed.), *Bourdieu, language and linguistics* (pp. 147–169). London, England: Bloomsbury Publishing.

Ministry of Education. (2016a). *School census preliminary reports 2016*. Retrieved from http://www.moe.gov.lk/english/ on October 20, 2017.

Ministry of Education. (2016b). *Content and language integrated learning handbook*. Ministry of Education. Isurupaya, Battaramulla: Sri Lanka.

Nadesan, S. (1957). Regional autonomy in a multi-national state 1957. *Ceylon Sunday Observer July 1957*. Retrieved from http://sangam.org/regional-autonomy-multi-national-state/ on August 15, 2018.

National Institute of Education. (2009). *Bilingual education: Teacher development manual*. Maharagama: Sri Lanka: National Institute of Education.

Noels, K. A., Kil, H., & Fang, Y. (2014). Ethnolinguistic orientation and language variation: Measuring and archiving ethnolinguistic vitality, attitudes, and identity. *Language and Linguistic Compass, 8*(11), 618–628. https://doi.org/10.1111/lnc3.12105.

Norton, B., & Toohey, K. (2011). Identity, language learning, and social change. *Language Teaching, 44*(4), 412–446. https://doi.org/10.1017/S0261444811000309.

Parliament Secretariat of Sri Lanka. (2015). *The constitution of Sri Lanka (Revised Edition 2015)*. Retrieved from www.parliament.lk/files/pdf/constitution.pdf.

Sayer, P. (2013). Translanguaging, TexMex, and bilingual pedagogy: Emergent bilingual learning through the vernacular. *TESOL Quarterly, 47*(1), 63–88.
Saunders, B. (2007). (Post) colonial language: English, Sinhala, and Tamil in Sri Lanka. Retrieved from http://homes.chass.utoronto.ca/~cpercy/courses/eng6365-saunders.htm.
Shammas, V. L., & Sandberg, S. (2016). Habitus, capital, and conflict: Bringing Bourdieusian field theory to criminology. *Criminology & Criminal Justice, 16*(20), 195–213. https://doi.org/10.1177/1748895815603774.
Spolsky, B. (2011). *Does the United States need a language policy?* Retrieved from http://www.cal.org/resource-center/briefs-digests/digests/%28offset%29/15.
Spolsky, B., & Hult, M. F. (2008). *The handbook of educational linguistics*. Malden, MA: Blackwell Publishing.
Tajfel, H. (1974). Social identity and intergroup behaviour. *Social Science Information, 13*(2), 65–93. https://doi.org/10.1177/053901847401300204.
Tajfel, H. (Ed.). (1978). *Differentiation between social groups: Studies in the social psychology of intergroup relations*. London, England: Academic Press.
Theobald, M. A., Busch, G., & Laraghy, M. (2019). Children's views and strategies for making friends in linguistically diverse English medium instruction settings. In I. Liyanage, & T. Walker (Eds.), *Mulitlingual education yearbook 2019: Media of instruction and multilingual settings*. Switzerland: Springer (In Press).
Tochon, F. V. (2019). Educational globalization and the creation of split identities. In I. Liyanage, & T. Walker (Eds.), *Mulitlingual education yearbook 2019: Media of instruction and multilingual settings*. Switzerland: Springer (In Press).
Tollefson, J. W. (2015). Language education policy in late modernity: Insights from situated approaches—commentary. *Language Policy, 14*(2), 183–189. https://doi.org/10.1007/s10993-014-9353-8.
Wickrema, A., & Colenso, P. (2003). *Respect for diversity in education publication—The Sri Lankan experience*. Washington, D.C.: Unpublished paper.
Wijesekera, H. D. (2011). Education as a tool of ethnic integration: Are we successful? In M. Jayawardene (Ed.), *Challenges of post conflict Sri Lanka*, (pp. 231–246). Colombo, Sri Lanka: Papers from the 4th International Symposium of General Sir John Kotelawela University.
Wijesekera, H. D. (2018). *Students' ethnolinguistic identities in multiethnic, bilingual education classrooms in Sri Lanka* (Doctoral dissertation). Queensland University of Technology, Brisbane, Queensland.
Wijesekera, H. D., Alford, J., & Mu, M. G. (2018). Forging inclusive practice in ethnically-segregated school systems: lessons from one multiethnic, bilingual education classroom in Sri Lanka. *International Journal of Inclusive Education*, 1–19. https://doi.org/10.1080/13603116.2018.1514730.
Wiley, T., & García, O. (2016). Language policy and planning in language education: Legacies, consequences, and possibilities. *Modern Language Journal, 100*(S1), 48–63. https://doi.org/10.1111/modl.12303.

Harsha Dulari Wijesekera (Ph.D.) is a Senior Lecturer at the Postgraduate Institute of English, Open University of Sri Lanka. Her research interests include bilingual education, sociolinguistics, social cohesion, assessment and evaluation in ELT, teacher education, and sociology of education. She started her teaching career as a teacher in public schools. At the tertiary level, she had worked in state, private and military universities, and as an Edexcel teacher trainer before she joined the PGIE.

Jennifer Alford (Ph.D.) is a Senior Lecturer and co-leader of the Literacies, Language, Texts and Technologies (LLTT) research group in the Faculty of Education, Queensland University of Technology, Australia. Her research interests include pedagogic models of literacy and English language education and what they afford; how English language education policies articulate, or otherwise, notions of criticality; and how teachers understand and mobilise approaches to literacy and language education amid increasingly narrow, test-related education priorities. She is also interested in: how schools provide equitable, robust English language education programs for culturally diverse learners; intercultural capacity for teachers; and bi/multilingual education policy and practice. Jennifer's Ph.D. thesis won the 2015 Penny McKay Memorial Award for Outstanding Thesis in Language Education, and a QUT Outstanding Thesis Award. She is the author of the forthcoming Routledge book called Critical Literacy with adolescent English language learners: Exploring policy and practice in global contexts.

CLIL for Who? Commodification of English-Medium Courses in Japan's Higher Education

Kayoko Hashimoto and Gregory Paul Glasgow

Abstract Content and Language Integrated Learning (CLIL), which had its origins in Europe in the 1990s, has been developed on the assumption that language learning is more effective if knowledge of content other than language is simultaneously acquired. Nowadays, however, CLIL tends to be considered more as one form of English-medium instruction, which symbolizes the current trend towards globalization in education. In Japan, where it is still in its early stages of development, CLIL-related practices are rarely documented and its potential effectiveness as a pedagogical approach is yet to be determined. This chapter situates CLIL within the context of Japan's higher education, with a particular focus on the Top Global University Project. While the government pushes the higher education sector to increase its international competitiveness by improving English proficiency levels and increasing the number of international students, there is an absence in government policies of acknowledgment of EMI and of the notion of bilingual education. This chapter examines how top Japanese universities have engaged in CLIL, analyses relevant documents published by universities and government offices, and identifies the problems and challenges in implementing CLIL or CLIL-influenced programs in Japan.

Keywords CLIL · EMI · Bilingual education · Top global university project · Japan's higher education

---

K. Hashimoto (✉)
The University of Queensland, Brisbane, Australia
e-mail: k.hashimoto@uq.edu.au

G. P. Glasgow
Kanda University of International Studies, Chiba, Japan
e-mail: gglinguist@gmail.com

1 Introduction

Since the term Content and Language Integrated Learning (CLIL) was coined in Europe in 1994 (Pérez-Canado, 2012), CLIL has been an increasingly popular type of bilingual education developed on "the assumption that the results of language learning are more sustainable if content other than language itself is simultaneously acquired with language skills" (Gogolin, 2013). Nowadays, however, even though the European Commission continues to emphasize the role of language education through CLIL in fostering European values such as social cohesion, democratic citizenship, and intercultural dialogue (Codó, 2018), it is also often seen primarily as another form of English-medium instruction (EMI). Dalton-Puffer (2007) explains the dominance of English as a target language in CLIL-type programs as the "trend towards internationalization and globalization, putting pressure on education systems to provide skills which will allow students to stand their ground in international contexts" (p. 1). While Nikula and Moore (2016) see the preparation of learners for the global community as a strength of this trend, they also point to the risk of diminishing the importance of other languages, and Codó (2018) sees the trend as "the effect of the commodification of language on intercultural dialogue" (p. 481). Yet research on CLIL, conducted predominantly in Europe, has generally been "acritical, embracing the inherent goodness of this approach, and centring on assessing its effectiveness for raising students' proficiency levels" (Codó, 2018, p. 475). The examination of CLIL from language policy perspectives is relatively new; Relaño-Pastor (2018), for example, brings a critical sociolinguistic ethnography approach to examining the complex relationship between policy and practice in CLIL-type bilingual programs, shedding light on the neoliberalization and commodification processes in language education in Europe.

CLIL has been spreading rapidly in Asia, but delivery modes and approaches vary, reflecting issues of EMI in the region. EMI in Asia has been extensively researched (Tollefson & Tsui, 2004; Hamid, Nguyen, & Baldauf, 2014; Fenton-Smith, Humphreys, & Walkinshaw, 2017) in a context in which many Asian countries have been seeking to enhance their English language capacities in order to cope with the impact of globalization on education and to establish their standing in the international community (see, e.g., Walker, Liyanage, Madya, & Hidayati, 2019). In Hong Kong, where EMI schools were in the majority before sovereignty reverted to China (Tsui, 2004), CLIL has been regarded as a variant of English-medium teaching (Lo, 2017). As Lo (2017) points out, in EMI secondary schools in Hong Kong, because subject specialists, rather than English language teachers, teach content-subjects in CLIL, the professional development (PD) of teachers is essential for the successful delivery of CLIL. In China, CLIL is used to teach non-language subjects at government schools in the context of Chinese-English bilingual education, which has been promoted by the government since the 1990s (Wei & Feng, 2015). Wei and Feng (2015) report that such CLIL-type bilingual education in China differs from immersion programs in that the exposure to the target language, in this case English, is usually somewhere between five and fifteen percent, whereas in prototypical immersion programs in any international setting, it normally exceeds fifty percent. This suggests that English is not a dominant language in bilingual programs in China, which has pursued a national language policy centred on Putonghua (Chen, 2018). This is in stark contrast to the situation in Malaysia where, as part of its nation-building efforts, the government reversed the medium of instruction (MOI) for Science and Mathematics from English to Bahasa Malaysia in 2008, which ironically prompted an increase in enrolments in EMI international schools (Gill, 2014).

In an era when "internationalization of education and neo-liberal ideology have gone hand-in-hand" (Liyanage, Tran, & Ata, 2018, p. 7), the Taiwanese government has encouraged the tertiary sector to establish CLIL programs for marketing purposes, mainly to attract international students, including native speakers of English and high proficiency English speakers. This is being done even though such a combination may have the potential to create sociocultural tensions in class between learners of different proficiencies and cultural backgrounds (Yang, 2015). Yang's study (2015) on the effectiveness of university CLIL courses in Taiwan reveals that students are unsure about the efficacy of CLIL courses in improving their productive skills (speaking and writing) in English and in enhancing their content knowledge, and argues that this is particularly evident in students of low English proficiency. The findings not only demonstrate a gap between the government initiative and actual implementation, but also the policy-makers' view that CLIL is a new and convenient tool for attracting students, regardless of their background. Increasing the number of international students is one of the major goals of Japan's internationalization of higher education (Burgess, Gibson, Kalphake, & Selzer, 2010; Chapple, 2014), but unlike in Taiwan and some other Asian countries, CLIL has not yet been explicitly identified as a new tool in the Japanese government's arsenal for the internationalization of higher education.

In 2018, the Japan CLIL Pedagogy Association held its first conference in Tokyo. Around thirty papers were presented at the conference by educators and teachers at all levels—from kindergarten to university—and from local Boards of Education. Given that this was a conference for CLIL practitioners and researchers, the program itself reflected certain aspects of local CLIL practices that characterize 'bilingual' education in Japan. The English title of the conference was *The 1st J-CLIL Annual Bilingual Conference*, while the original Japanese was 日本CLIL教育学会 (J-CLIL) 第一回大会, literally, *Japan CLIL Education Association (J-CLIL) First Congress* (Japan CLIL Pedagogy Association, 2018). Strangely, there is no equivalent of 'bilingual' in the original Japanese. The gap between English and Japanese is also evident in the conference program. The program uses both Japanese and English but does not do so consistently. For example, it gives the names of presenters, their affiliations, and paper titles only in one language—Japanese or English. Presumably, if the information is given in Japanese, the paper will be presented in Japanese. In English-speaking countries, such as Australia, the description 'bilingual conference' normally implies that all information will be available in both languages, but that is not the case here. Interestingly, only the *Reception Exhibition*, *Opening*, and *Closing* are marked as 'bilingual' using English in the timetable for the conference. This suggests that 'bilingual' must include English and that the conference has two difference audiences—Japanese speakers and English-speaking foreigners who do not necessarily speak Japanese.

In Japanese government policy documents, 'bilingualism' is only attributed to foreigners (Hashimoto, 2013a), and this relates to the fact that the so-called 'English-only' curriculum, promoted by the Ministry of Education, Culture, Sports, Science and Technology (MEXT) for primary, secondary and tertiary programs, has never been officially identified as an EMI policy or a bilingual education policy (Hashimoto, 2013a, 2018a, 2018b). How does this kind of ambivalent attitude towards EMI and bilingualism affect the way the tertiary sector introduces CLIL in its programs as part of its internationalization strategies? In critiquing language policy and planning in Europe and Asia, Diallo and Liddicoat (2014) argue that pedagogical issues tend to be delegated to teachers while there is silence on the macro level. Does this apply to CLIL pedagogy in higher education in Japan? And, if so, what are the implications for learners and teachers?

This chapter explores these questions by examining policy documents on Japan's internationalization of higher education as well as CLIL-related information available on the websites of universities participating in the Top Global University Project (hereafter TGUP). TGUP, a government-funded project that replaced the Global 30 Project in 2014, aims to "enhance the international compatibility and competitiveness of higher education in Japan" by providing "prioritised support for the world-class and innovative universities that lead the internationalization of Japanese universities" (MEXT, 2014c). To improve the "ratio of foreign faculty and students" and to increase the number of "lectures in English" (MEXT, 2014c, original English) were priority targets for participating universities. In the 2018 interim reports on the performance of each university (Japan Society for the Promotion of Science, 2018; MEXT, 2018a, 2018b), the number of courses offered in English remained as a key item for measuring achievement. This study applies Critical Discourse Analysis as a methodological tool for analysing these documents (Fairclough, 2001; van Dijk, 2008; Blackledge, 2009). When documents are available in both Japanese and English, we identify any differences between them and discuss the implications of the differences.

2 Japan's Education System: CLIL, but not EMI or Bilingual Education

As stated earlier, while CLIL has been increasingly known as a form of EMI in Europe and Asia, MEXT has not yet begun to promote CLIL as a means of enhancing English language teaching (ELT) for primary, secondary and tertiary education. There are a number of reasons for this, but the absence of the notion of bilingualism in Japanese society and the lack of a definition of MOI in educational policies have been significant factors in the way CLIL has been introduced in Japan's education system.

In the government's policy documents, bilingualism is attributed only to foreigners, and the specific way the Japanese terms are used to describe 'bilingual' and 'bilingualism' reflects the ambiguous notion of MOI in curriculum documents. The terms 'bilingual" and 'bilingualism' are mostly written in *katakana* (a type of Japanese character used for loanwords) even though Japanese equivalents exist. The ubiquity of *katakana* words in Japanese society is widely acknowledged and has been documented as a cultural phenomenon (Stanlaw, 2004; Backhaus, 2007; Agency of Cultural Affairs, 2014). Critics such as Kato (2006) argue that *katakana* words are often used in order to obscure meaning. While the *katakana* word for 'bilingual' functions to label English-speaking foreigners (Hashimoto, 2018c), the kanji equivalents such as 二言語 (two languages), 二ヵ国語 (languages of two countries), 二言語使用 (use of two languages) or 二言語使用者 (user of two languages) draw attention to the two languages, which are given equal weight. In Japan, the two languages are usually Japanese and a foreign language, but a foreign language is unlikely to be given the same importance as the national language, particularly when the foreign language is not identified. As discussed later in this chapter, MEXT has maintained the term 'foreign language' in its educational policies when it actually means English, not to allow for the possibility that it might refer to other languages but, in an effort to avoid giving official status to English in Japanese society.

As with 'bilingual' and 'bilingualism', the term 'medium of instruction' (指導言語, lit. instruction language) is only found in documents that refer to foreign and returnee children on the MEXT website. The annual reports, 2014–2016, of one local government on support projects for foreign and returnee children (Hashimoto, 2013b) states that "because the *instruction languages* vary often it is not possible to send instructors who speak their mother tongues" (Yokosuka-City, 2017, original Japanese, authors' translation and emphasis). In the document, the term 'instruction languages' is used in reference to the mother tongues of the children, rather than to provide information about which languages are actually used to teach the children in the schools in question. It could be interpreted that, since the children speak many different mother tongues, the term 'instruction language' is used to represent them all without identifying the languages. In fact, the report claims that there are eleven different languages but does not list the languages.

In contrast to this, there are numerous entries for the Japanese term for 'English' in the public documents available on the MEXT website, but these are often under the category of foreign languages, rather than MOI. In 2010, the Office for Promoting Foreign Language Education (Elementary and Secondary Education Bureau, International Education Division) set up a study panel for the improvement of foreign language proficiency as one of its research collaboration panels. This panel consists of twelve members—five are university academics, four are from the business sector (trade and banking), two are from the education industry and one from the sport sector, but there is no representation of primary or secondary schools. According to the minutes of the panel's first meeting, one of the university academics reported that his university had incorporated CLIL in the undergraduate curriculum partly because it had been chosen to participate in the Global 30 Project. He advised the panel that CLIL is a way to teach specialist content in easy language using supporting materials (often visuals), and that it was developed in Europe mainly for primary and secondary education. He explained that CLIL programs are available for both domestic and international students at his university:

> … it is difficult for international students to master Japanese, and that is why we want to provide an environment for them to study hard mixing with Japanese students. In order to do that, we need to create a mutual space. Unless we create some middle ground between a place only for Japanese and a place only for Americans, they are not able to mix with each other. CLIL is one of the arrangements for achieving this.
>
> … Since we offer the courses [CLIL] in English, students who are fluent in English, such as international students, can take them. At the same time, Japanese students whose English is not as proficient can also study the content in English in CLIL programs.
>
> (MEXT, 2010, Authors' translation)

This statement highlights several issues. First, CLIL is understood as a way to teach content to students who do not have a high level of language proficiency. If CLIL is offered using English, certainly Japanese students who want to improve their English will benefit from attending CLIL programs, but what are the implications for American international students? Do they want to study the content in a program if it is designed for or targeted at students with lower English proficiency? Given that the catchphrase of the Global 30 Project for international students was 'Study in English at Japanese universities' (Hashimoto, 2013a), this private university responded to the government's expectations by offering what they call CLIL programs for both domestic and international students. Burgess et al. (2010) blame the 'closedness' of the Japanese tertiary sector for the isolation of international students, and the post-project evaluation of the Global 30 Project made the point that most degree courses offered in English are isolated from the rest of the university curricula (MEXT, 2015). Is CLIL an appropriate response to this problem? How will the level of academic content be reconciled with language instruction pitched at students with lower level proficiency? How will students with different levels of language proficiency be assessed in the same course, particularly if lower proficiency students, as language learners, struggle to reconcile language and content? By allowing both domestic students developing their English language proficiency and English-dominant international students to enrol in CLIL programs, the original intention behind CLIL—content is simultaneously acquired with language skills—is totally lost, or is maintained at the expense of international students who do not need CLIL.

In 2014, CLIL was mentioned at a meeting of another research collaboration panel of the Office for Promoting Foreign Language Education (Elementary and Secondary Education Bureau) on 'Setting targets for achievement using a 'can-do list' for foreign language education' (MEXT, 2014a). The panel consisted of eight university academics, two high school teachers, and one representative from a local Board of Education. Although, historically, Japan is a highly examination-oriented society (Zeng, 1999), setting clear goals for each level of language proficiency in the four skills and assessing learners' proficiency accordingly is a new challenge for Japan. At the ninth meeting of the study panel, one panel member commented in relation to CLIL that:

> Like Finland, if efforts are made to incorporate a CLIL-type element—learning a foreign language with content from other subjects - into the class, it would be possible to set a high [proficiency] goal. Increasing the number of class hours is not enough. It is necessary to change the quality as well.
>
> (MEXT, 2014a, authors' translation)

This comment suggests that CLIL is seen as a way of utilising a different teaching method that will enhance the effectiveness of foreign language teaching. This echoes such expectations as that "CLIL can complement the traditional EFL (English as a Foreign Language) methodologies, such as the grammar translation and audiolingual methods, and CLT [Communicative Language Teaching]" (Ikeda, Pinner, Mehisto, & Marsh, 2013, p. 1) and that "the concept of CLIL seems to have the potential to revitalize and expand EFL teaching in Japan" (Sasajima, 2013, p. 56).

CLIL is also mentioned in the 2017 interim report of Super-Global High Schools (SGH). SGH is a funding scheme that was created to "nurture global leaders who can compete internationally from the high school stage" (MEXT, 2012), and "the designated schools are expected to design a profile of their ideal leader, set specific research topics and education content in consideration of their regional characteristics and features of the schools" (Super Global High School, 2018, original English). Since 2014, both public and private schools have been chosen for five-year funding—56 schools in 2014, 56 schools in 2015, and 11 schools in 2016. In 2017, MEXT set up a panel to review the SGH project. In the interim report, two schools (one of them attached to a top national university) were praised for incorporating CLIL into the curriculum, including collaboration between English language subjects and other content subjects (MEXT, 2017a). CLIL is also incorporated in one primary school, which is a MEXT nominated research development school that is attached to a top national university. The school reports that in order to enhance students' communication skills, CLIL has been introduced to English classes in all grades (1–6) by allowing students to learn content from other subjects and about school events in English (MEXT, 2017b). These examples suggest that CLIL is still very new to school-level education, and introducing it into the school curriculum depends on local initiatives, including relationships with local universities, rather than on government guidance. The next section presents findings of analysis of documents related to how top Japanese universities have embraced CLIL as an opportunity for curriculum development.

3 CLIL and Top Global Universities

The original Japanese name of TGUP is スーパーグローバル大学創成支援 (lit. creation and support of super global universities). Although 'Top Global University Project' is the official English term, the direct translation of the Japanese is used in the section on "University Education and Global Human Resource Development for the Future" in the English version of the 2013 White Paper: "MEXT has been promoting projects, such as pushing for studying abroad, *super global* universities and high schools" (MEXT, 2013, original English, authors' emphasis). The term 'super' seems to have particular importance for the government. It is also applied to other government-funded schemes for high schools, such as SGH, as discussed in the previous section, and 'Super Professional High Schools' (SPH), which were introduced in 2014 in order to promote vocational training (MEXT, 2014b). Unlike TGUP, the English name for SGH has remained the same as the original Japanese—it was not changed to 'Top Global High Schools'. This kind of usage of the term 'super' can be explained as an example of Japanese-English, which indicates that a series of government-funded 'super' projects are decidedly domestic in nature (Chapple, 2014).

Thirty-seven universities were selected to participate in TGUP in 2014. Type A universities (Top Type) are institutions (eleven national and two private) that are "world-class universities that have the potential to be ranked in the top 100 in world university rankings" (MEXT, 2014c), and Type B (Global Traction Type) are institutions (ten national, two prefectural, and twelve private) that are "innovative universities that lead the internationalization of Japanese society, based on continuous improvement of their current efforts" (MEXT, 2014c). The funding period is up to ten years, depending on the nation's financial circumstances, and the funding for each university is determined by the outcome of progress reviews, which are carried out every fiscal year. Of the thirty-seven universities, two (both Type B) included CLIL in their proposed initiatives when they applied. Sophia University (private) claimed that it offered CLIL subjects that allow students to learn specialized content in English, and proposed to conduct TEAP (Test of English for Academic Purposes) to measure the effectiveness of CLIL-based English teaching, as well as CLIL subjects in Japanese for international students. The other university that made reference to CLIL is Aizu University (prefectural), which claimed that it has been a bilingual university since its establishment. It proposed to deliver advanced EMI courses using a CLIL-based approach, allowing international students to study alongside Japanese students.

MEXT has planned to conduct interim assessments in the fourth and seventh years of funding. In 2018, MEXT published the outcome of the first assessment in various forms. Before analysing the interim assessment, this section first examines how each TGUP university has engaged with CLIL, based on the information available on their university websites. For the website search, any CLIL-related information was grouped into three categories: curriculum, staff profiles (including publications and presentations), and events and PD such as conferences and seminars. As Tables 1 and 2 show, there is interest in CLIL—almost half of the universities have academic staff members who are engaged in CLIL and half of the Type A universities have organized CLIL-related events. Another interesting aspect is that all but one of the universities that offer CLIL-related courses are private universities. This could reflect the fact that the majority of Type A universities are research-oriented national universities that attract international students mainly for graduate study, whereas private universities tend to attract international students to their undergraduate programs and, as a result, their programs are more varied.

Table 1 CLIL and Type A Top Global Universities (July 2018)

	University	Curriculum	Staff profile/publication	Events/professional development
National				
1	Hokkaido			
2	Tohoku		✓	✓
3	Tsukuba		✓	
4	Tokyo		✓	✓
5	Tokyo, medical & dental		✓	
6	Tokyo, technology			✓
7	Nagoya		✓	
8	Kyoto			✓
9	Osaka			
10	Hiroshima		✓	
11	Kyushu		✓	✓
Private				
12	Keio			
13	Waseda	✓ Study abroad pre-departure	✓	✓

As for PD, Tohoku University (Type A, national) organized a PD program on 'Theory and Practice of CLIL' in October 2017. According the promotional flyer, English classes for improving practical skills offered at the university would be introduced along with CLIL theories. Another Type A university (Tokyo Institute of Technology, national) has regularly run a series of PD seminars on CLIL (delivered by a language centre attached to a university in Australia) since 2015. Interestingly, this PD program has been promoted as 'Teaching in English Seminar'. In terms of undergraduate programs, only Waseda University (Type A, private) offers a program using CLIL in preparation for study-abroad, which forms part of 'Area Studies and Plurilgual/Multicultural education'.

Among Type B universities, Kyoto Institute of Technology (national) offers 'Active English CLIL' as part of its elite program. No information is available on the content of this course, but the university states that, as one of the TGUP universities, it aims to train students to reach a Test of English for International Communication [Listening and Reading] score of 730 upon graduation. Sophia University (private) uses a CLIL approach in its academic communication course, which is part of the English for Academic Purposes program, as well as in the fourth-year courses for students majoring in English literature. At Hosei University (private), the Department of Global and Interdisciplinary Studies offers all of its courses in English. It claims that upon completion of one of the courses, Education for Children III, students should be able to design and conduct foreign language activities using a project-

Table 2 CLIL and Type B Top Global Universities (July 2018)

	University	Curriculum	Staff profile/publication	Events/professional development
National				
1	Chiba		✓	
2	Tokyo, foreign studies		✓	
3	Tokyo, arts			
4	Nagaoka, technology			
5	Kanazawa		✓	
6	Toyohashi, technology			
7	Kyoto, technology	✓ Active english		
8	Nara, science & technology			
9	Okayama		✓	✓
10	Kumamoto			
Prefectural				
11	Akita international			
12	Aizu			
Private				
13	ICU			
14	Shibaura, technology			
15	Sophia	✓ English literature; academic communication	✓	✓
16	Toyo		✓	
17	Hosei	✓ Education for children		
18	Meiji		✓	
19	Rikkyo	✓ Study abroad program (UK)	✓	
20	Soka		✓	
21	International			
22	Ritsumeikan	✓ English teacher training courses	✓	✓
23	Kwansei		✓	
24	Ritsumeikan Asia Pacific			

based approach or CLIL. Rikkyo University (private) reports that its 'Short-Term Study Abroad Program in Economics' includes 'English for Economics' in CLIL offered by a university in the UK. It is worth noting that no CLIL-related information is available on the websites of Akita International, which offers all courses in English, ICU, whose students are fully bilingual, or Aizu University, which conducts university business bilingually. As mentioned earlier, Aizu University initially proposed to offer some courses using a CLIL-based approach, but these do not appear on the current website. Perhaps these universities' indifference to CLIL demonstrates that, as Fortanet-Gomez (2013) points out, teaching a subject in a foreign language is not the same as the integration of language instruction and content.

In 2018, MEXT published a summary report on the interim review of TGUP. Among the thirty-seven universities, six (16%) were given a rating of 'S', signifying good progress and the likelihood of completing their proposed projects. Twenty-five universities (68%) were given an 'A', indicating the probability that they would achieve their goals if they continued their current efforts, and six universities (16%) received a 'B', on the grounds that they needed to make further efforts in order to achieve the proposed targets (MEXT, 2018a). The summary highlights the increase in the number of courses offered using foreign languages as MOI, the number of Japanese students who have studied abroad, and the number of international students, as follows:

> …the number of courses offered in *foreign language(s)* has increased 1.7 times compared to the year before the project started (19,533 course in 2013; 32,846 courses in 2016), and there are 873 degree courses that can be completed only in *foreign language(s)*, which is an increase of 221 compared to the year before the project started. … Student mobility has also increased: the number of students who studied abroad for credit has increased 1.5 times (16,055 in 2013; 23,532 in 2016), and the number of [*foreign*] international students has increased 1.4 times (49,618 in 2013; 69,119 in 2016). Although there is some progress in the number of students who satisfy the expected level of *language proficiency*, further efforts are expected to achieve the final goals.
>
> (MEXT, 2018a, authors' translation and emphasis)

Clearly, numbers matter as a measure of achievement of TGUP, but in contrast to the detailed information on the numbers, the content of key features remains ambiguous because the foreign language(s) are not identified. In fact, the four-page document does not contain the word 'English' anywhere. The summary states that Japanese students' language proficiency has not improved as expected, but the document does not say that this refers to English proficiency. This complete absence of the term 'English' in the document suggests that its omission is not accidental. As additional information to the interim report, MEXT produced a document entitled スーパーグローバル大学創成支援事業グッドプラクティス集 [Top Global University Project Good Practice Collection] (MEXT, 2018b). MEXT explains that the purpose of this publication is to share information on the various excellent projects conducted by the universities with the general public, but it is rather strange to see that the term 'good practice' is written as a loanword in *katakana*.

In the collection, 'Efforts to increase language proficiency' and 'Courses offered in foreign languages and degree courses that can be completed only in foreign languages' are among the eleven items on the good practice list. Contrary to the government's insistence on using the term 'foreign language(s)', rather than English, each university uses expressions such as 'offer in English', 'take in English', 'conduct in English', 'provide in English', 'Englishnisation of minutes', 'Englishnisation of courses', and 'Englishnisation of teaching materials'. No other languages are mentioned, apart from Sophia University's reference to its system for recording individual students' language progress. Throughout the Collection, there is no term that refers to CLIL or bilingual. In terms of MOI or EMI, only one university (Soka University) uses the term 'English Medium Programs' in English, which is explained in Japanese as 'courses that can be completed only in English'. Another interesting feature is that English-only courses are often described or named as 'global' in English: 'Super Global Course', in which all courses are offered in English (Kyoto); the 'Global Liberal Arts Program' (GLAP) in which a degree can be obtained by taking courses only in English (Rikkyo); 'Global Communication Workshop', which is an English negotiation practice workshop (Tokyo Medical & Dental); and 'Global Studies in Japanese Cultures Program', which is an English degree program (Waseda).

Rose and McKinley (2018) argue that TGUP seems to emphasize the development of EMI courses for both the domestic and international student bodies. In fact, an emphasis on EMI as a space for integrating Japanese and foreign students can be observed in some of the statements: "The percentage of international students is 43%" (Super Global Course, Kyoto); "Japanese students take the classes in English with international students" (Kumamoto); and, "International students study their specialized courses offered in English with Japanese undergraduate students" (Akita). However, in 2017 93.3% of international students studying in Japan were from Asia, most notably 40% from China and 23% from Vietnam (Japan Student Services Organisation, 2017). International students are never identified by their nationality—only their 'foreignness' is emphasized. Strategic engagement and cooperation with overseas universities is predominantly about universities in the UK, USA and Australia. This presents a very curious picture of Japan's internationalization strategies in higher education if we consider the future development of CLIL. 'Strategic engagement', therefore, seems to be less focused on engagement that reflects broader cultural pluralism and corresponds with the current international student body in Japanese universities. On the contrary, CLIL appears to be utilized more narrowly as a means to commodify EMI courses in Japanese higher education under the guise of 'internationalization', which in the Japanese sense seems to remain a vision that is narrowly restricted to North American, British and Australian varieties of English (Kubota, 2002).

4 Conclusion

Morizumi (2015) observes that MEXT's ambiguous definition of MOI left the tertiary sector to interpret and implement the government initiative to promote 'English courses' in their own ways, which has implications for how CLIL is perceived and implemented in Japanese higher education. As examined in this chapter, there seem to be three different types of English-medium courses offered under this initiative: one for Japanese students, one for international students, and one for both Japanese and international students. The first type is courses to enhance Japanese students' English proficiency effectively. This reflects another MEXT initiative of 'teaching English classes in English' similar to the one at upper secondary school level This, in fact, was *not* a CLIL initiative and nor did not constitute EMI because it only referred to the amount of English that teachers use in class, depending on students' proficiency levels, and did not apply to teaching materials or assessment (Hashimoto, 2013a). CLIL in Japanese higher education, however, seems to be welcomed as a new tool that offers different teaching models for this type of English course. Although acquiring language skills is the main purpose in this type of study context, content is also important because students' motivation to learn a language also depends on their interest in the content. If, however, the content relates to already-familiar topics the issue is how to describe and explain familiar matters in English.

The second type of English-medium courses are offered to international students. The expression 'degree courses that can be completed only in English' suggests that these courses are for foreign students who do not have sufficient Japanese language skills to study in Japanese. Why, then, would international students, mostly from Asia, want to study specialized subjects in English in Japan where English is not a common language? Given that increasing the number of foreign academics is another goal of TGUP, presumably these academics would be expected to teach such English degree courses. At the same time, however, Japanese academics have also been encouraged to teach their courses in English, which is reflected in various PD programs featured in the TGUP Good Practice Collection. In this sense, provided that PD is sufficient, CLIL seems to provide an opportunity for Japanese specialist teachers with English proficiency to further develop their content teaching skills and language proficiency. While this may raise questions about ensuring the quality of such courses, and about the attraction for multilingual international students of courses taught in English by Japanese academics, this may be the beginning of a new era in which English is used in Asia as a common language for education. Haberland (2011) argues that staff and student mobility has brought changes in English as a lingua franca—no longer is it about the English of native speakers. Does CLIL open up new opportunities for English to be used as a common language among multilingual speakers of English from other parts of Asia in Japan?

The third type of English MOI courses are those that cater to both Japanese and international students in order to create a mutual space for them to mix, but if their language proficiency levels are not the same, guaranteeing quality of delivery becomes the crucial question?

Issues relating to the commodification of language and of international students have been identified in relation to global economic development (Liyanage et al., 2018). International students are consumers, who must bear the cost of their education/tuition, but the quality of the education they receive is not necessarily guaranteed as long as the providers' main interest is meeting numerical targets, which Phillipson (2017) describes as the economic and geopolitical agenda behind the current English teaching business. Given that the world ranking of Japanese universities has been declining (Nikkei, 2017) and Japanese people's English language proficiency has worsened (Aoki, 2017; EF, 2017), the commodification of both foreign students and Japanese students, which is framed with the numerical targets set in relation to this government-funded project, does not seem to have benefits for any of the parties involved. Englishization (Kirkpatrick, 2012) is an important aspect of the Japanese government's international strategies, but the lack of acknowledgment of the language and of the users of the language is one of its fundamental weaknesses. CLIL has the potential to bring positive changes to Japan's higher education, but if the government sees international students as a future source of skilled labour (Nikkei, 2018), it needs to formulate and present clear language in education policies and guidelines for MOI in the tertiary sector.

References

Agency of Cultural Affairs (ACA). (2014). 平成25年度「国語に関する世論調査」の概要 [*2013 Fiscal year opinion survey on the national language overview*]. Retrieved from www.bunka.go.jp/tokei_hakusho_shuppan/tokeichosa/kokugo_yoronchosa/pdf/h25_chosa_kekka.pdf.
Aoki, M. (2017, April 6). Japan's latest English-proficiency scores disappoint. *The Japan Times*. Retrieved from www.japantimes.co.jp/news/2017/04/06/national/japans-latest-english-proficiency-scores-disappoint/#.WiT7YtOCxPY.
Blackledge, A. (2009). *Discourse and power in a multilingual world*. Amsterdam: John Benjamins Publishing Company.
Backhaus, P. (2007). *Linguistic landscapes: A comparative study of urban multilingualism in Tokyo*. Clevedon: Multilingual Matters.
Burgess, C., Gibson, I., Kalphake, J., & Selzer, M. (2010). The "Global 30" Project and Japanese higher education reform: An example of a "closing in" or an "opening up"? *Globalisation, Sciences and Education, 8*(4), 461–475. https://doi.org/10.1080/14767724.2010.537931.
Chapple, J. (2014). Finally feasible or fresh façade? Analysing the internationalisation plans of Japanese universities. *International Journal of Research Studies in Education, 3*(4), 15–28. https://doi.org/10.5861/ijrse.2014.794.
Chen, K. H. Y. (2018). Ideologies of language standardization: The case of Cantonese in Hong Kong. In J. W. Tollefson & M. Pérez-Milans (Eds.), *The Oxford handbook of language policy and planning* (pp. 202–220). New York: Oxford University Press.
Codó, E. (2018). Language policy and planning, institutions, and neoliberalisation. In J. W. Tollefson & M. Pérez-Milans (Eds.), *The Oxford handbook of language policy and planning* (pp. 467–484). New York: Oxford University Press.
Dalton-Puffer, C. (2007). *Discourse in content and language integrated learning (CLIL) classrooms*. Amsterdam, Netherland: John Benjamins.
Diallo, I., & Liddicoat, A. (2014). Planning language teaching: An argument for the place of pedagogy in language policy and planning. *International Journal of Pedagogies and Learning, 9*(2), 110–117.
EF. (2017). *EF English proficiency index*. Retrieved from www.ef-australia.com.au/epi/.
Fairclough, N. (2001). Critical discourse analysis as a method in social scientific research. In R. Wodak & M. Meyer (Eds.), *Methods of critical discourse analysis* (pp. 121–138). London: Sage Publications.
Fenton-Smith, B., Humphreys, P., & Walkinshaw, I. (Eds.). (2017). *English medium instruction in higher education in Asia-Pacific: From policy to pedagogy*. Cham, Switzerland: Springer.

Fortanet-Gomez, I. (2013). *CLIL in higher education*. Bristol, UK: Multilingual Matters.
Gill, S. K. (2014). *Language policy challenges in multi-ethnic Malaysia*. Dordrecht: Springer.
Gogolin, I. (2013). Bilingual education. In J. Simpson (Ed.), *The Routledge handbook of applied linguistics* (pp. 229–242). New York: Routledge.
Haberland, H. (2011). Ownership and maintenance of a language in transnational use: Should we leave our lingua franca alone? *Journal of Pragmatics, 43,* 937–949.
Hamid, M. O., Nguyen, H. T. M., & Baldauf, R. B. (Eds.). (2014). *Language planning for medium of instruction in Asia*. London: Routledge.
Hashimoto, K. (2013a). "English-only", but not a medium-of-instruction policy: The Japanese way of internationalising education for both domestic and overseas students. *Current Issues in Language Planning, 14*(1), 16–33. https://doi.org/10.1080/14664208.2013.789956.
Hashimoto, K. (2013b). The Japanisation of English language education: Promotion of the national language within foreign language policy. In J. W. Tollefson (Ed.), *Language policies in education: Critical issues, Second edition edited* (pp. 175–190). London and New York: Routledge.
Hashimoto, K. (2018a). Japan's "super global universities" scheme: Why does the number of "foreign" students matter? In A. W. Ata, L. T. Tran, & I. Liyanage (Eds.), *Educational reciprocity and adaptivity: International students and stakeholders* (pp. 25–44). New York: Routledge.
Hashimoto, K. (2018b). Teaching license renewal and the professional development of Japanese primary school teachers of English. In K. Hashimoto & V. Nguyen (Eds.), *Professional development of English language teachers in Asia: Lessons from Japan and Vietnam* (pp. 29–44). London and New York: Routledge.
Hashimoto, K. (2018c). Construction of the native speaker of Japanese. In S. A. Houghton, D. J. Rivers, & K. Hashimoto (Eds.), *Beyond native-speakerism: Current explorations and future visions* (pp. 99–114). New York: Routledge.
Ikeda, M., Pinner, R. S., Mehisto, P., & Marsh, D. (2013). Editorial. *International CLIL Research Journal, 2*(1), 1–2. http://www.icrj.eu/21/editorial.html.
Japan CLIL Pedagogy Association. (2018). *The 1st J-CLIL Annual Bilingual Conference*. https://docs.wixstatic.com/ugd/d705d2_4a89217c8f9f4c459443ebcde15a2520.pdf.
Japan Society for the Promotion of Science. (2018). スーパーグローバル大学創成支援事業中間評価結果の総括 [*Top Global University Project interim assessment summary*]. Retrieved from https://www.jsps.go.jp/jsgu/chukan_hyoka_kekka.html.
Japan Student Services Organisation. (2017). 平成29年度外国人留学生在籍状況調査結果 [*2017 Fiscal year, survey results on foreign students enrolment*]. Retrieved from https://www.jasso.go.jp/about/statistics/intl_student_e/2017/index.html.
Kato, S. (2006, April 19). 悲しいカタカナ語 [Sad *katakana* words]. *Asahi Shimbun*, evening edition, p. 10.
Kirkpatrick, A. (2012). English in ASEAN: Implication for regional multilingualism. *Journal of Multilingual and Multicultural Development, 33*(4), 331–344.
Kubota, R. (2002). The impact of globalization on language teaching in Japan. In D. Block & D. Cameron (Eds.), *Globalization and language teaching* (pp. 13–28). London: Routledge.
Liyanage, I., Tran, L. T., & Ata, A. W. (2018). Re-examining reciprocity in international education. In A. W. Ata, L. T. Tran, & I. Liyanage (Eds.), *Educational reciprocity and adaptivity: International students and stakeholders* (pp. 3–22). New York: Routledge.
Lo, Y. Y. (2017). Development of the beliefs and language awareness of content subject teachers in CLIL: Does professional development help? *International Journal of Bilingual Education and Bilingualism*. Advance online publication. https://doi.org/10.1080/13670050.2017.1318821.
MEXT. (2010). 外国語能力の向上に関する検討会(第一回)議事要旨 [*Study panel for improvement of foreign language proficiency (the first meeting): Summary proceedings*]. Retrieved from http://www.mext.go.jp/b_menu/shingi/chousa/shotou/082/gijigaiyou/1301500.htm.
MEXT. (2012). *2012 White paper on education, culture, sports, science and technology*. Retrieved from http://www.mext.go.jp/b_menu/hakusho/html/hpab201201/detail/1344908.htm.
MEXT. (2013). *2013 White paper on education, culture, sports, science and technology*. Retrieved from http://www.mext.go.jp/b_menu/hakusho/html/hpab201301/detail/1360701.htm.

MEXT. (2014a). 外国語教育における「CAN-DOリスト」の形での学習到達目標設定に関する検討会議(第9回)主な意見 [*Study panel for achievement target setting by using "can-do list" for foreign language education (the ninth meeting): Major comments*]. Retrieved from http://www.mext.go.jp/b_menu/shingi/chousa/shotou/092/shiryo/attach/1344701.htm.

MEXT. (2014b). 平成26年度「スーパー・プロフェッショナル・ハイスクール」(SPH)指定校について [*2014 "Super Professional High School" (SPH) designated schools*]. Retrieved from http://www.mext.go.jp/b_menu/h2014oudou/26/04/1346420.htm.

MEXT. (2014c). *Press release 'Selection for the FY2014 top global university project'*. Retrieved from www.mext.go.jp/b_menu/houdou/26/09/__icsFiles/afieldfile/2014/10/07/1352218_02.pdf.

MEXT. (2015).「大学の国際化のためのネットワーク形成推進事業」の事後評価結果について[*Post-project evaluation report on the Global 30 Program*]. Retrieved from http://www.mext.go.jp/a_menu/koutou/kaikaku/1355917.htm.

MEXT. (2017a). スーパーグローバルハイスクール(平成27年度指定)の中間評価について [*Super Global High Schools (designated in 2015) interim assessment*]. Retrieved from http://www.mext.go.jp/b_menu/houdou/29/09/1396726.htm.

MEXT. (2017b). 広島大学附属小学校 [*Hiroshima University attached primary school*]. Retrieved from http://www.mext.go.jp/a_menu/shotou/kenkyu/htm/08_news/1401003.htm.

MEXT. (2018a).「スーパーグローバル大学創成支援事業」(平成26年度採択)の中間評価について [*Top Global University Project (2014 selection) interim assessment*]. Retrieved from http://www.mext.go.jp/a_menu/koutou/kaikaku/sekaitenkai/1401770.htm.

MEXT. (2018b). スーパーグローバル大学創成支援事業グッドプラクティス集 [*Top Global University Project Good Practice Collection*]. Retrieved from https://tgu.mext.go.jp/downloads/index.html.

Morizumi, F. (2015). EMI in Japan: Current status and its implications. *Educational Studies, 57*, 119–128.

Nikkei. (2017, September 5). 東大、過去最低46位に 英紙の世界大学ランキング [*Tokyo University record-low 46th. English journal world university ranking*]. Retrieved from https://www.nikkei.com/article/DGXLASDG05H8I_V00C17A9000000/.

Nikkei. (2018, 26 March). 共通テストの英語民間試験、7種認定 公平性など課題多く[*Seven English commercial tests were approved for the centre test: Problems in fairness*]. Retrieved from https://www.nikkei.com/article/DGXMZO28577840W8A320C1CR8000/.

Nikula, T., & Moore, P. (2016). Exploring translanguaging in CLIL. *International Journal of Bilingual Education and Bilingualism*. Advance online publication. https://doi.org/10.1080/13670050.2016.1254151.

Pérez-Cañado, M. (2012). CLIL research in Europe: Past, present and future. *International Journal of Bilingual Education and Bilingualism, 15*(3), 315–341.

Phillipson, R. (2017). Myths and realities of "global" English. *Language Policy, 16,* 313–331.

Relaño-Pastor, A. M. (2018). Bilingual education policy and neoliberal content and language integrated learning practices. In J. W. Tollefson & M. Pérez-Milans (Eds.), *The Oxford handbook of language policy and planning* (pp. 505–525). New York: Oxford University Press.

Rose, H., & McKinley, J. (2018). Japan's English-medium instruction initiatives and the globalization of higher education. *Higher Education, 75*(1), 111–129.

Sasajima, S. (2013). How CLIL can impact on EFL teachers' mindsets about teaching and learning: An exploratory study on teacher cognition. *International CLIL Research Journal, 2*(1), 55–66. http://www.icrj.eu/21/article5.html.

Stanlaw, J. (2004). *Japanese English: Language and culture contact*. Hong Kong: Hong Kong University Press.

Super Global High School. (2018). *Outline of Super Global High School Program*. Retrieved from http://www.sghc.jp/en/.

Tollefson, J. W., & Tsui, A. B. M. (2004). *Medium of instruction policies: Which agenda? Whose agenda?*. Mahwah, NJ: Lawrence Erlbaum Associates.

Tsui, A. B. M. (2004). Medium of instruction in Hong Kong: One country, two systems, whose language? In J. W. Tollefson & A. B. M. Tsui (Eds.), *Medium of instruction policies: Which agenda? Whose agenda?* (pp. 97–116). Mahwah, N.J.: Lawrence Erlbaum Associates.

van Dijk, T. A. (2008). *Discourse and power*. New York: Palgrave Macmillan.

Walker, T., Liyanage, I., Madya, S., & Hidayati, S. (2019). Media of instruction in Indonesia: Implications for bi/multilingual education. In I. Liyanage & T. Walker (Eds.), *Multilingual education yearbook 2019: Media of instruction & multilingual settings* (pp. 209–229). New York: Springer.

Wei, R., & Feng, J. (2015). Implementing CLIL for young learners in an EFL context beyond Europe. *English Today, 31*(1), 55–60.

Yang, W. (2015). Content and language integrated learning next in Asia: Evidence of learners' achievement in CLIL education from a Taiwan tertiary degree programme. *International Journal of Bilingual Education and Bilingualism, 18*(4), 361–382. https://doi.org/10.1080/13670050.2014.904840.

Yokosuka-City. (2017). 平成29年度「公立学校における帰国・外国人児童生徒に対するきめ細かな支援事業」に係る昱告書の概要(橫須賀市)[*Summary of a report on "Support projects for returnee and foreign children at public schools"*]. Retrieved from http://www.mext.go.jp/a_menu/shotou/clarinet/003/001/1405579.htm.

Zeng, K. (1999). *Dragon gate: Competitive examinations and their consequences*. London and New York: Cassell.

Kayoko Hashimoto is Senior Lecturer at School of Languages and Cultures, The University of Queensland, Brisbane, Australia. Her main research areas are language policy, English language teaching in Japan, internationalisation and higher education, and Japanese language teaching in Asia. Her latest publications include a co-authored book, *Beyond Native-Speakerism: Current Explorations and Future Visions* (2018, Routledge, with Stephanie. A. Houghton & Damian J. Rivers), a co-edited book *Professional Development of English Language Teachers in Asia: Lessons from Japan and Vietnam* (2018, Routledge, with Van-Trao Nguyen), and an edited book *Japanese Language and Soft Power in Asia* (2017, Palgrave Macmillan). She is a thematic editor (language and education) of *Asian Studies Review*.

Gregory Paul Glasgow is Associate Professor in the Department of English at Kanda University of International Studies in Chiba, Japan. His research interests are agency in language policy and planning and the impact of language education curriculum reform on pedagogical practice in the Japanese education system. Dr. Glasgow is also a specialist in second language teacher education and professional development. He has previously organized and conducted workshops in professional development seminars for Japanese teachers of English in collaboration with the Embassy of the United States in Tokyo. His latest co-edited volume (2018, Routledge) is entitled *Researching Agency in Language Policy and Planning*.

Benefits of Translanguaging and Transculturation Exchanges Between International Higher Degree Research Students and English Medium Research Supervisors

Minglin Li and Beryl Exley

Abstract Discussions around internationalisation in Higher Degree Research (HDR) supervision have advocated a "deparochialising" (Lingard in Globalisation, Societies and Education 4(2):287–302, 2006, p. 187) of research education for international students via approaches that make use of students' existing language, culture and theoretical knowledge. Ideas include taking up reflexive and collaborative learning (Ryan in Teachers and Teaching 17(6):631–648, 2011) and HDR supervisors of international students being open to translanguaging (Li & García in Research methods in language and education. Encyclopedia of Language and Education. Springer, Cham, Switzerland, pp. 1–14, 2016) and transculturation practices (Choy, Singh, & Li in Education Sciences, 7(19), 2017). We explore interview data from international HDR students from language backgrounds other than English and some English speaking HDR supervisors working with international HDR students to document their assumptions about translanguaging and transculturation practices. The transcripts reveal these are regular practices for these participants. Both sets of participants agree that translanguaging and transculturation practices (i) enhance the specificity of the communication, (ii) promote the expertise of the HDR student, (iii) provide two-way learning, and (iv) feed into new knowledge generating practices. Translanguaging and transculturation practices are thus more than the reciprocal exchange of ideas; they are new forms of pedagogic processes whereby communicative work changes research processes, practices and systems of knowledge production, transfer, and acquisition that benefit both the HDR student and the HDR supervisor.

Keywords Higher Degree Research (HDR) · Cross-cultural HDR supervision · Translanguaging and transculturation · Internationalisation in HDR education

---

M. Li (✉)
School of Humanities, Languages and Social Sciences, Griffith University, Brisbane, Australia
e-mail: minglin.li@griffith.edu.au

B. Exley
School of Education and Professional Studies, Griffith University, Brisbane, Australia
e-mail: b.exley@griffith.edu.au

1 Cross-Cultural Higher Degree Research Supervision

Given the burgeoning uptake of Higher Degree Research (HDR) students studying in a language and culture other than their own, it is prudent to focus on the pedagogic practices of this interaction. Many international HDR students seek to develop their understanding of global interrelatedness, connect to international research communities and contribute positively to these communities as well as their own (Choy, Singh, & Li, 2017). Research literature has already documented the challenges of cross-linguistic and cross-cultural HDR supervision. For example, in a multi-institutional semi-structured interview-based study with HDR students and supervisors who had experience in cross-cultural/cross-linguistic supervision, Winchester-Seeto et al. (2014) identified challenges including separation from the familiar, language and communication difficulties, and cultural differences in dealing with the hierarchy of the supervisor/student relationship.

From another viewpoint, Manathunga's (2017) Australian-based research illustrates "the negative consequences of adopting assimilationist approaches to doctoral pedagogies" (p. 114). She calls on international HDR students to widen "what comes to count as knowledge globally" (p. 114) by integrating their own cultural and linguistic knowledge into their studies. She explains that "mutual respect, dialogic approaches to supervision and the recognition of the intellectual resources diverse students bring with them represent the core principles of empowering and effective intercultural supervision" (p. 115). She also argues for the take up of translanguaging and transculturation practices within HDR supervision so as to "develop more empowering intercultural communication and pedagogy" (p. 114). In addition, Wisker and Robinson (2014) conceive of cultural difference as an opportunity to engage with "different learning behaviours, imperatives and concerns and different ways of constructing and expressing knowledge" (p. 19). These authors argue that when all parties appreciate cultural difference, learning from different perspectives is enabled.

In recent decades, discussions around internationalisation in HDR supervision have advocated a "deparochialising" (Lingard, 2006) of research education for international students and called for new approaches to supervision that harness the languages, culture and theoretical knowledge of HDR students via a process of reflexive and collaborative learning (Ryan, 2011). As Wisker and Robinson (2014) assert, global cultural flows can facilitate recognition of silenced voices of Indigenous, international and immigrant researchers and their topics, expressions, methodology and methods. Dooley, Exley and Poulus (2016), Manathunga (2011), and Singh, Manathunga, Bunda and Qi (2016) have reported on the experiences of research teams whose members come from disparate linguistic, cultural and knowledge positions. Similarly, Exley, Davis and Dooley (2016) document their personal experiences of the need to make their individual cultural positions explicit. Davis, a strong and proud Australian Aboriginal man, teacher and researcher, moves with ease between Indigenous and non-Indigenous worlds and world views. Exley and Dooley, however, are white, non-Indigenous teacher educators and researchers with long histories of teaching and researching in and for schools in communities marked by diversity and disadvantage. In their accounts, they acknowledge Davis' role in transmitting to them the principles of Indigenous research which includes "giving up the Western researcher-educator's illusion of the right to 'know all'" (p. 40). Exley and Dooley also document that they do not always fully participate in some yarning (community talking) sessions because it is sometimes culturally inappropriate to do so. In another case, Exley, Whatman and Singh (2018) recount the tension-ridden processes of negotiating Western educational research ethics policies and procedures and ways of knowing and being in Indigenous contexts. For example, Exley identifies the "hegemonic University Research Ethics policies and procedures, in particular their officious consent forms, sequencing dilemmas and the dilemma with confidentiality and acknowledgement" (p. 535). Whatman confirmed the "unpredictableness of qualitative data collection and that issues of ethics can be a protracted process" when undertaken in a culturally appropriate way (p. 535).

Other research literature explores Western HDR supervisors working with international HDR students who have English as an Additional Language (EAL) and non-Western backgrounds (see, for example, Choy et al. 2017; Manathunga, 2011, 2013; Singh, 2009; Singh & Chen, 2012). In this chapter, we explore interview data from international HDR candidates with Asian backgrounds whose first language is not English and some English speaking HDR supervisors working within a large city-based Australian university. All participants self-identified as engaging in translanguaging and transculturation practices. We hone in on four productive outcomes for the international HDR students and the HDR supervisors. Before we do so, the next section overviews the definitions of translanguaging and transculturation used in this chapter.

2 Translanguaging and Transculturation Practices in Education

Translanguaging is a linguistic practice used in multilingual situations, as well as a pedagogical practice used in educational settings. The term translanguaging was coined by Williams (1994), popularized by Baker (2001/2011), and extended by researchers in diverse linguistic and cultural contexts (see, e.g., Li & García, 2016). Translanguaging offers a unique way of conceptualizing bilingualism as "a new and transformed linguistic system rather than the addition of two" languages (Li & García, 2016, p. 5). Translanguaging emphasizes that the bilingual speaker is not two monolinguals in one (Grosjean, 1982), but that at its very core, the psycholinguistic system of a bilingual speaker is different to that of monolingual speakers (de Bot, Lowie, & Verspoor, 2007). According to Velasco and García (2014), the languages of bilingual speakers are not separate linguistic systems, but one linguistic system—an integrated linguistic repertoire from which bilingual speakers choose the language or choose to switch or alternate (Filipi, 2019) between the languages to communicate with others.

Research undertaken by García and Kano (2014) documents students and teachers engaging in complex discursive practices that cycle between the language practices of each. When activated, these "complex and fluid discursive practices" span a range of multimodal texts, such as those produced through "reading, writing, listening, discussing, taking notes, writing reports and essays, and taking exams" (García, 2014, p. 74). Creese and Blackledge (2010) refer to these practices as translanguaging, a flexible bilingualism, used as instructional strategies that also "make links for classroom participants between the social, cultural, community, and linguistic domains of their lives" (p. 112).

Translanguaging practices serve to sustain existing language practices, develop new language practices and facilitate the communication of appropriate knowledge, thus giving voice to "new sociopolitical realities" (García & Kano, 2014, p. 261). In examining the translanguaging pedagogies used in language classrooms, Creese and Blackledge (2010) stated:

> Both languages are needed simultaneously to convey the information ... each language is used to convey a different informational message, but it is in the bilingualism of the text that the full message is conveyed. (p. 108)

García (2009) also refers to *"multiple discursive practices* in which bilinguals engage in order to *make sense of their bilingual worlds"* (p. 45, italics in original). Baker (2001/2011) highlights the multimodality of translanguaging as well, noting that when topics are read or heard in one language, and then written or discussed in another language, the subject matter has to be "digested" (p. 289). Translanguaging also implicates an individual's capacity to "think, reflect, and extend their inner speech" (García & Kleifgen, 2010, p. 63) and to explore the representation of values, identities and relationships (Li, 2011).

Li (2011) refers to translanguaging space as "a space for the act of translanguaging as well as a space created through translanguaging" (p. 1223). He asserts that translanguaging space has its own "transformative power" (p. 1223). It is not a space where different identities, values and practices simply co-exist, but a space where the process of "cultural translation" (Bhabha, 1994) between traditions takes place with the possibility of generating new identities, values and practices. Translanguaging spaces are a special form of pedagogy with their own cognitive processes and rules for interaction and interpretation situated within unique socio-historical dimensions (Li, 2011).

An increasing number of HDR students are writing in multilingual contexts, and the varieties of linguistic and cultural resources brought by multilingual students to their academic writing has been recognised by a growing number of researchers (see, for example, Canagarajah, 2011; Kaufhold, 2018; Mazak, 2017; Singh, 2009). Research has acknowledged the contribution translanguaging makes to students' academic learning (see, for example, Lewis, Jones, & Baker, 2013), and academic writing (see e.g., Canagarajah, 2011; Kaufhold, 2018; Velasco & García, 2014). Li (2011) proposes that translanguaging advances creativity via choosing "between following and flouting the rules and norms of behaviour, including the use of language" and "pushing and breaking the boundaries between the old and the new, the conventional and the original, and the acceptable and the challenging" (p. 1223). Li (2011) also proposes that translanguaging advances criticality via bringing insights of various cultural, social and linguistic phenomena to question and problematize received wisdom and to express a position. Processes of translanguaging, however, are not without points of tension due to the ranges of ideologies, policies and practices being brought into the encounter (Li, 2011).

We use transculturation to refer to the use of cultural concepts from international HDR students' home countries in their research while studying in Western countries. The term transculturation was coined in 1940 by the Cuban anthropologist Fernando Ortiz in opposition of the term acculturation that had been coined by anthropologists in the United States in 1936 (Taylor, 1991). Taylor (1991) considers transculturation as the phenomenon of emerging and converging of cultures, the transformative process involved in the acquisition of foreign cultural material—"the loss or displacement of a society's culture due to the acquisition or imposition of foreign material, and the fusion of the indigenous and the foreign to create a new, original cultural product" (p. 91). The theory of transculturation "delineates the process by which symbols, discourse, and ideology are transformed as one culture changes through the imposition or adoption of another, and examines the historic and socio-political forces that produce local meanings" (Taylor, 1991, p. 92). Transculturation is thus a political process as the consciousness of one society's histories and manifestations comes into contact with the histories and manifestations from other societies. Pratt (1991) explains how members of marginalized groups do not unthinkingly imitate or reproduce the language of the dominant culture, but to varying extents choose what is appropriated and how it gets used. Zamel (1997) emphasizes the nature of transculturation which "assumes and celebrates the selective, generative, and inventive nature of linguistic and cultural adaptation and thus reflects precisely how languages and cultures develop and change—infused, invigorated, and challenged by variation and innovation" (p. 350). Therefore, she encourages the transculturation model that recognizes this process of adaptation as dynamic, involving both active engagement and resistance.

Singh et al. (2016) argue for a theoretical model of transcultural co-research practice in research education. Singh et al. (2016) point to the necessity of the transcultural approach given the contradictory processes produced by globalization that "promote the movement of people and ideas across geographical and epistemological boundaries yet continue to reinforce the dominance of White, Western knowledge production" (p. 54). The Indian-Australian, Irish-Australian, Aboriginal and Chinese researchers on this team grappled with cultural differences as they undertook their research work. Working together, they examined how "renegade knowledge" (Singh et al., 2016, p. 59) can be included in doctoral supervision using a process of intellectual contestation, dissensus and dialogue. In their transcultural co-research, they strove to nurture a dynamic meaning-making through self-reflexive learning based on each author's intellectual contributions and (trans)cultural dispositions. Grounding their transcultural co-research in "a reconceptualization of intellectual power in a globalized and technology-driven world" they argue that "intellectual power today can no longer simply take the point of advantage on knowledge hierarchies, but should be actualized through mutual learning, intellectual responsibility and a transcultural research disposition" (Singh et al., 2016, p. 60). They regard this transcultural practice as a departure from one-way mentoring to a pedagogic process that mobilizes the expertise of all team members. Encouraged by Singh et al.'s (2016) conceptualization, Choy et al. (2017) call into question the need for the prefix "trans", stating that cultures are neither fixed, static nor tightly bounded and transcultural practice involves incorporation of cultural knowledge and theories from other intellectual traditions based on the assumption of an equality of intelligences.

In this chapter, we explore the assumptions of international HDR students from language backgrounds other than English and their English-speaking research supervisors as they use translanguaging and transculturation practices. To contribute to the emerging research theory in internationalising HDR education, we draw on international HDR students and HDR supervisor recounts where Western and native languages, and cultural knowledge and theories have been synthesised.

3 Research Methods

Using a two-phase multi-method research design, our study explores how multilingual international HDR students from Asian linguistic and cultural backgrounds (hereafter EAL HDR students) and English-speaking research supervisors (hereafter HDR supervisors) recount their use of translanguaging and transculturation for positive gains.

Upon receipt of ethical approval from the University's Human Research Ethics Committee, HDR coordinators in this large city-based teaching and research-intensive university in Australia were contacted to assist with sending email invitations and the requisite Information Sheet and Consent Form to prospective participants who had completed their HDR confirmation (usually at the end of the first full year of HDR study). We also emailed invitation letters, and the requisite Information Sheet and Consent Form to HDR supervisors who have supervised and/or are supervising EAL HDR students. All potential participants were asked to engage in two tasks: an individual interview of up to 60 min, and confirmation of the written transcript of the individual interview.

Seven EAL HDR students from Asian linguistic and cultural backgrounds and ten HDR supervisors from a range of disciplinary fields agreed to participate in this research. The participants confirmed that the EAL HDR students were studying with Australian universities as the students wanted to learn from the West and because of a perceived benefit of acquiring Western knowledge. All participating HDR supervisors reported that they encouraged their EAL HDR students to utilize, where appropriate in their dissertation, the language, cultural concepts and philosophical ideas from their home countries on the proviso that the dissertation continued to meet the examination requirements. In all cases except one, the EAL HDR students who attended the interviews could not be matched to a HDR supervisor participant. In almost all cases, the HDR supervisors were recounting experiences with EAL HDR students who had already graduated.

In the first phase of the study, semi-structured interviews were carried out by the first author in places selected by the participants. These semi-structured interviews proved to be useful for gathering in-depth information about participants' accounts of their experiences and assumptions. In addition, these semi-structured interviews allowed for good interpretive validity (Gay & Airasian, 2003; Johnson & Turner, 2003). The semi-structured interview questions were based around demographic data, research topic, use of translanguaging and transculturation practice, and reasons for using or not using translanguaging and transculturation practices. These semi-structured interview questions were derived from our knowledge of the research literature and were supplemented with probing questions during the interview (Robson, 2002). The audio recordings of the interviews were then transcribed by a professional transcribing service. In the second phase of the study, the interview transcripts were sent to participants for content review and additional comments. No participants requested any changes.

A thematic approach was adopted to analyse the edited transcripts to derive a list of assumptions when using translanguaging and transculturation practices in HDR supervision. After reading the transcripts several times, the first author identified some major themes which were then coded using both descriptive and interpretive codes (Miles & Huberman, 1994). These codes were then utilized to retrieve details from the transcripts about the benefits of translanguaging and transculturation practices for further analysis, presentation and discussion.

In the next section of this chapter, we present the four reported benefits of translanguaging and transculturation practices between EAL HDR students and their English medium supervisors during HDR supervision at this Australian university. In what follows, we draw on data provided by a range of participants. When presenting the participants' recounts, false starts and long pauses were removed to ensure a more fluent reading experience. Italics are used to show verbatim data transcripts and ellipses show where data were removed because of a topic shift. When speech was unclear, the transcription is shown in square brackets. When data included details that could potentially identify the interview participant or another person, the words were removed and replaced with [[removed]].

4 Reported Benefits of Translanguaging and Transculturation Practices in HDR Supervision

4.1 Enhances the Specificity of Communication

The seven EAL HDR students and the ten HDR supervisors reported that translanguaging and transculturation practices enhanced the specificity of the communication between the EAL HDR students and the HDR supervisors. Participants reported using specific words from EAL HDR students' first language (L1) when finding an equivalent word in English proved difficult or impossible. Taking up L1 words enhanced the presentation and interpretation of the meaning, particularly when the point of discussion referred to cultural implications, local literature, or when data were generated and collected in the L1 of the EAL HDR student. One of the EAL HDR students explained using L1 words when presenting data:

> So in my thesis I tend to use the way how … the participants express themselves. So I would put directly or literally in their own languages, in their own words, and then I would explain in English what that means. For example, there is a specific term, one of (the participants) say, this kind of curriculum design or planning is called "Liang Zhang Pi". (Student 1)

Student 1 explained that *Liang Zhang Pi* has two layers of meaning, or *two different/separate systems like that,* and justified that using *Liang Zhang Pi* instead of a translated English term conveyed underlying meanings associated with the cultural background. Student 1 also explained that the HDR supervisor encouraged the use of translanguaging and transculturation practices.

Supervisor 1 recalled that some of her EAL HDR students *definitely had to use their own language because they've had to take primary source materials written in [[removed]] or [[removed]] and translate them into English for the purpose of the thesis.* Supervisor 1 emphasized that the EAL HDR students had to bring their own understandings of their culture to their research work when commenting on the cultural, social and political contexts of their home countries. Supervisor 1 commented on the value of EAL HDR students' translanguaging and transculturation practices, saying that:

> It adds a lot of depth to their thesis so they're able to combine their own language, their own culture, with what they learn here, in order to, I think, hopefully, produce very high quality, in-depth theses. And I think it adds value to the whole process, that they come in … with that different perspective. (Supervisor 1)

4.2 Promotes the Expertise of the EAL HDR Student

In separate interviews, Supervisors 1 and 2 explained that they had to encourage their EAL HDR students to take on an expert role via translanguaging and transculturation practices. Excerpts from the interview data provided by these supervisors are as follows:

> I have had to say a few times, no, you're the expert, you tell me, because … I don't have expertise in [[removed]] regulation. I can help with writing a good thesis, but … you are the expert, you have to be. (Supervisor 1)
>
> I think that in many ways the students are more confident if they are talking, not only more confident, I think they feel that they have more to contribute if they're trying to make those relationships work between what their culture's thinking and saying and what other cultures are thinking and saying. (Supervisor 2)

Supervisor 3 described having to work with the EAL HDR students to shift their thinking about being *afraid of displeasing* their supervisors by not following their supervisor's Western research orientation, instead taking the initiative to introduce transculturation practices. Supervisor 3 identified that, under the consistent encouragement of their HDR supervisors, the EAL HDR students were becoming familiar with taking some responsibility for their own Ph.D. and in the process becoming independent researchers. Supervisor 1 recalled that her Asian students were *quite pleased* and *a bit surprised but happy* as they recognised their growing status as experts.

Supervisor 1 reflected on recurring discussions centred on the constant points of discussion centred on the EAL HDR students being encouraged to shift their previously held cultural position of the supervisor as the expert, to the new position of the EAL HDR student as the expert on the topic of their dissertation.

> It's great to be respected but you have to tell them though it's your thesis, you have to take control and ownership of it and you make decisions about [it], and I will guide you and we can talk it through but at the end of the day, you have to decide. … it is important sometimes for these students to make sure they feel empowered to take control of their own thesis and the direction because they know more than I do about, really, what they need to say in that thesis. … I think they liked the idea that I said, no, you're the expert, you tell me. Or, I'll constantly reiterate, I'll give feedback and I'll say, look, I would do this way and I would change the structure and include this here, but will that be right, you know, and I'll keep asking them for their input and I think they like that. I think they've come to like it. … I guess, as well as empowering them, giving them a sense of responsibility for their own learning. (Supervisor 1)

4.3 Encourages Two-Way Learning

Interview data also explored the realisation that HDR supervisors sometimes lacked certain content knowledge, or sometimes pretended to lack certain content knowledge that seemed crucial to the research study. Supervisor 3 described themselves as *ignorant* about *culture of another kind,* or in some cases pretending to be ignorant about *culture of another kind*, therefore relying on the EAL HDR student to fill the knowledge gap. Supervisor 3 homed in on the difficulty of the task besetting the EAL HDR student whilst also discussing the benefits of two-way learning.

> When you come from one kind of culture to another kind of culture and the value systems or the scholarly structures are different, there is adjustment that has to be made to produce a thesis in that culture and, I mean, it was a hard thing. It must be a terribly hard thing. … But I don't think it's a bad thing to do; I think it's a great thing to do but it does involve a different level of learning and it also involves working with a supervisor in such a way that you can kind of educate them, and this is another role of the student. I hate to admit it but I'm ignorant. When I get a student from Malaysia or Iran or Iraq or from Africa, those students come with their own set of expert knowledges but they don't have my expert knowledge, and I don't have theirs, so when they come to me with a way of thinking about a topic, I have to try and make sense of it and they have to try and help me to make sense of it by teaching me what they're thinking about. (Supervisor 3)

Supervisor 1 also indicated that transculturation practices added valued to the supervisor's knowledge base.

> So, before they started, I probably didn't know very much but we've had interesting discussions about it, so it's been more about developing an understanding.... It's me learning from them. Yeah, very much. So, they brought that knowledge and as I said, it adds value and depth to their thesis and they explain it to me. (Supervisor 1)

Student 2 overtly labelled the transculturation practices as *two ways learning*, explaining the simultaneous benefit to the HDR supervisor and the EAL HDR student.

> So it is like two-ways learning because that surprised them in what occurred in the workplace in [[removed]] and then they feed in with me what happened in the workplace in Australia. So, it's two-ways learning; they learn about what happen in my culture and then learn about what happened in the [Australian] culture and I use the differences and similarity in order to better explain or clarify the results I use. (Student 2)

Following on from the theme of two-way learning, Student 3 explained how the HDR supervisor's interest in the HDR study motivated the EAL HDR student to continue their studies.

> I think I became more motivated in trying to get the message across and so even though it was a part of my reading for my thesis but after such a discussion, I was trying to read more about how people wrote about [[removed]] culture in those situations. Yeah, so it's like more reading for me but I was trying because I was more motivated by my supervisor's interest in that part of the results so I just read more and tried to improve my writing so that I can actually get the message across. Yes, so I think it's helped to improve my writing, also my reading. (Student 3)

4.4 New Knowledge Generating Practices

A point borne out of Supervisor 3's interview data was the realisation that both the EAL HDR student and the HDR supervisor used translanguaging and transculturation practices to generate new knowledge. In talking about an EAL HDR student's English language proficiency, Supervisor 3 homed in on the need to develop a common language for the purpose of speaking in *scholarly terms* and establishing intellectual commonality. Supervisor 3 acknowledged the complexity of these discussions, not only because of the translanguaging but also because of the transculturation practices. Supervisor 3 recounted that it was quite hard to *tease out a way to approach and understand that complexity*. After a number of meetings with plenty of explanations and discussions, Supervisor 3 would search for more relevant materials. Although it took a lot of time, by the end of the project, a much richer cross-cultural analysis was undertaken.

Supervisor 3 recounted an EAL HDR student's use of translanguaging and transculturation practices in a dissertation that explored published editions of folktales from a particular Asian country. Supervisor 3 commented:

> So one of the things I found challenging was to understand how the stories had layers of meaning. So they weren't just stories in which things happen, you know, a fisherman looks at the moon and then a magic spirit comes out of the moon and comes down to earth and something changes, you know, it wasn't just that. For me, there had to be a symbolic value but I found it very difficult to understand what that symbolic value was and I think my student found it hard to articulate that for me because for her it was intuitive. She felt she'd learnt it from childhood and she understood it, but how to express it in English to me was extremely difficult. ... So it was quite elusive or slippery kind of thing to get hold of, as you say, the implied meaning or the underlying meaning of a set of things that happen. (Supervisor 3)

Supervisor 3 reported that the strategy agreed upon with the EAL HDR student was to present some of the folk stories in L1 with English translation and an appendix as needed. According to Supervisor 3, this approach involved not only linguistic translation but cultural translation also. Supervisor 3 acknowledged that translation is a stressful and *an extremely hard thing*, but that the process brings rewards because it *involves a different level of learning*.

Supervisor 1 provided an example of how translanguaging and transculturation practices generated a major change to the theoretical framework for the student's dissertation. The supervisor and students went to a conference together and attended a paper presentation discussing cultural comparison, something with potential for the student's thesis. Supervisor 1 recounted that that framework:

> really explained what's happening in [[removed]]. So it actually allows you to culturally position ... and actually figuratively draw this and explain ... the weakness we are finding are real weaknesses. They are not weaknesses in what you should do, but they won't work until you do these things. (Supervisor 1)

Supervisor 1 emphasized the importance of learning and knowing about EAL candidates' background cultural knowledge, saying *to supervise that you have to actually understand it* and in this case *really understanding where [[removed]] Higher Education fits in the world as well, and what are the implications*. Given the uniqueness of each individual research setting in Asian countries, it is highly likely that a theoretical framework developed in Western countries is not applicable in Asian countries. For this reason, Supervisor 1 asserted that:

> So we have to also be careful that as Australian supervisors we don't try and impose Australian cultural values on an Asian setting where the research is being done. We have to acknowledge where it is. So I mean I've found out so much that I didn't know, and it's interesting, ... and it's sort of developing ... mutual respect and making sure students know that they are becoming the expert, and we work with them to help them look at an issue, make sure they're doing it rigorously, ... [choosing] the framework for what they are doing. (Supervisor 1)

Student 3 detailed how they and the supervisors have both enriched their cultural repertoire through translanguaging and transculturation practice and how together they have developed the appropriate research instrument for interviews carried out in Student 3's home country. Student 3 was thinking about using a survey designed in another country and used widely internationally, but as Student 3 explained, *there is no cultural evaluation of the scale whether the scale using Asian culture is different from that used in European or Western culture*. Student 3 identified some dimensions that were consistent across cultural groups, but also a dimension with a very high level of uncertainty when compared across cultural groups. After extensive analysis, Student 3 chose to use a cultural concept to explain the results.

5 Concluding Discussion

As Manathunga (2013) asserts, "the pressure towards assimilation to Western research norms and ways of knowing remains very strong in Western universities" (p. 78), including universities in Australia. Findings that highlight the use of translanguaging and transculturation practices is therefore important. Our analysis shows that our participants made four positive assumptions about translanguaging and transculturation practices. The first positive outcome of translanguaging and transculturation practices within HDR supervision was enhancement of the specificity of communication, an outcome reported in Velasco and García's (2014) earlier work. The second positive outcome of translanguaging and transculturation practices was the elevation of the EAL HDR student as an expert. Singh (2009) has long advocated that HDR supervisors must recognize and acknowledge their own cross-cultural ignorance and in doing so acknowledge the expertise of the EAL HDR student. Manathunga (2011) supports this view and points out that "supervisors may have to accept that there is a great deal they do not or cannot know" (p. 368). Singh (2009) claims that when HDR supervisors acknowledge their own ignorance, the reward is that they have an "incentive for learning" (p. 187). Thus, ignorance leads to the third positive outcome of translanguaging and transculturation practices, that of two-way learning that value-adds to the HDR supervisor's knowledge base. The fourth positive outcome of translanguaging and transculturation practices within HDR supervision is new knowledge generation practices. Manathunga (2007) identifies this as moments of "creativity", where "culturally diverse students may carefully select those parts of Western knowledge that they find useful and seek to blend them with their own knowledge and ways of thinking" (pp. 97–98).

Thus, when translanguaging and transculturation practices are permitted into the HDR supervision encounter, they have the potential to bring with them their own "transformative power" (Li, 2011, p. 1223) that benefits both the EAL HDR student and the HDR supervisor. The translanguaging and transculturation practices that specify communication, position the EAL HDR student as the expert, provide for two-way learning and produce new knowledge generating practices create the space for creativity in HDR supervision. In this way, the findings reported here suggest that translanguaging and transculturation practices take HDR supervision beyond its mundane pedagogies of teaching students about using theoretical concepts, research methods and the analysis of findings. As a point of difference, our findings indicate that HDR supervision that adopts translanguaging and transculturation practices has the potential to build connections between the intellectual resources of EAL HDR students and their disparate worldviews to inform the knowledge base of the HDR supervisor in unanticipated and unexpected ways. This suggests that translanguaging and transculturation practices are more than the reciprocal exchange of ideas; they are pedagogic and curriculum processes where communicative work leads to change in research processes, practices and systems of knowledge production, transfer and acquisition that benefit both the EAL HDR student and the HDR supervisor.

We, however, do not finish our discussion here. It would be remiss of us to not return to the broader discussion already mentioned earlier in this chapter, that whereby participating HDR supervisors asserted the proviso that the dissertation continued to meet the Western examination requirements. Despite some reported benefits of translanguaging and transculturation practices, there is no escaping the ongoing impact of Western imperialism on EAL HDR students' linguistic, ideological, cultural, and technological form. Yet again, as Merriam and Kim (2008) point out, EAL HDR students still need to give way to Western norms as they finalise their dissertation for examination; Western knowledge seems to be forsaking nothing in the processes outlined. In this sense, the call for further research into translanguaging and transculturation practices in international HDR supervision seems timely.

References

Baker, C. (2001/2011). *Foundations of bilingual education and bilingualism* (3rd ed.). Clevedon: Multilingual Matters.
Bhabha, H. (1994). *The location of culture*. London: Routledge.
Canagarajah, S. (2011). Codemeshing in academic writing: Identifying teachable strategies of translanguaging. *The Modern Language Journal, 95*(3), 401–417.
Choy, S., Singh, P., & Li, M. (2017). Trans-cultural, trans-language practices: Potentialities for rethinking doctoral education pedagogies. *Education Sciences, 7*(19). https://doi.org/10.3390/educsci7010019.
Creese, A., & Blackledge, A. (2010). Translanguaging in the bilingual classroom: A pedagogy for learning and teaching? *Modern Language Journal, 94*(1), 103–115.
de Bot, K., Lowie, W., & Verspoor, M. (2007). A dynamic systems theory approach to second language acquisition. *Bilingualism: Language and Cognition, 10*(1), 7–21.
Dooley, K., Exley, B., & Poulus, D. (2016). Research on critical EFL literacies: An illustrative analysis of some college level programs in Taiwan. *English Teaching & Learning, 40*(4), 39–64.
Exley, B., Davis, J., & Dooley, K. (2016). Empirical reference points for Bernstein's model of pedagogic rights: Recontextualising the reconciliation agenda to Australian schooling. In P. Vitale & B. Exley (Eds.), *Pedagogic rights and democratic education: Bernsteinian explorations of curriculum, pedagogy and assessment* (pp. 33–46). London: Routledge.
Exley, B., Whatman, S., & Singh, P. (2018). Postcolonial, decolonial research dilemmas: Fieldwork in Australian Indigenous contexts. *Qualitative Research, 18*(5), 526–537.
Filipi, A. (2019). Language alternation as an interactional practice in the foreign language classroom. In I. Liyanage & T. Walker (Eds.), *Multilingual education yearbook 2019: Media of instruction & multilingual settings* (pp. 25–42). New York: Springer.
García, O. (2009). *Bilingual education in the 21st century: A global perspective*. Malden: Wiley/Blackwell.
García, O. (2014). U.S. Spanish and Education: Global and Local Intersections. *Language Policy, Politics, and Diversity in Education: Review of Research in Education, 38*(1), 58–80.
Garcia, O., & Kano, N. (2014). Translanguaging as process and pedagogy: Developing the English writing of Japanese students in the US. In J. Conteh & G. Meier (Eds.), *The multilingual turn*

in languages education: Opportunities and challenges (pp. 258–277). Bristol, UK: Multilingual Matters.

García, O., & Kleifgen, J. A. (2010). *Educating emergent bilinguals: Policies, programs, and practices for English language learners*. New York, NY: Teachers College Press.

Gay, L. R., & Airasian, P. (2003). *Educational research: Competencies for analysis and applications* (7th ed.). Upper Saddle River, New Jersey: Merrill-Prentice Hall.

Grosjean, F. (1982). *Life with two languages: An introduction to bilingualism*. Cambridge, MA: Harvard University Press.

Johnson, B., & Turner, L. (2003). Data collection strategies in mixed methods research. In A. Tashakkori & C. Teddlie (Eds.), *Handbook of mixed methods in social and behavioral research* (pp. 297–319). Thousand Oaks, CA: Sage.

Kaufhold, K. (2018). Creating translanguaging spaces in students' academic writing practices. *Linguistics and Education, 45*(2018), 1–9.

Lewis, G., Jones, B., & Baker, C. (2013). 100 bilingual lessons: Distributing two languages in classrooms. In C. Abello-Contesse, P. Chandler, M. López-Jiménez, M. Torreblanca-López, & R. Chacón-Beltrán (Eds.), *Bilingualism and multilingualism in school settings* (pp. 107–135). Bristol: Multilingual Matters.

Li, W. (2011). Moment analysis and translanguaging space: Discursive construction of identities by multilingual Chinese youth in Britain. *Journal of Pragmatics, 43*, 1222–1235.

Li, W., & García, O. (2016). From researching translanguaging to translanguaging research. In K. King, Y. Lai, & S. May (Eds.), *Research methods in language and education. Encyclopedia of Language and Education* (3rd ed., pp. 1–14). Cham, Switzerland: Springer. https://doi.org/10.1007/978-3-319-02329-8_16-1.

Lingard, B. (2006). Globalisation, the research imagination and deparochialising the study of education. *Globalisation, Societies and Education, 4*(2), 287–302.

Manathunga, C. (2007). Intercultural postgraduate supervision: Ethnographic journeys of identity and power. In D. Palfreyman & D. McBride (Eds.), *Learning and teaching across cultures in higher education* (pp. 93–113). New York: Palgrave Macmillan.

Manathunga, C. (2011). Moments of transculturation and assimilation: Post-colonial explorations of supervision and culture. *Innovations in Education & Teaching International, 48*(4), 367–376.

Manathunga, C. (2013). Culture as a place of thought: Supervising diverse candidates. In A. Engels-Schwarzpaul & M. Peters (Eds.), *Of other thoughts: Non-traditional ways to the Doctorate: A guidebook for candidates and supervisor* (pp. 67–82). Rotterdam: Sense Publishers.

Manathunga, C. (2017). Intercultural doctoral supervision: The centrality of place, time and other forms of knowledge. *Arts and Humanities in Higher Education, 16*(1), 113–124.

Mazak, C. (2017). Introduction: Theorizing translanguaging practices in higher education. In C. Mazak & K. Carroll (Eds.), *Translanguaging in higher education: Beyond monolingual ideologies* (pp. 1–28). Bristol: Multilingual Matters.

Merriam, S., & Kim, Y. S. (2008). Non-Western perspectives on learning and knowing. *New Directions for Adult and Continuing Education, 119*, 71–81.

Miles, M. B., & Huberman, A. M. (1994). *Qualitative data analysis: An expanded sourcebook* (2nd ed.). Thousand Oaks, CA: Sage.

Pratt, M. L. (1991). Arts of the contact zone. *Profession, 91*, 33–40.

Robson, C. (2002). *Real world research: A resource for social scientists and practitioner-researchers*. Oxford, UK; Madden, MASS.: Blackwell Publishers.

Ryan, J. (2011). Teaching and learning for international students: Towards a transcultural approach. *Teachers and Teaching, 17*(6), 631–648. https://doi.org/10.1080/13540602.2011.625138.

Singh, M. (2009). Using Chinese knowledge in internationalising research education: Jacques Rancière, an ignorant supervisor and doctoral students from China. *Globalisation, Societies and Education, 7*(2), 185–201.

Singh, M., & Chen, X. (2012). Ignorance and pedagogies of intellectual equality: Internationalising Australian HDR education programs and pedagogies through engaging Chinese theoretical tools.

In A. Lee & S. Danby (Eds.), *Reshaping HDR education: Changing programs and pedagogies* (pp. 187–203). London: Routledge.
Singh, M., Manathunga, C., Bunda, T., & Qi, J. (2016). Mobilising Indigenous and non-western theoretic-linguistic knowledge in HDR education. *Knowledge Cultures, 4*(1), 54–68.
Taylor, D. (1991). Transculturating transculturation. *Performing Arts Journal, 13*(2), 90–104.
Velasco, P., & García, O. (2014). Translanguaging and the writing of bilingual learners. *Bilingual Research Journal, 37,* 6–23.
Williams, C. (1994). *Arfarniad o ddulliau dysgu ac addysgu yng nghyd-destun addysg uwchradd ddwyieithog* [Evaluation of teaching and learning methods in the context of bilingual secondary education]. (Unpublished Ph.D. thesis). University of Wales, Bangor, UK.
Winchester-Seeto, T., Homewood, J., Thogersen, J., Jacenyik-Trawoger, C., Manathunga, C., Reid, A., & Holbrook, A. (2014). Doctoral supervision in a cross-cultural context: Issues affecting supervisors and candidates. *Higher Education Research & Development, 33*(3), 610–626.
Wisker, G., & Robinson, G. (2014). Examiner practices and culturally inflected doctoral theses. *Discourse, 35,* 190–205.
Zamel, V. (1997). Toward a model of transculturation. *TESOL Quarterly, 31*(2), 341–352.

Minglin Li is a Senior Lecturer in TESOL/Educational Linguistics in the School of Humanities, Languages and Social Science at Griffith University in Australia. Her research is in the area of Educational Linguistics with a particular focus on English language education policy and planning for Chinese schools where English is taught and learned as a foreign language (EFL). She explores how EFL teachers are actively involved in EFL education policy enactment in their teaching practice and how their practices impact on student learning. She also investigates factors influencing effective EFL teaching and learning in China at the school and tertiary level. Her recent work examines learners' dictionaries in order to assist EFL learners to maximize their learning. Minglin Li has a strong interest in Higher Degree Research (HDR) student supervision, exploring HDR curriculum and trans-cultural and trans-language practice in Higher Degree Research education.

Beryl Exley specialises in English Curriculum and Literacies Education within the School of Education and Professional Studies at Griffith University, Queensland, Australia. Her Ph.D. examined English language teaching in cross-cultural contexts from the viewpoint of offshore English teachers from Australia and the United Kingdom and from Indonesian language institution managers. Her research work applies a socio-cultural lens to examine the inherent features of language and literacy curricula, pedagogy and assessment in school and tertiary contexts, both in face-to-face and social media interactions. She also explores new pedagogical applications of system functional linguistics in early years, primary and secondary schooling contexts so that students are better resourced to enact a pedagogy of language inquiry for reading/viewing and writing/composing multimodal texts. She is interested in language and literacy as matters of social-justice for students and their teachers and how different processes of curricula, pedagogy and assessment provide access to disparate possibilities.

Trilingualism and Medium of Instruction Models in Minority Schools in Qinghai Province, China

Ma Fu

Abstract Multilingual education for students belonging to China's 55 ethnic minority groups presents challenges of learning their home language, the national language (Mandarin) and a foreign language (usually English). The difficulties faced by such students in coping with multilingualism are exacerbated by the demands that are placed on the education system for coherent policy implementation; adequate financial, infrastructural and human resources; and ensuring community understanding and support. The language-in-education practices that have been observed across the nation have been found to vary according to local conditions. This chapter focuses on practices in schools in Qinghai Province, in Western China, where a number of ethnic minority languages are spoken. In particular, it investigates how the choice of medium of instruction in individual schools is a product of contextual factors including the role and status of the different languages, beliefs about language learning, and the systemic support available. Two main models are identified: one is to use the dominant local ethnic language as the medium of instruction, with Mandarin and English as curricular subjects; the other model involves the use of Mandarin as the medium of instruction, with the ethnic language and English being taught as subjects. The chapter evaluates the achievements and shortcomings of each model and argues that effective implementation of multilingual education in Qinghai Province is hampered by weak infrastructure and policy frameworks.

Keywords Medium of instruction · Language policy · Minority education · Multilingual education · Curriculum

1 Introduction

Multilingual education is a feature of school life in mainland China, especially for students belonging to the country's 55 ethnic minority groups, who grapple with the challenge of learning their home language, the national language, and a foreign lan-

Ma Fu (✉)
Qinghai Nationalities University, Qinghai, China
e-mail: ibrahimmafu@aliance.com

guage. The difficulties confronted by such students in coping with multilingualism are exacerbated by the challenges that are faced by the education system in striving to ensure coherent policy implementation; adequate financial, infrastructural and human resources; and community understanding and support. Research into multilingual education (e.g., Feng & Adamson, 2015a, 2015b, 2018) demonstrates that contextual factors such as ethnolinguistic vitality of the various languages, socioeconomics, geopolitics, and historical beliefs, attitudes and practices all contribute to the local decisions regarding language-in-education. Across China, the manifestations of multilingual education are diverse because the contexts of minority groups are so different (Adamson & Feng, 2009). Some groups possess flourishing languages with a long and respected oral and written tradition, other minority languages struggle to survive; some groups are closely assimilated with the mainstream Han, others perceive their identity to be distinct; some groups have ready access to significant economic, political, and social capital, others do not. Four major models of multilingual education were identified in a recent nationwide project (see Feng & Adamson, 2015a), ranging from one that strongly promotes competence in at least three languages to models that privilege one or more language to the detriment of others—usually it is the minority languages that suffer.

This chapter presents a policy study of language-in-education practices that have emerged in schools in Qinghai Province, in Western China. By doing so, it offers insights into policy dilemmas in promoting multilingualism through effective medium of instruction (MOI) practices in less developed areas. Two main models are identified: one is to use the dominant local ethnic language as the MOI, with Chinese and English as curricular subjects; the other model involves the use of Chinese as the MOI, with the ethnic language and English being taught as subjects. The chapter presents the context and rationale for these practices and assesses their achievements and shortcomings. It argues that weak infrastructure and policy frameworks for education in Qinghai make the implementation of multilingual education very challenging, especially when considering the array of minority languages spoken.

2 Multilingual Education in China

Multilingual education, for the purposes of this study, refers to the development of linguistic competence in at least three languages through formal schooling. In China, the requirement in basic education is for students to learn at least two languages, Chinese and a foreign language (usually English). Many, but not all, ethnic minority areas also teach their own languages as well. The choice of MOI in support of multilingual education is a key component, along with other decisions such as when each language is introduced and, in some cases, removed from the curriculum; the number of hours allocated to each language at different levels; the offering of any contiguous subject (such as cultural studies or supplementary reading lessons); and the role and nature of assessment.

In this chapter, 'Chinese' refers to the northern variety of spoken Mandarin Chinese known as Putonghua (which means 'standard language') and standard written Chinese (also based on northern forms of Mandarin grammar and vocabulary, with simplified characters). These forms of Chinese are strongly promoted by the central government for national unity. Chinese is the default MOI in most primary and secondary schools across China, although some local variations are found, as this chapter will show. Ethnic minority groups are generally supportive of Chinese being a prominent feature of schooling, as they believe that proficiency in the language will improve the life chances of students. In some regions, parents have expressed willingness to relinquish the use of the minority language in schools to ensure that their children can have increased exposure to Chinese; in other regions, a more balanced linguistic arrangement may be found (Adamson & Feng, 2015).

Foreign language education has traditionally been based on pragmatic choices reflecting government priorities in China. For example, Russian was emphasized during the period of Sino-Soviet cooperation in the 1950s, whereas English has been the preferred foreign language since China opened her doors to international investment and trade. Other foreign languages are taught in some areas, particularly border regions, but English currently predominates by a considerable margin (Gil & Adamson, 2011) In some parts of the country, there have been experiments with using English as the MOI (see Feng, 2007) in schools, and many universities require students to take a number of English-medium courses in their undergraduate programmes. The use of English-medium teaching has proved controversial: advocates point to the need for China to develop human capital for a globalized world, while critics are concerned about the effects on student learning and the possible loss of Chinese cultural values (e.g., Xu, 2003; Yan, 2004). Ethnic minority regions have embraced English language learning where resources permit because of its associations with tourism and international trade (Blachford & Jones, 2011; Huang, 2011; Sunuodula & Feng, 2011; Yi & Adamson, 2019), as well as the opportunities the language offers for closing the social and educational inequities that exist between minority groups and the majority Han (Beckett & MacPherson, 2005; Sunuodula, Feng, & Adamson, 2015).

Policies and practices concerning the presence of minority languages in the school curriculum (as the MOI or as an individual subject) vary according to local conditions. While the central government has enshrined support for minority languages in the state constitution, specific decisions have been devolved to provincial and local education bureaux, resulting in a range of policy responses.

This chapter is derived from a recent study of multilingual education in eleven ethnic minority regions of China, including Qinghai. The research comprised analysis of policy and curriculum documents, visits to schools and their neighbourhoods, and interviews with administrators in education bureaux, school leaders, teachers, parents and students. The aim of the research was to uncover models of multilingual education and the factors that helped to shape them. Follow-up research was also conducted into aspects of particular interest in specific contexts; in the case of Qinghai, choices of the MOI in ethnic minority schools were the focus. The main project identified four prevalent models (Adamson & Feng, 2014, 2015; Dong et al. 2015), which were labelled the Accretive Model, Balanced Model, Transitional Model and Depreciative Model.

The Accretive Model promotes a strong version of multilingualism by focusing, in the early years of primary education, on developing the students' mother tongue (the ethnic minority language) through the study of the language and its use as the MOI. Chinese and English are also accorded a generous proportion of curriculum space to enable the students to develop a high level of competence in the former, and a developing level of competence in the latter. An example was found in Yanji City, in the Yanbian Korean Autonomous Prefecture in north-eastern China. The students studied the Korean language and learnt other subjects through the medium of Korean. Their knowledge of Korean was leveraged to help them learn Chinese, and these two languages were then deployed to support the learning of English—hence the 'accretive' characteristic of the approach to multilingualism (Zhang, Li, & Wen, 2015).

The Balanced Model is found in areas where there is a significant presence of students for whom Chinese is the first language alongside the students whose mother tongue is the ethnic minority language. To accommodate the two profiles, a school offers two parallel streams: one uses Chinese as the MOI while the ethnic minority language is learnt as a subject, the other uses the ethnic minority language as the MOI while Chinese is learnt as a subject. Outside the classroom, the school supports a bilingual environment. English, meanwhile, is taught through the medium of the respective stream.

The Transitional Model is less favourable to multilingualism in that it is designed to facilitate the development of Chinese competence at the expense of the minority language. According to this model, the minority language is used as the MOI for one or two years in primary schools before it is replaced by Chinese. The minority language then tends to disappear from the school curriculum altogether from this stage onwards. English, which is typically introduced in primary schools in Year 3, is taught through the medium of Chinese. (This has the advantage that the national textbooks can be used in English lessons, rather than tailored materials being required.)

Finally, the Depreciative Model is the weakest in terms of supporting multilingualism but it is the model most commonly found by the research team in the nationwide study (Adamson & Feng, 2015). It is found in schools that claim to be multilingual but, in reality, only use Chinese as the MOI. Chinese and a foreign language, usually English, is taught. However, the ethnic minority language has no presence in the school curriculum. Such schools often justify their 'multilingual' label by pointing out the ethnic diversity of their students (Adamson & Feng, 2014). The lack of support for ethnic minority languages in schools adopting this model means that the students' competence in these languages tends to wither.

The diversity of models reflects different levels of commitment to ensuring the well-being of ethnic minority language. It is not just political will and investment of resources by education bureaux that influence the choice of model: the ethnolinguistic vitality of the minority languages in local communities is also a key determining factor. The next section of this chapter presents snapshot of the situation in Qinghai

Province by identifying the prevalent models of multilingualism that are in operation and looking at some of the factors that shape and sustain them.

3 The Case of Qinghai

Qinghai is a large province, located on the Qinghai-Tibet Plateau in western China. Although possessing rich natural resources, the province is economically underdeveloped in comparison with the rest of the country. It covers an area of over 720 thousand square kilometres with a population is about 5.62 million people, around 46% of whom belong to ethnic minorities such as Tibetans (22%), Hui (16%), Tu (4%), Sala (2%) and Mongolians (2%). There are six ethnic minority autonomous prefectures and one autonomous region in Qinghai, allowing the local government a greater control of local education policies. The provincial government has prioritized education for development, and has paid attention to the educational challenges facing the minority groups. In its thirteenth five-year plan released in 2015, the government of Qinghai called on education bureaux at all levels to follow specified principles for education in ethnic minority regions, namely to promote and continually improve 'bilingual' education; to strengthen the provision of textbooks for schools in minority areas, and to provide high-quality education resources for pastoral areas where farming and cattle herding predominate. The plan mandated the establishment of partnerships between the bureaux in high resource and low resource areas to foster cooperation and communication; the trialling of Chinese tests for ethnic minorities; and the provision of boarding schools for students from agricultural and pastoral areas. As a result of this investment, the scale of schooling in the autonomous prefectures and counties is expanding, the efficiency of school management has been significantly improved, and the infrastructure greatly modernized. According to statistics of minority education collated by Qinghai officials, there are now over half-a-million minority students enrolled in basic education and about 780 minority primary schools in total; about 500 schools offer Tibetan and Chinese or Mongolian and Chinese, and more than 190,000 students in primary and secondary schools experience this form of bilingual education. In terms of trilingual education, English is by far the foreign language that is most commonly offered in schools.

As can be judged from this overview, the provision of multilingual education in Qinghai is both complex and problematic. The following sections examine how schools resolve the issues. Two teaching models are commonly adopted in bilingual minority schools in Qinghai: the first model involves the use of the minority students' mother tongue as the MOI, with Chinese being learnt as a subject; while the second model uses Chinese as the MOI, with the mother tongue as a subject. In Qinghai, at the time of the study, 288 primary and secondary schools (57% of bilingual schools) had adopted the first model. The vast majority (284 schools) use Tibetan as the MOI. The remaining four primary and secondary schools in Haixi prefecture deploy Mongolian as the MOI. Meanwhile, 210 other schools (42%) use Chinese as the

MOI, 208 of which teach Tibetan as the second language. In Haixi prefecture one of the other two schools starts with Mongolian as the MOI in early primary school years but then switches to Chinese; and one is a Kazak school that uses Chinese as the MOI.

4 Ethnic Language as MOI

As noted earlier, Qinghai province has an array of different ethnic minority groups, of which by far the largest are the Tibetans. In regions where the Tibetan community predominates, one finds a very strong ethnolinguistic vitality manifested in the widespread use of the Tibetan language for daily life, trade, and some official communications. In the past ten years our site visits to Tongren County in Huangnan Tibetan Autonomous prefecture reveal that this vitality is evident within the confines of the schools as well as the broader surroundings. For example, in the Tongren Ethnic School, the Tibetan language could be heard being spoken for a variety of school activities inside the classroom and in the playground, while many of the administrative notices were written in Tibetan script, with just a few in Chinese. Most of the staff and students were first-language Tibetan speakers, although they also demonstrated a high degree of competence in Chinese. Another feature of the school was the presence of Tibetan cultural activities, such as dance and music, as an integral part of the students' learning experiences.

The school has modernized its infrastructure since the implementation of the central government policy to stimulate the large-scale development of western China. A large amount of funds has been invested in the construction of new buildings, to produce a well-resourced school with modern facilities. Tongren Ethnic School has adopted Tibetan as the MOI from the first grade in primary school. The students study the language as an individual subject as well. Seven class hours per week were allocated for this purpose in Grade 1, nine in Grade 2, eight in Grade 3, nine in Grade 4, seven in Grade 5 and eight in Grade 6. The national language, Chinese, was viewed as an important subject, and was also allocated considerable amounts of classroom time: seven hours in Grade 1, rising to nine (Grade 2), ten (Grades 3 and 4) and nine in Grade 5, before dropping down to six hours a week in Grade 6. English first appears in Grade 3, with two hours per week in Grades 3 and 4, five in Grade 5 and six in Grade 6. This relatively generous allocation of time to both subjects suggests a genuine attempt to foster trilingualism, bolstered by the use of the mother tongue as the MOI, which facilitated the work of the teachers and students alike. In this regard, the school's model matches that of the Accretive Model, which is characterised by being located in areas of strong ethnolinguistic vitality, cultural heritage, and ethnic identity (Adamson & Feng, 2015). There is a functional differentiation between Tibetan and Chinese on the one hand and English on the other—the aim is to achieve a high level of competence in the first two languages (for cultural identity and local use in the case of Tibetan and for national and increasing international opportunities afforded by Chinese) and initial competence in the foreign language, which has lower immediate value.

5 Chinese as MOI

The bilingual schools that use Chinese as the MOI are, for the most part, located in the regions of Qinghai where the Tibetan minority groups predominate. In the schools in Yushu prefecture where the Tibetan students use the Kangba dialect, the Tibetan language is taught as a curriculum subject. Chinese is used as the MOI for other courses. For the purposes of this chapter, our research team visited a number of schools in Yushu prefecture. One location for our site visits was Qumalai county in Yushu. In this county, the population is over 20,000 people, of whom 98% are Tibetans. The county has 16 schools, scattered around the various towns and villages. One of the schools is the designated Ethnic School in the county. It has 600 students on the roll and employs 29 teachers, made up of 24 Tibetans, three Han, one Mongolian and one Sala.

The school has chosen Chinese as the MOI in order to facilitate the students' access to mainstream opportunities across China, while also paying attention to the development of competence in Tibetan. Teacher recruitment has ensured that the school is well equipped to achieve its goal: approximately 80% of the teachers have acquired certification in Chinese proficiency at the second grade or higher and therefore they can speak very fluent Putonghua. According to the school timetable, five periods of Tibetan, five periods of Chinese and four periods of English are allocated for every grade every week. The teachers try to use the target language in the respective classes. The maths, politics, history, physics, and chemistry classes are taught in Chinese.

During our visit to the school, we found that every student we met could communicate well in Chinese, while the Kangba dialect of Tibetan was the first language of the majority. The students displayed beginner competence in English. Although the school only offered a single stream (as there was no parallel classes that used Tibetan as the MOI), it can be classified as a form of Balanced Model. The use of Chinese was not intended to replace or reduce the importance of Tibetan, as found in school curricula that implement Transitional or Depreciative Models of multilingual education. Indeed, the two languages are seen as complementary elements of the students' education, with English being developed as circumstances permitted. The language environment supports the students' acquisition of a high level of Chinese, which suggests that their education is not being impeded through the use of a less familiar second language as MOI.

6 English as a Foreign Language

When one goes beyond bilingual education to consider multilingual education—that is, including the study of one or more foreign languages—the challenges mount exponentially. The landlocked location of Qinghai means that there are no international borders, and the preferred foreign languages (generally English and Russian) are distant both geographically and linguistically. Arabic is more accessible because of the Islamic connections between minority groups such as the Hui and Arabic-speaking nations, but the language only has a small presence in education in Qinghai, usually in non-formal settings. Lack of resources historically has handicapped the development of multilingual education in Qinghai. After the Cultural Revolution, the instigation of economic reforms in the late 1970s resulted in some bilingual schools offering a foreign language (usually English) at the secondary level. It has only been two decades since multilingual education became a regular feature, when the province sought to comply with the national-level policy initiated by the State Council to deepen and strengthen education reforms in minority regions. One component of this policy was the decision that a foreign language should be offered where sufficient resources allowed. However, the flexibility afforded to Qinghai to adapt or develop policies according to local contexts is not strongly evident, with none of the autonomous prefectures establishing specific policy guidelines for schools in offering foreign languages. The same applies to resources: for instance, the English course syllabus and textbooks used in minority schools are the same as the ones used nationwide.

In general, bilingual schools in Qinghai offer English as the main foreign language. However, this is a relatively recent trend as English has only been regularly appearing in the curriculum in Qinghai over the past two decades due to a dearth of resources. Nowadays, more than 90% of bilingual schools have offered English for more than 10 years. The English curriculum varies from school to school. In some, English is introduced in the third year of primary school with two lessons a week being allocated, increasing to five in the fifth grade. In others, English only appears in grade 5 in primary school. In another variation found in Xunhua county, where almost all the primary schools are bilingual schools with Tibetans forming the major ethnic minority group, two or three English lessons are offered every week from grade three to six. In Zadoi County in Yushu prefecture, there are more than one thousand students and 95 teachers in the Second Nationalities Secondary School; 98% of the students and 50% of the teachers are Tibetan. Since English courses were first offered in 2000, each class of students has two English lessons every week every semester. In Tongde county, a nine-year boarding school, covering primary to junior high school education, has about 1300 students and 100 teachers; 99% of the students and 95% of the teachers are Tibetan. English courses started in 2010, and there are four to five English lessons provided for each class of students every week. These variations reflect the availability of resources and English teachers in individual schools.

English is not a compulsory subject in the examinations for entering a school or a higher grade (such as from junior secondary to senior secondary school); however, if a student's English grade is high, the grade can be included in the calculation of the overall final score. In an examination-oriented education system like the one prevailing in Qinghai, English is thus perceived to be a minor subject that does not merit much attention. The number of English teachers available for deployment in bilingual schools in Qinghai is still insufficient for every school to offer English in the curriculum, and, furthermore, as English has a relatively low status compared with other subjects in the curriculum, the quality of English teaching has been correspondingly poor. Due to the lack of qualified teachers, the provincial education bureau has been forced to recruit teachers without an English major to teach the language. Statistics show that of the more than 200 English teachers employed in bilingual junior high schools, only 50% majored in English in college. Furthermore, the percentage of English teachers who are fluent in both Chinese and Tibetan is very small in bilingual schools.

Site visits found that the English syllabus in bilingual schools is exactly the same as the one designed for schools across the whole of China, as are the English textbooks, the *New Target English Go for it!* series published by the People's Education Press (the curriculum publishing section of the Ministry of Education in Beijing) in October 2012. Every bilingual school is equipped with sufficient resources and equipment for English teaching and learning. From the site visits it appears that exposure to English is limited to inside the classroom; there is a noticeable gap between the pedagogy utilised in these English classes and the expectations underpinning the textbooks, which have adopted task-based learning and incorporates themes, communicative functions, and language structures. In the schools, however, English classes tended to be teacher-centred and focus mainly on linguistic aspects rather than communication. Teachers' limited professional knowledge and lack of teaching experience tend to impede good English learning in terms of curriculum requirements. Qinghai Nationalities University is the only university in Qinghai that caters specifically for ethnic minority students; every year, about one thousand students from these bilingual schools enter the university, and the English grades of about 90% of these students are so low that they require substantial remedial work to learn communicative forms of English when they enter college.

The circumstances observed during the site visits reveal the dilemma surrounding the offering of English as a foreign language in Qinghai province, particularly in the more rural areas. On the one hand, learning English provides ethnic minority students with opportunities to access social and economic capital in terms of increased employment and educational prospects in mainstream society. In this way it offers social equity in that the minority students have the same access as the majority Han. The benefits are recognised by minority students as evidenced by the fact that each year around one hundred students enrol in foreign language majors in tertiary institutions in the province. On the other hand, the relatively poor quality of English teaching at primary and secondary level reflect the difficulties associated with English as an international language. English is linguistically distant from both Chinese and many ethnic minority languages, including Tibetan, in terms of written script, grammar, phonology, and lexis. The challenge of teaching and learning the language is so daunting it is perhaps unsurprising that achievements are low and many minority students do not possess strong motivation or interest to study foreign languages.

Following official concerns about the deficient quality of foreign language teaching and learning in bilingual schools, a nationally-funded teacher professional development programme has been running in some higher education institutes since 2011, offering a twenty-day course for about fifty English teachers from bilingual schools each year. Qinghai province also included measures to improve teaching quality in minority schools in its thirteenth five-year plan for 2016–2020.

In 2012, the School of Foreign Languages of Qinghai Nationalities University was authorized by the Qinghai provincial education bureau to undertake the training programme for English teachers in junior high schools; during the training programme, the School of Foreign Languages also evaluates the qualifications of English teachers from bilingual schools in Qinghai. About fifty English teachers participate in the programme every year. The English placement test results show that the language competence of teachers who had not taken an English major is comparably weak. The teaching quality of bilingual minority schools is also related to English teachers' professional knowledge. According to a survey of about 200 English teachers who participated in the training, about 50% of them reported little knowledge of English linguistics, and a severe lack of systematic training in language skills (listening, speaking, reading, and writing). Teachers' views on how to teach English suggest that they largely rely on the mother tongue. A small-scale qualitative survey of thirty English teachers from secondary schools in prefectures and counties reveals that 56% of teachers think the best way to understand a reading passage in English is to translate it into the students' mother tongue; 45% of teachers agree that it would better to study the content through mother tongue before speaking in English; while 48% of teachers consider the best way to write a good essay as to draft the content in the mother tongue before translating it into English.

In order to provide the teachers with a broader choice of pedagogical options, the training programme focuses on theoretical understanding and practical techniques for using the textbooks and for using oral English in the classroom, and with other aspects of linguistic and pedagogical knowledge. Meanwhile, selected English teachers from secondary schools are sent to study in top universities in countries like the United Kingdom, Singapore, and Australia with the support of the China Scholarship Council.

There is also a growing cohort of university graduates who are capable of undertaking English teaching in bilingual schools. As part of their degree programme, they spend some time studying in English-speaking countries. Many become English teachers across the range of bilingual schools through competitive recruitment, while some concentrate on specialising in Tibetan-English translation.

These measures are beginning to show promising results. In an annual English speech contest held in Qinghai, the author has noted a steady rise in the quality of performances by students from bilingual schools. In the *Xiwang Yingyu zhi Xing* (Hope English Star) contest in 2014, three primary students from bilingual schools in Yushu prefecture were highly praised by the judges for the fluency of their oral English and excellent performance skills, and were nominated for the national final of the contest. Nonetheless, significant improvements will take time to manifest themselves. Multilingualism is important for the social and educational development of Qinghai as China embarks upon its major programmes of economic development, so it is vital that the issue of teacher quality for foreign language learning continues to be addressed.

7 Challenges and Ways Forward

This chapter outlines the progress made in Qinghai in recent decades in enabling students to access enhanced educational opportunities through a multilingual curriculum. Flexibility in the MOI means that students can—at least in most circumstances—learn through a familiar language that is either their mother tongue or a commonly used second language, and the balanced offering of both Chinese and the ethnic minority language (e.g., Tibetan) ensures that students can learn the national language as well as a relevant local language. In addition, the minority students are assisted in developing their cultural identity within the larger context of China. In terms of foreign language, much work has been done in facilitating the learning of English (and other languages) in the province.

However, as acknowledged by officials and academics in Qinghai, there are major challenges to be faced. First, although the Tibetan language might be seen as a good platform for developing multilingualism, given the language's very strong ethnolinguistic vitality in local communities, its long history and rich cultural heritage, the robustness of the written form of the language, and a codified grammar and vocabulary, its presence in the school curriculum rarely extends beyond primary schooling. The reason for this phenomenon is pragmatic: Chinese is the key language for social, academic, and professional success. A foreign language—especially English—is also deemed to be important. However, other ethnic languages lack the robustness of Tibetan and all (including Tibetan) are seen as having lower economic and social value than either Chinese or English, Hence the ethnic language tends to lose out when more curriculum time is devoted to Chinese and when the latter is used as the MOI. The presence of English, too, has proved detrimental to the sustainability of weaker languages, although it has proved supportive of strong ethnic languages in other minority regions, such as Korean in the Yanbian Korean Autonomous Prefecture.

The absence of the ethnic language (as MOI and as a subject for study) from many secondary schools can result in the students acquiring competence in just the social domains of the language, and they miss out on academic and professional domains, which can have a negative impact on the long-tern sustainability of the language. Second, the resources (both human and material) to support a strong model of trilingualism are lacking. There is a shortage of trained teachers who are able to operate bilingually or trilingually. Suitable textbooks are rarely available. Systematic support for teacher development is still in its infancy. Local policies to promote trilingualism in education are lacking. Further steps are required to address these challenges.

In terms of future directions, the findings of this chapter suggest that the provincial local government officials (and decision-makers in less developed areas of language diversity inside and beyond China) need to make some considered choices if they are to fully espouse the goal of multilingualism. The Balanced Model is appropriate by catering for a degree of demographic diversity: students can learn through their preferred MOI and they can access the major local, national, and international languages that improve their life chances. This model can be bolstered by training teachers who understand the rationale underpinning the model and who have the linguistic and pedagogical capacity to implement it effectively. It requires the development of locally-relevant learning materials and experiences for all three languages, with care being paid to the MOI, which is not just a matter of selecting the appropriate language (Tibetan or Chinese) to deliver content—it also involves the judicious use of the chosen language to support student learning. Consideration needs to be given to ensuring the continued study of Tibetan, Mongolian and other ethnic minority languages in secondary education, so that students can have the opportunity (if they wish) to develop their competence in the professional and academic domains of the language.

These approaches require a reasonable attitude towards multilingualism, based on the capacity of the education system to deliver adequate learning opportunities. Expecting students to achieve full trilingualism is unrealistic. The goal could be to establish a very strong grounding in their first and second languages (Chinese or ethnic minority language) and beginner-to-intermediate competence in a foreign language. Such a goal would need to be supported by a positive attitude towards the value of ethnic languages and engagement by communities in the education process. If successful, the policy could furnish the human capital to help the economic development of the province, while also contributing to the sense of cultural identity of the minority groups in the Chinese context.

References

Adamson, B., & Feng, A. (2009). A comparison of trilingual education policies for ethnic minorities in China. *Compare, 39*(3), 321–333.
Adamson, B., & Feng, A. W. (2014). Models for trilingual education in the People's Republic of China. In D. Gorter, V. Zenotz, & J. Cenoz (Eds.), *Minority languages and multilingual education* (pp. 25–44). Dordrecht, The Netherlands: Springer.
Adamson, B., & Feng, A. W. (2015). Trilingualism in education: Models and challenges. In A. W. Feng & B. Adamson (Eds.), *Trilingualism in education in China: Models and challenges* (pp. 243–258). Dordrecht, The Netherlands: Springer.
Beckett, G. H., & MacPherson, S. (2005). Researching the impact of English on minority, and indigenous languages in non-western contexts. *TESOL Quarterly, 39*, 299–307.
Blachford, D. Y. R., & Jones, M. (2011). Trilingual education policy ideals and realities for the Naxi in Yunnan. In A. W. Feng (Ed.), *English language across Greater China* (pp. 228–259). Clevedon, UK: Multilingual Matters.

Dong, F., Narisu, Gou, Y. H., Wang, X. G., & Qiu, J. (2015). Four models of Mongolian nationality schools in the Inner Mongolia Autonomous Region. In Feng, A. W., & Adamson, B. (Eds.), *Trilingualism in education in China: Models and challenges* (pp. 25–45). Dordrecht, The Netherlands: Springer.

Feng, A. W. (Ed.). (2007). *Bilingual education in China: Policies, practices and concepts.* Clevedon, UK: Multilingual Matters.

Feng, A. W., & Adamson, B. (Eds.). (2015a). *Trilingualism in education in China: Models and challenges.* Dordrecht, The Netherlands: Springer.

Feng, A. W., & Adamson, B. (2015b). Contested notions of bilingualism and trilingualism in the People's Republic of China. In W. E. Wright, S. Boun, & O. Garcia (Eds.), *Handbook of bilingual and multilingual education* (pp. 484–494). Oxford, UK: Wiley-Blackwell.

Feng, A. W., & Adamson, B. (2018). Language policies and sociolinguistic domains in the context of minority groups in China. *Journal of Multilingual and Multicultural Development, 39*(2), 169–180.

Gil, J., & Adamson, B. (2011). The English language in China: A sociolinguistic profile. In A. W. Feng (Ed.), *English language education across Greater China* (pp. 23–45). Clevedon, UK: Multilingual Matters.

Huang, B. L. (2011). Economic development and growing importance of the English language in Guangxi. In Feng, A. W. (Ed.), *English language education across Greater China* (pp. 212–227). Clevedon, UK: Multilingual Matters.

Sunuodula, M., & Feng, A. W. (2011). Learning a third language by Uyghur students in Xinjiang: A blessing in disguise? In A. W. Feng (Ed.), *English language in education and societies across Greater China* (pp. 260–283). Clevedon, UK: Multilingual Matters.

Sunuodula, M., Feng, A. W., & Adamson, B. (2015). Trilingualism and Uyghur identity in the People's Republic of China. In Evans, D. (Ed.), *Language and identity: Discourse in the world* (pp. 81–104). London, UK: Continuum.

Xu, K. Q. (2003). 'Shuangyu Jiaoxue' Rezhong Yinguangzhu Zhonghua Minzu Wenhua Yishi Wenti [Beware of the loss of Chinese culture in the clamour for 'bilingual schooling']. *Waiyu Jiaoxue [Foreign Language Education], 25*(3), 86–89.

Yan, C. C. (2004). Zhiyi Shuangyu Jiaoyu [Reservations about bilingual education]. *Tanshuo yu Zhengming [Exploration and Argumentation], 8,* 16–18.

Yi, Y., & Adamson, B. (2019). English in a Mongolian ethnic minority primary school. In I. Liyanage & T. Walker (Eds.), *Multilingual education yearbook 2019: Media of instruction & multilingual settings* (pp. 175–188). New York: Springer.

Zhang, Z. A., Li, G. H., & Wen, L. T. (2015). Trilingual education in China's Korean communities. In A. W. Feng & B. Adamson (Eds.), *Trilingualism in education in China: Models and challenges* (pp. 47–64). Dordrecht, The Netherlands: Springer.

Ma Fu is Professor and Dean of the School of Asian Studies in Qinghai Nationalities University in Xining, Qinghai Province in western China. He specialises in the study of language policy and practices regarding ethnic minority languages, and has produced a large number of national and international journal articles and book chapters. Professor Ma is a founder-member of a major research network in China established to identify and compare models of multilingual education. For many years, he has also been active in organising training programmes in multilingual education for teachers from rural areas of the province, as well as a number of school-based projects.

Children's Views and Strategies for Making Friends in Linguistically Diverse English Medium Instruction Settings

Maryanne Theobald, Gillian Busch and Megan Laraghy

Abstract Despite one in four children in Australia entering preschool using English as an additional language or dialect (EAL/D) (Australian Bureau of Statistics (ABS) in Migration 2015–16. Retrieved from http://www.abs.gov.au/ausstats/abs@.nsf/Latestproducts/3412.0MediaRelease12015-16, 2017), Australian classrooms are predominantly monolingual English-speaking. This mismatch in languages may affect how participation and relationships are established. This chapter explores children's strategies for making friends in settings characterised by linguistic diversity but where the medium of instruction is English. Child-friendly video-recorded interviews with 72 preschool-aged children, 3–4 years, were conducted in a preschool at an inner-city centre. Children were asked to talk and draw a picture about making friends when there are language differences. Children's responses not only revealed their competencies in using non-verbal strategies to communicate with each other but also reflected inclusive attitudes. The importance of using a variety of languages as media of instruction, such as including songs and words representative of the minority languages of the classroom, and having positive conversations with children about language difference are highlighted.

Keywords Friendships · Preschool · Cultural and linguistic diversity · Medium of instruction · Inclusion · Children's views

M. Theobald (✉)
Queensland University of Technology, Brisbane City, QLD, Australia
e-mail: m.theobald@qut.edu.au

G. Busch
Central Queensland University, Norman Gardens, QLD, Australia

M. Laraghy
Lady Gowrie Love Street Community Kindergarten, Fortitude Valley, QLD, Australia

1 Introduction

With increased migration and transnational movements, classrooms across the world are becoming increasingly diverse to include children from a range of cultural and linguistic backgrounds. Such diversity globally has led to the medium of instruction (MOI) for children being the centre of much debate for educational settings. In Australia, on average, one quarter of children use English as an additional language/dialect (EAL/D) when they enter school (Australian Bureau of Statistics (ABS), 2017). The MOI and interaction in Australian classrooms, however, is predominantly monolingual, English (Fielding, 2015). In reality, this means that children who use EAL/D are being spoken to at school in a language that is not their dominant language and this may create challenges for participation and belonging.

Play is how young children learn, participate and make friends in preschool classrooms. Being proficient in the dominant language of the setting provides valuable capital (McDonnell, 2017) in peer interaction and is attributed to later success in academic aspects of schooling (Halle, Hair, Wandner, McNamara, & Chien, 2012). The categorisation of children with EAL/D or with a Language Background Other than English (LBOTE) has become, albeit unwittingly, synonymous with difficulties in learning (Liyanage, Singh, & Walker, 2016). Consequently, the multilingual child, as a "second language learner", may be constructed as a "problem" (Stafford & Drury, 2013, p. 70). With a focus on learning through play, social relationships are increasingly important in preschool classrooms. A mismatch in languages may influence children's participation in classroom activities and consequently how they may make friends.

2 Language and Inclusive Policies for Educational Settings in Australia

Educational settings in the prior-to-school years in Australia are regulated by a National Quality Standard (NQS) (Australian Children's Education & Care Quality Authority (ACECQA), 2018), that sets a national benchmark for quality care and education. In particular, Quality Area Six, "Collaborative partnerships with families and communities," seeks to foster belonging for all children, including those from diverse cultures, through collaborative partnerships with families so that each child has the capacity to participate fully in the program (ACECQA, 2018). The accompanying curriculum framework for educational settings, *Early Years Learning Framework: Being, Belonging and Becoming* (Department of Education, Employment and Workplace Relations (DEEWR), 2009), proposes that quality early childhood programs support children to develop communication skills and have cultural competence in order to have successful relationships with others (DEEWR, 2009). Another policy that has been introduced in the compulsory years of schooling in Queensland, *Global Schools—Creating Successful Global Citizens* (Department of Education, Training and Employment (DETE), 2014), is an initiative based around the premise that language provides a medium for people to engage with others. The policy outlines that learning a language other than English and having a global outlook aids empathy and intercultural competence (DETE, 2014, p. 4). These policies, focusing on inclusive and global outlooks, may sit alongside policies to do with the MOI, however, they are not necessarily in companion with MOI policies. It is not well reported on how policies that promote inclusivity are reflected in practice or experienced by children as they go about making friends in preschool settings.

3 The Importance of Having Friends

Having a friend provides children with social and emotional support (Danby, 2008; Dunn, 2004), is closely related to success in school activities (Buhs & Ladd, 2001), and can help with language acquisition (Piker, 2013). Children learn to communicate, talk to others, and share their ideas through friendships. Studies of friendship have found that making friends means having things in common, such as interests (Hartup, 1992) and "doing things together" (Corsaro & Molinari, 1990, p. 221). There is a tendency to overlook the complexity of friendships because of the view that childhood is a 'natural' state, a developmental view of childhood that has dominated education and psychology (García-Sánchez, 2017). More contemporary views of childhood suggest, however, that childhood is socially constructed (Corsaro, 2017; Prout & James, 1997). When viewed as a social construction the concept of childhood, and thus follows, friendship, is located in the here and now, in relation to social context, "situated and interactionally produced in everyday communicative and social practices" (García-Sánchez, 2017, p. 3). Such a view embraces that children's experiences of childhood are diverse, according to their lived experiences and the unique relationships that occur with a local social order (Danby & Baker, 1998).

Few studies have invited children themselves to share their views on making friends and fewer still have sought the perspectives of younger children. One exception is an Australian study by Danby, Thompson, Theobald and Thorpe (2012) of young children's own views about making friends when starting school. These researchers found that children used strategies that could be sorted into three categories: (1) making requests; (2) joining a group: and, (3) involving an action (Danby et al., 2012). Extending analysis of the same data, Theobald, Danby, Thompson and Thorpe (2017b) found that children defined being a friend as someone who included others, showed concern, and was supportive. These elements help overcome loneliness and contribute to feelings of wellbeing (Dunn, 2004).

4 Friendships in Settings with Linguistic Diversity

There has been a lack of attention on the concept of friendships in settings with linguistic diversity, with a few exceptions examining friendship with older children or adults. Some of these studies have found that speaking the same language and having the same ethnicity does have a part to play in making friends (Pica-Smith, Antognazza, Marland & Crescentini, 2017) and that bilingual practices support friendship (Watson & Hua, 2017; Wijesekera & Alford, 2019). Hopf, McLeod and McDonagh's (2017) study of Fijian school children's language choices found that even though the school had a multilingual MOI policy, most students made friends with peers of the same language background but showed respect to inter-ethnic peers. Barley's (2017) study of older children in an Irish school, identified that language and identity played an integral part in making friends with others. Similarly to Cromdal's (2004) earlier Swedish study, Barley identified that language was used as a way to bully and exclude other children from games. Lanza and Svendsen's (2007) study of multilingual communities in Oslo, Norway, found, however, that having things in common promoted friendship and belonging more than having the same language.

5 Talk: A Gateway for Belonging and Inclusion

"Talk is a gateway" (Theobald, 2017a, p. xix) for making connections that can create experiences of belonging and inclusion. Children's experiences of belonging, being included or excluded in play, have consequences for their ongoing participation. Being seen as a participating member of the peer culture of the dominant language may take some time (Rydland, Grøver & Laurence, 2014) and language competence is revealed or may be hidden depending on the changing social hierarchies of local peer groups (Cekaite & Björk-Willén, 2013). A longitudinal study of two monolingual English-speaking Australian children (a boy, aged 7–8, and his sister, aged 9–10) attending a German school, found that code-switching was used as a way to exclude others, even when there were strict rules in place about the MOI used in the playground (McLeod, Verdon & Theobald, 2015). Over time, being fluent in the dominant language became more important for both children's participation. Similarly, Björk-Willén (2007) found that crossing to another language was an effective strategy to 'lose' children as they tried to enter the peer group. These studies suggest that, despite the MOI, children work out ways to bypass such policies.

Play and games are times when children actively co-create peer culture (Corsaro, 2017). The dynamic nature of the interactions in educational settings means that other factors have the potential to shape relationship trajectories. For example, Scholtz and Gilligan's (2017) study of the perspectives of 12-year-old girls in a culturally diverse school in Dublin, Ireland, suggest that emotional ties have a role to play. They also found that while children identified others as 'nice' they felt fulfilled with their own circle of friends. Theobald, Bateman, Busch, Laraghy and Danby's

(2017a) study of play among children in a preschool characterized by cultural and linguistic diversity found that cultural knowledge, that is, an understanding of local games, the interests of the peer group, and being responsive to the social agendas of peers, is important for making friends. These studies indicate that having common interests and understanding the local peer culture are also important for how children make friends where there are language differences. To date there is little research that reports very young children's voices about MOI and how views of inclusion and friendship are enacted in educational settings. This chapter investigates making friends in settings rich with cultural and linguistic diversity by asking the key stakeholders—very young children.

6 The Study

Data presented in this chapter came from a study, *Better Friends, Better Lives,* that used video-ethnography and child-friendly interviews to explore how children make friends at preschool. The central research questions were: What role does language play in children's interactions when making friends and keeping friends? and; What strategies, social cues and signs do children use to interact when there are language differences?

6.1 The Setting

This study was conducted in an inner-city preschool centre in South-East Queensland, Australia, over a six-week period in the first year and in the following year over a two-week period. Research participants were children, aged four to five years, and one teacher. In total, 72 children participated in the study across three classes. Approximately 30% of the children in each class identified as having a first language other than English. Languages included Greek, Japanese, Arabic, Spanish, Afrikaans, French, and languages used in India (and some neighbouring nations) including Gujarati, Tamil, Bengali, and Telugu.

6.2 Ethical Procedures

The study gained approval from the university research ethics board and the director of the preschool centre. Ethical procedures were followed at all times. Prior to data being collected the first author visited the preschool and met with teacher, guardians, and children. A research pack was provided that included a child-friendly information letter and consent forms. Respecting the rights of the children to make decisions about matters in their life meant that the consent form included a place for children to indicate their consent by a mark or circling a smiley face (Danby & Farrell, 2004). An interpreter assisted the children as needed.

6.3 Data

Data for analysis are derived from two sources. The first source of data is extracts of children's responses from child-friendly interviews. The interviews with children were semi-structured and held in small groups of children with a researcher and interpreter at a table during the everyday play activities of the children. Using a conversational approach, the children were invited to the table and asked about friends, how they made friends, and how they might make friends if they do not share the same language with someone else. The children were then asked to draw a picture about friends. The drawing activity was intended to make children feel at ease and to give children another medium to provide their views (Einarsdottir, Dockett & Perry, 2009), however, the drawings are not presented in this chapter.

Conversations were held in small groups so each child was asked individually to provide their views. The small group context fostered dialogue among children and the researcher in more extended conversations. The conversations lasted anywhere from 5 to 30 min and were video-recorded. The researchers were flexible in their approach to conducting the research conversations. While the drawing generally commenced after most questions were asked, children who were more reserved were asked to draw about making friends and then the researcher's questions overlapped with the activity of drawing. Conversations with children extended into other times during the day, as researchers spent time in the setting. Such an approach adhered to research indicating children's participation is contingent on research design and methods (Danby, Ewing & Thorpe, 2011; Theobald, 2017b).

The views of children who have a first language other than the MOI are often missing from research of children's perspectives, despite moves in research to position children as active participants and to gain a child's standpoint (Mayall, 2002; Theobald, Danby & Ailwood, 2011). To empower all children to share their views, the teacher advised researchers of the children's language backgrounds and language preferences. Following the teacher's advice, two interpreters were employed, one who spoke Japanese and English and one who spoke the languages of India and English. Both interpreters had experience working with children and held police background checks for working with children in Australia. Children in the group who spoke Greek, Arabic, Spanish, Afrikaan or French were identified as not requiring interpreter assistance and participated in the research by speaking English with the researcher.

A second source of data is comprised of (1) researcher-teacher discussions and (2) an extended conversation between children and the researcher. The teacher's reflections about her teaching philosophy were collated in written form. This teaching philosophy sets the context for the ways languages are used in the setting, beyond the official English MOI policy. The project acknowledges the collaboratively produced accounts, assembled from the questions asked, the context in which the research is conducted, and influenced by institutional roles regarding adults and children in an educational setting (Baker, 1997).

6.4 Analytical Methods

When data collection was completed the recordings of the conversations were transcribed verbatim and pseudonyms substituted for participant names. Transcription is in itself an analytical process as the researcher identifies the key extracts for selection, relevant for the research question at hand (Davidson, 2009). The extracts selected here focused on the children's responses about making friends where there were language differences. Following transcription, selected extracts were collated as the data pool. Summative Content Analysis was then conducted. In Summative Content Analysis (Hsieh & Shannon, 2005), two members of the research team first read the collection of transcripts. Each researcher used inductive analysis to identify and code the children's responses of suggested methods to make friends where there are language differences. These were then considered for similarities and differences and three general categories emerged.

An interpretative approach informed by the sociology of childhood studies (Corsaro, 2017) is used to examine the children's accounts of making friends where there were language differences. An interactional focus is a shift away from an individualist perspective of development. Researchers considered co-constructed elements of interactional practices (Corsaro, 2017).

7 Results

The results are presented in two parts. Part One presents the thematic results of the children's accounts and provides extracts of the conversations. Part Two of the results focuses on the teaching philosophy and pedagogical approach of the setting. It presents an extract from the teacher's reflections about this teaching philosophy and pedagogical approach beyond the MOI of the setting. This part also unpacks an extended conversation that occurs between children and researcher to investigate how children oriented to the teaching philosophy or did not orient to it.

8 Part 1: Children's Accounts

In total, 101 responses were provided by the children regarding ways to make friends when there were language differences. Some children proposed a variety of suggestions as the conversations extended. Content analysis of the children's responses identified three key themes. These are: (1) Strategies with *interactive and non-verbal elements* (63 responses); (2) Strategies with *linguistic focus* (38 responses); and (3) Strategies that indicated *Inclusive attitudes* (5 responses). Underpinning many of the responses were characteristics of persistence and a willingness to be connected. The three themes and subsequent sub-themes are presented below, with selected extracts of the conversation to illustrate the *types* of responses that were categorised under each sub-theme.

9 Theme 1: Interactive and Non-verbal Strategies

In this theme, responses focused on the interactional and non-verbal strategies that would enable children to make connections with others. This theme has four sub-themes, namely (1) Toys and resources, (2) Games, (3) Multimodal, and (4) Gestures of friendship. The sub-theme, Gestures of friendship involved three categories: (a) Giving gifts; (b) Intimate actions; and (c) Reading emotions. Games provide children with opportunities to connect and find similarities, and also to learn the fundamental organization of their peer culture (Corsaro, 2017). The non-verbal actions were presented as 'friendly' actions. For example, children suggested using gestures, waving hello, or hugging,

9.1 Sub-theme 1: Toys and Resources

Children named toys or resources that were available in the preschool contexts, such as trains, Lego and Playdoh, as a way of doing something "together".

Extract 1:

Interpreter:	What if you started talking and someone couldn't understand what you were saying or you couldn't understand what they were saying? What could you do then to make friends?
Samir:	Then we play trainset and the Lego.
Researcher:	You do the Lego, all right.
Interpreter:	If your friend doesn't understand you…Do something together?
Samir:	Yes.
Researcher:	How would you show that you're going to do it together?
Samir:	I get the Playdoh.

In this account, Samir suggests a non-verbal action of sharing toys and materials, such as Playdoh, is an effective tool to make friends. Using a toy would be a technique that teachers model and encourage as a way for children to enter play, or shadow each other, and are resources easily accessible to children in preschool settings (Björk-Willén, 2007; Theobald et al., 2017).

9.2 Sub-theme 2: Games

Games were common responses across the interviews. Children named games that involved actions, turn-taking, or moves such as musical statues, hide and seek, soccer, or snakes and ladders. They also named pretence as important for playing together.

Extract 2

Researcher:	Sometimes friends use different words or languages. How would you make friends then?... What would you do instead of talking if that didn't work?
Matt:	Play snakes and ladders.
Researcher:	Play snakes and ladders? Do a game?
Matt:	Play with a ball.
Researcher:	What game are you playing with the ball?
Matt:	Soccer.
Daniel:	I'm playing soccer too.

The child identifies that games such as soccer or snakes and ladders as ways to overcome language differences. These games usually do not require talk to be exchanged in order for them to be played. Soccer (football) is a game that is known across the world. This child reinforced the strategy of playing soccer in the drawing he produced.

9.3 Sub-theme 3: Multimodal

Children identified multimodal ways to make connections with others such as waving, actions, or using hands and feet.

Extract 3

Researcher:	What if they didn't understand? What would you do then?
May:	I would say, I'll show you what I'm telling you.
Researcher:	Show you what I'm telling you? Okay. What would—what could you do if that didn't work?
May:	You can explain with your hands or feet.
Researcher:	Explain with your hands and your feet, oh. Can you tell me more about that? What things might you do?
May:	I'm not sure.

This account illustrates how children show awareness of multimodal strategies to communicate (Mondada, 2014), with May suggesting using her hands and feet. Her drawing also showed figures holding out their hands and feet. In early childhood settings, signs and symbols are often used to accompany spoken language, providing multiple ways that children can both access and present information. For example, a teacher may hold up their hand to indicate Stop or Look and actions are often used to accompany songs and rhymes.

9.4 Sub-theme 4.1: Gestures of Friendship: Giving Gifts

Children suggested friendly gestures, such as giving flowers, gifts or presents.

Extract 4

Researcher:	Has that happened here at kindy, where you've used other ways to make friends?
Elly:	Yeah.
Researcher:	Other than talking? Can you tell me about that?
Elly:	Sometimes with my friends at kindy, I be nice with them and give—one-time Laura and me—Laura gave me stickers and I gave her a picture.
Researcher:	So that's another way of showing friends?
Elly:	Yeah. I went to Laura's place and I saw that she hung up the picture that I gave her.
Researcher:	How did that make you feel?
Elly:	Good.
Researcher:	So, friends go to each other's house.

This account identified "friendly" strategies of giving gifts and visiting each other. The account reflects the action of giving something as a gesture of friendship. Elly's explanation of her friend Laura hanging up Elly's picture in her house as illustrating their friendship reflects the reciprocal nature of friendship identified by Dunn (2004). Here, children propose a cultural practice, giving gifts, that they may have seen or experienced as part of their everyday life.

9.5 Sub-theme 4.2: Gestures of Friendship: Intimate Actions

Children proposed gestures of friendship that included intimate activities such as visiting others' homes as a way of making friends.

Extract 5

Researcher:	What could you do to make friends instead of talking?
Wal:	When you can make them … you could give them presents to make friends.
Researcher:	Give them presents ?

Wal:	Yeah, and then have sleepovers and invite them to your party.
Researcher:	Yes, that's some ideas.

The personal intimate nature of being a friend is illustrated here in the reference to coming to one's party and sleeping over. Invitations to and participation in birthday parties are often used as evidence for friendship. For children perhaps the making of friends is a bit unclear until they have opportunities for activities to become common interests can be consolidated.

9.6 Sub-theme 4.3: Gestures of Friendship: Reading Emotions

Children proposed activities to enact that responded to how another child might be feeling.

Extract 6

Researcher:	If you or if somebody couldn't understand what you said and you couldn't understand what they said, how would you be friends?
Sol:	You would say if someone hurt you, you would say sorry and I think that will be…
Researcher:	What if they didn't understand?
Sol:	Maybe…you could go to the zoo with them and cheer them up if they were crying.

Sol's account highlights an awareness of others' emotions and a desire to support others in making them feel better. Being able to read others' emotions is a resource for social interaction and being friends. Many emotional signals such as crying are universal and transferable across cultures.

10 Theme 2: Linguistic Focus

In this theme, the children's responses focused on how they might find particular words that could be taught or learnt to find a common language (lingua franca) to connect with each other. There are four sub-themes: (1) Teaching the dominant language; (2) Speaking another's language; (3) Sharing and exchanging language; and (4) Using written language.

10.1 Sub-theme 1: Teaching or Using the Dominant Language (MOI)

Extract 7

Shey:	The best way to make a friend is to ask them to play with you? Would you like to play with me?
Researcher:	And what if they didn't understand what you said.
Shey:	You can just you can you can teach them how them talk.
Researcher:	What language would you teach them
Shey:	I would teach them English if they didn't know English.
Researcher:	Yes. Do you talk in other languages? …
Shey:	Yes sometimes I talk in I talk in Telagul and Hindi, and Tamil.
Researcher:	Three languages?
Shey:	and I talk in English so it's all four languages.
Researcher:	Who do you talk in different languages to?
Shey:	I talk all these languages to my grandparents
Researcher:	What about when you came to kindy?
Shey:	The first time I came I was shy but I tried to make friends with Amy and I said her name and she said I'm Amy. I asked her to play and she said yes. A few days later we become best friends.

In this account, Shey identifies that learning English is helpful for forming friendships, suggesting that she would teach another child how to speak English if they did not speak English. As the account shows, the child also shows an awareness of the way in which context influences the language spoken. For example, the child gestures towards English being the preferred language at kindy, whereas, when speaking with grandparents, any of the four languages spoken by the grandparents would be appropriate.

Extract 8

Researcher:	What if they didn't understand what you were saying or you didn't understand what they said back to you?
Bailey:	I would say, beg your pardon?
Researcher:	Right. If that didn't work, what would you do then?
Bailey:	I would say, what did you say?
Researcher:	yeah. If they couldn't understand what you were saying, what would you do then?
Bailey:	I would maybe just say to them what? I will tell them what? if they don't listen to me I'll just – I'll just say their name and I'll tell you that
Researcher:	Okay. How do the teachers help you make friends?
Bailey:	By telling us to meet them. I played with him a long time.

This account by Bailey highlights a linguistic strategy of using the dominant language. However, the account also demonstrates the boy's persistence and expressed desire to overcome a language barrier, as he reports he would try again and again to communicate. He names also the teacher as important in helping children to meet each other, making the first introduction. Teachers can guide and scaffold children's participation in peer play without disrupting the unique qualities of the play.

Extract 9

Interpreter:	Can you tell me how you made friends?
Hal:	*Datte Daddy to ippaisa ippai shabetterukara eigo dakarasa dondon wakattekita.*
	Because, I talked with Daddy a lot in English, so understood more and more.
Interpreter:	*A, sokka. Eigo dondon wakattekitara otomodachimo dekitanoka.*
	Oh, I see. More you spoke English, more you made friends.
Hal:	*Ippai shabettakara eigo.*
	Spoke a lot of English.

This child's account outlines that, when becoming bilingual in Japanese and English, it was important for him to learn to speak the dominant language of the setting. Here Hal identifies strategies of practicing talking in the language and this helped him to make friends. This account emphasises that having bilingual communication outside of the preschool, in this case with his Dad, greatly assisted him to become better at using the dominant language of the setting, English. Translation between languages has been found to promote language acquisition, biliteracy development, and foster a greater sense of self and has implications for implementing one MOI (Cummins, 2007).

10.2 Sub-theme 2: Speaking in Another's Language

Extract 10

Researcher:	How do you make friends when you speak different languages?
Lena:	Well the teacher tells us some different language and we say them. And in Kumi's language to speak mummy its Okaasan. It means that it's your mummy. It's to say mummy in a different language. Japanese

The teacher's role is highlighted in this account. Here, the teacher provides children with key words in other languages, external to the MOI. This strategy is reported as a key way for making friends.

Extract 11

Researcher:	How would you make friends?
Oprah:	Just say what kind of language they're in … You could talk the language.

Researcher:	… Okay. What else might you do if that didn't work—in the meantime when you're still learning the language? How else would you show them you want to be friends?
Oprah:	You could hug them…and say will you be my friend.

Initially Oprah reported that learning and talking in the first language of another child would be the best strategy. The researcher's response suggests that it may take some time to learn the language, problematising this potential solution. In response, one of the children suggests a physical action of hugging them, to *show* friendship.

Extract 12

Moana:	To understand their language, I need to go on holidays to a different country and learn a different language, but it is not Spanish because my babysitter is from Colombia.
Researcher:	Really? So you know some Spanish?…
Moana:	Hola.
Researcher:	Hola, hello.
Moana:	I know buenos dias; that means good morning.
	I know amigo; that means friend.
	I know chico de oro, that means golden boy if I don't know their name…

Moana's account emphasises that language is important to communicate with others and she suggests using another's language for a greeting. Such an account shows an alignment with the idea that language does play an important role for rituals such as when you meet someone for the first time. Moana seems to be reporting on a past experience of where she met someone who spoke Spanish, perhaps a child in the preschool group. This account also suggests it is important to use the words that might be associated with friends, such as amigo.

10.3 Sub-theme 3: *Sharing and Exchanging Language*

Children suggested that exchanging languages by saying words from each child's first language is a way of learning each other's language.

Extract 13

Researcher:	What if somebody went up to them and said something and they couldn't understand what you said and they said something to you and you couldn't understand what they said?
Daniel:	You'd say something what they say and say something what you say.

The willingness to share and exchange languages is evident in this child's account. There is a display of valuing and respect for others.

Extract 14

Interpreter:	Kotoba ga wakaranakutemo otomodachi to.
	Do you think you can play with someone who does not know the language?
Kumi:	Kae-chan wa darekani kikaretara shabennai.
	I won't talk if someone talks to me in the language that I don't understand.
Kumi:	Imawa nihon no otomodachi. Rita-ch an toka Hal-kun shika Inaikedo.
	Right now, there are only Japanese friends, Rita and Hal.
Interpreter:	Unun, sokka. Jya, Eigo dattara otomo dachi dekinainokana?
	Yes, I see. Is it hard to make friends if they speak English?
Kumi:	Un.
	Yes.

Kumi's account suggests that, from her standpoint as child who uses English as an additional language, the MOI of English only is a barrier to her making friends. She reports that she does not talk if someone does not speak in her first language, Japanese. This lack of communication is affecting her social connections as she is making friends with Japanese-speaking children but not friends with children who speak English, the MOI.

10.4 Sub-theme 4: Using Written Language

Extract 15

Connor:	There is some people that speak a different language…
	I know all of their names.
Researcher:	How did you make friends with them? How did you get to know all their names?
Connor:	The teacher told us.
Researcher:	Can you make friends without talking?
Connor:	I know how to make friends without talking.
Researcher:	How?
Connor:	Write notes.
Researcher:	Write some notes?
Sammy:	Write our name on a piece of paper and then…
Jenny:	But what if they don't know how to read?
Researcher:	Right, what if they don't know how to read? What would you do then?
Connor:	I know how to read.
Researcher:	Not everybody does.

In this extract, Connor identifies that the teacher was an important resource for helping the children to know each other's names as a first step in making friends.

Making notes by writing their name on a piece of paper is offered as a way of making friends. However, Jenny contests this strategy by indicating that it might not work if they do not know how to read. Jenny's suggestion could be seen as a recognition that there are different forms that written language takes, and that a child who cannot speak English might not be able to read English. Thus, more discussion about what multilingualism means and that language comes in many forms, spoken and written, is required.

11 Theme 3: Inclusive Attitudes

Responses associated with the theme of Inclusive attitudes were less common (5 responses), however, some children did explicitly highlight the importance of including others. For example, children focused on the consequences of making friends with everyone to make a better world.

Extract 16

Researcher:	How would it feel not to have friends?
Lizzie:	if you didn't friends you wouldn't have any love and then who would you be happy with? …Very sad and lonely…
Amy:	You could play by your own.
Lizzie:	…because nobody would like want you…
Oprah:	It sure would make me sad and I would play…
Lizzie:	…or need you or doesn't want to be friend with you. So if Elsa didn't want to be friends with me or my mum and dad didn't want to be mum and dad with me, what would I do? I'd just stay out there by myself. It wouldn't be very fair. No one would come over to me.
Researcher:	No. What would you do then?
Lizzie:	I'd be very sad.
Amy:	I would never do that.
Lizzie:	I would probably make a better world and I would try and make friends with everyone.

In this account, Lizzie, Amy and Oprah discuss whether friends are needed or not and how they would feel if they were on their own without friends. Lizzie's last statement, "I would try to make friends with everyone", highlights the inclusive attitudes that are reinforced in the setting and outlined in the guidelines accompanying curriculum for early childhood education in Australia (DEEWR, 2009).

Extract 17

Researcher:	What if you didn't speak the same language, how would you make friends?
Aahna:	We could—we don't have to speak the same language if we don't want to

Researcher:	No?
Aahna:	So if we—so if we find one we- that be nice—we can be friends for ever and ever and they come to your house.

Contrary to the earlier accounts (extracts 12–14), Aahna proposes that speaking the same language is *not* a necessary condition for making friends. As a multilingual child, Aahna suggests that interpersonal aspects such as to "be nice" as a necessary condition. This account is underpinned by an inclusive ideology and it shows the importance placed on the longevity and the closeness of the relationship of friends. Dunn (2004), Hartup (1992) and Theobald et al. (2017) also observed that friends share intimate times. The account also highlights that different contexts, school to home, are important for making friends and for deepening interaction.

12 Part 2: Exploring Pedagogical Approaches Beyond the Medium Instruction Setting

In this section, we examine the pedagogy of the setting beyond the MOI from the teacher's reflection on the teaching philosophy, and then examine an extended conversation to investigate if the pedagogy is oriented to by the children.

12.1 Teaching Philosophy

Extract 18

Working with families and laying a solid foundation for inclusion involves learning about family's cultural beliefs and language. The staff adopt a family project approach that involved using pictures to support the learning of English in conjunction with the use of their home language. It is a tool for interaction whether linguistic or interactively through gesture. Parents were also invited to stay for an hour in morning to help with routine so that I as the teacher could learn the routine words in the child's first language. In this way I was able to use the language support the child in the routine more effectively.

Teachers and peers can learn songs, words and simple phrases to support children with English as an additional language. Also important is the teacher valuing inclusive ideologies and for the child feeling valued and gaining the confidence to engage to their new environment. When this occurs, children start to normalise languages other than English being spoken in the class and seek opportunities to share the children's culture alongside them. An example of this is that the children prefer to sing Twinkle Twinkle Little Star in Mandarin rather than English.

The teacher here reports on educational philosophy. In particular, she highlights how the language backgrounds of the children in the class are incorporated into the program. This inclusion of the languages of children in the group is a demonstration of how educators might value children's home language by themselves learning the children's first languages, presenting routines, playing games or including instructional dialogue in languages other than English. Such actions follow inclusive guidelines outlined in the *Early Years Curriculum Guidelines* (DEEWR, 2009). While the MOI of the setting was English, the teaching philosophy and pedagogical approaches demonstrated that children's language backgrounds were valued.

12.2 Extended Conversation

The next extract presents one extended conversation between a small group and the researcher. One child's initial response represented a monolingual mindset about language and making friends. However, as the conversation progressed the teaching philosophy of incorporating languages beyond the MOI, was oriented to by the children.

Extract 19

Researcher:	Who can be friends?
Jenny:	No idea.
	Definitely not people who speak in a different language. Otherwise you don't understand what they're saying and they may be saying, will you like to be my friend?
Researcher:	What would you do? You have lots of people here who speak other languages…So how would you make friends?…
Jenny:	I don't know…(Shrugs)
Researcher:	Your teacher—what would Mrs L say to do, do you think?
Jenny:	She would probably say—you would probably say, then don't worry about it.
Researcher:	How would—if someone didn't have a friend…
Jenny:	Get a friend.
Researcher:	What would they do?
Jenny:	You could just find a English friend.
Researcher:	Can you be friends with all people?
Jenny:	Yeah, but not much people in other countries have enough money to fly here.
Researcher:	But you've got lots of friends here who speak different languages.
Jenny:	That's because they learnt how to speak English language.
Researcher:	Are there some words that you know?
Jenny:	Okaasan.
Researcher:	What does that mean?
Sammy:	Mummy.
Jenny:	I know a song in one of the languages
Connor:	Yeah, it's in Chinese

Jenny, Connor and Sammy:	Atama no kata no hiza to tsumasaki hiza to tsumasaki, atama no kata no hiza to tsumasaki, hiza to tsumasaki
	(children touch heads, shoulders, knees and toes)
	Me to mimi to kuchi to hana
	(children touch eyes, ears and mouth and nose)
	Atama no kata no hiza to tsumasaki no hiza to tsumasaki
	(children touch heads, shoulders, knees and toes)
Researcher:	…How does that make everyone feel when you sing that together?
Jenny:	I don't know.
Researcher:	How does it make you feel when you sing it together?
Jenny:	Not really anything.
Researcher:	What about you Sammy?
Sammy:	It makes me feel happy when everyone sings…
Jenny:	Yeah. It makes me feel like that too.

The emphasis placed on language is highlighted in this account. Jenny initially suggests that making friends with children who are not English speakers is not possible. Despite having high cultural and linguistic diversity in the setting, a monolingual mindset is apparent in this discussion. When faced with the response, the researcher pushes a moral discourse of being inclusive by asking what the teacher, a dominant adult in the preschool, would suggest. This is a reminder about the preschool policy and seems to prompt the children to evoke the classroom culture about being inclusive. As the conversation progresses, the children remind each other of a strategy that they had been taught at preschool, using some of the children's first language to sing a song together. The teacher's pedagogical practice of introducing songs in languages other than English has been successful here in promoting a the beginnings of a positive attitude toward making friends despite language difference. Sharing a song in a common language, promotes commonality among the children. Having something in common is identified as a key element for making friends (Hartup, 1992) and "doing things together" (Corsaro & Molinari, 1990, p. 221). The accounts also named learning each other's language as a useful strategy for making friends. This extract demonstrates the importance of having open discussions about language differences and the teacher's role in supporting children's friendships.

13 Discussion

Analysis of children's accounts identified a variety of strategies for making friends when there were language differences. Three themes (1) *interactive and non-verbal strategies,* (2) *linguistic strategies,* and (3) *inclusive attitudes* were identified. Theme 1, *interactional and non-verbal strategies,* accounted for the greatest number of responses, nearly double to the second theme, linguistic strategies. This result suggests that children showed they were willing to overcome potential barriers of language differences as they strived to make friends. Speaking English, the language that was used as the medium of instruction, was identified as important in forming friendships by both multilingual and English-only speaking children in Theme 2, *linguistic strategies*, however, children also named the importance of using another's language. Theme 3, *Inclusive attitudes* were referred to explicitly by a few children.

The children's accounts demonstrated a determination and willingness to make connections. They reported strategies that were underpinned by taking on the perspective of others, gestures of friendship, expressions of emotion and a willingness to share languages, similar to findings of McLeod et al. (2015) and Danby et al. (2012). These features of making friendships reflected some of the inclusive beliefs articulated by the teacher of incorporating the children's languages beyond the MOI for routines and interactional language, as well as reflecting aspects of the curriculum framework (DEEWR, 2009) and the National Quality Standards (ACECQA, 2018) regarding fostering relationships and inclusion.

The importance of valuing diversity by talking about and making attempts in normalizing diversity as part of the fabric of our culture rather than dismissing difference, is important particularly in monolingual MOI settings. In Extract 14, one child suggested that she would not speak using the MOI. As the last extract showed, one child suggested that making friends with children who did not speak the language of the MOI was difficult and could not be done, however, as the conversation evolved she and her peers identified particular strategies that reflected an inclusive ideology to overcome potential problems. The last account highlights that attitudes regarding inclusion are not automatic. Children may need to discuss more openly such topics of language difference in order to deconstruct their own assumptions of this.

14 Conclusion

Friendship and language learning are intertwined. A play environment that is language-rich encourages language acquisition (Cummins, 1984, 2007) and as discussed in this chapter, assists in friendship development. In linguistically diverse early years settings, supporting children to play games that incorporate non-verbal communication such as soccer, musical statues; find common interests; use objects such as Lego; and share songs in other languages can help to foster friendships and in turn may help to expedite the task of language learning. Increased opportunities for play and enabling time to make connections has a cumulative effect in encouraging children communicate with others, and if learning a second language this interaction ultimately assists them to become more confident and skilled at using language.

Adults had an important role in helping children make friends. The teacher was mentioned as a support to help children make initial introductions and find common interests to support children's ongoing peer play. These accounts reflected the philosophy that the teacher promoted through her activities in the classroom. For example, including songs translated to various languages is a linguistic strategy to foster belonging and legitimizing use of a variety of languages for facilitating communication between children. In this way, the medium of instruction, English, was interjected with other languages so that English was not the only language heard within the education setting. Acknowledging multilingualism and using it as a teaching resource can support children's efforts to learn the language of instruction and to make friends. A few children spoke about the importance of practising the language of instruction with family members or people outside of the setting. Other adults, such as parents, grandparents, siblings or babysitters, were named as influential in becoming fluent speakers of the dominant language and this consequently helped them to make friends.

Given these findings, we make the following recommendations:

- Educators who integrate key words of languages that reflect the first language of the children in the class beyond MOI may help children to make initial contact with each other.
- Educators can introduce objects and games that do not rely on language to foster interactions. In turn, this builds a play language and expedites language learning.
- Educators might assist children to find common interests and learn the local peer culture as this is a key aspect of making friends.
- Conversations and explicit discussion about making friends where there are language differences, even with very young children, are important in addressing preconceived ideas and bias toward a monolingual mindset, especially important where there is a monolingual MOI.
- There may be some benefit for children to have 'play advocates' who speak the children's first language.

The findings from this chapter show that children display a desire to overcome linguistic barriers to make friends, and, when provided opportunities, can name a diverse range of strategies for doing so. Children report their willingness to try to find a communicative 'lingua franca', in addition to, and despite of, the MOI of the setting. While there are still some challenges faced by educators to overcome monolingual mindsets, pedagogical actions are identified as important. Pedagogical actions include acknowledging and valuing the multilingual resources of children by incorporating children's home languages in daily activities, and having conversations about language. Such actions can support children in linguistically diverse early years education settings to negotiate cross-linguistic friendships and participate in opportunities to learn through play.

References

Australian Bureau of Statistics (ABS). (2017). *Migration 2015–16*. Retrieved from http://www.abs.gov.au/ausstats/abs@.nsf/Latestproducts/3412.0MediaRelease12015-16.

Australian Children's Education & Care Quality Authority (ACECQA). (2018). *National quality standard and assessment and rating*. Canberra: Australian Children's Education & Care Quality Authority.

Baker, C. (1997). Membership categorization and interview accounts. In D. Silverman (Ed.), *Qualitative research: Theory, method and practice* (pp. 130–143). London: Sage.

Barley, R. (2017). Language identify and peer interaction at a linguistically diverse school. In M. Theobald (Ed.), *Friendship and peer culture in multilingual settings* (pp. 89–112). London: Emerald.

Björk-Willén, P. (2007). Participation in multilingual preschool play: Shadowing and crossing as interactional resources. *Journal of Pragmatics, 39*(2), 2133–2158. https://doi.org/10.1016/j.pragma.2007.05.010.

Buhs, E. S., & Ladd, G. W. (2001). Peer rejection as antecedent of young children's school adjustment: An examination of mediating processes. *Developmental Psychology, 37*(4), 550–560.

Cekaite, A., & Björk-Willén, P. (2013). Peer group interactions in multilingual educational settings: Co-constructing social order and norms for language use. *International Journal of Bilingualism, 17*(2), 174–188. https://doi.org/10.1177/1367006912441417.

Corsaro, W. A. (2017). *The sociology of childhood*. London: Sage.

Corsaro, W. A., & Molinari, L. (1990). From seggiolini to discussione: The generation and extension of peer culture among Italian preschool children. *International Journal of Qualitative Studies in Education, 3*(3), 213–230.

Cromdal, J. (2004). Building bilingual oppositions: Code switching in children's disputes. *Language in Society, 33*(1), 33–58.

Cummins, J. (1984). *Bilingualism and special education: Issues in assessment and pedagogy*. San Francisco, CA: College-Hill Press.

Cummins, J. (2007). Rethinking monolingual instructional strategies in multilingual classrooms. *Canadian Journal of Applied Linguistics/Revue canadienne de linguistique appliquée, 10*(2), 221–240.

Danby, S. J. (2008). The importance of friends; the value of friends; friendships within peer cultures. In L. Brooker & M. Woodhead (Eds.), *Developing positive identities: Diversity and young children* (pp. 36–41). Milton Keynes: Open University.

Danby, S., & Baker, C. (1998). What's the problem?: Restoring social order in the preschool classroom. In I. Hutchby & J. Moran-Ellis (Eds.), *Children and social competence: Arenas of action* (pp. 157–186). London: Falmer Press.

Danby, S., Ewing, L., & Thorpe, K. (2011). The novice researcher: Interviewing young children. *Qualitative Inquiry, 17*(1), 74–84. https://doi.org/10.1177/1077800410389754.

Danby, S., & Farrell, A. (2004). Accounting for young children's competence in educational research: New perspectives on research ethics. *The Australian Educational Researcher, 31*(3), 35–49.

Danby, S., Thompson, C., Theobald, M., & Thorpe, K. (2012). Children's strategies for making friends when starting school. *Australasian Journal of Early Childhood, 37*(2), 63–71.

Davidson, C. (2009). Transcription: Imperatives for qualitative research. *International Journal of Qualitative Methods, 8*(2), 35–52.

Department of Education, Education & Workplace Relations (DEEWR). (2009). *Belonging, being and becoming: The early years learning framework for Australia*. Canberra: Commonwealth of Australia.

Department of Education, Training and Employment (DETE). (2014). *Global schools—creating successful global citizens*. Canberra: Commonwealth of Australia.

Dunn, J. (2004). *Children's friendships: The beginnings of intimacy*. Malden, MA: Blackwell.

Einarsdottir, J., Dockett, S., & Perry, B. (2009). Making meaning: Children's perspectives expressed through drawings. *Early Child Development and Care, 179*(2), 217–232.

Fielding, R. (2015). *Multilingualism in the Australian Suburbs: A framework for exploring bilingual identity*. Singapore: Springer.

García-Sánchez, I. (2017). Friendship, participation and multimodality in Moroccan immigrant girls' peer groups. In M. Theobald (Ed.), *Friendship and peer culture in multilingual settings* (pp. 1–32). London: Emerald.
Halle, T., Hair, E., Wandner, L., McNamara, M., & Chien, N. (2012). Predictors and outcomes of early vs. later English language proficiency among English language learners. *Early Childhood Research Quarterly, 27*(1), 1–20. https://doi.org/10.1016/j.ecresq.2011.07.00.
Hartup, W. W. (1992). *Having friends, making friends and keeping friends: Relationships as educational contexts*. ERIC Digest. Retrieved from http://ericeece.org/pubs/digests/1992/hartup92.html.
Hopf, S. C., McLeod, S., & McDonagh, S. H. (2017). Fiji school students' multilingual language choices when talking with friends. In M. Theobald (Ed.), *Friendship and peer culture in multilingual settings* (pp. 55–88). London: Emerald.
Hsieh, H. F., & Shannon, S. E. (2005). Three approaches to qualitative content analysis. *Qualitative Health Research, 15*(9), 1277–1288.
Lanza, E., & Svendsen, B. A. (2007). Tell me who your friends are and I might be able to tell you what language(s) you speak: Social network analysis, multilingualism, and identity. *International Journal of Bilingualism, 11*(3), 275–300.
Liyanage, I., Singh, P., & Walker, T. (2016). Ethnolinguistic diversity within Australian schools: Call for a participant perspective in teacher learning. *International Journal of Pedagogies & Learning, 11*(3), 211–224. https://doi.org/10.1080/22040552.2016.127259.
Mayall, B. (2002). Towards a child standpoint. In B. Mayall (Ed.), *Towards a sociology for childhood: Thinking from children's lives* (pp. 112–139). Buckingham, UK: Open University Press.
McDonnell, S. (2017). Speaking distance: Language, friendship and spaces of belonging in Irish primary schools. In M. Theobald (Ed.), *Friendship and peer culture in multilingual settings* (pp. 33–54). London: Emerald.
McLeod, S., Verdon, S., & Theobald, M. (2015). Becoming bilingual: Children's insights about sequential bilingualism and its influence on friendships. *International Journal of Early Childhood (IJEC), 47*(3), 385–402.
Mondada, L. (2014). The local constitution of multimodal resources for social interaction. *Journal of Pragmatics, 65*, 137–156.
Pica-Smith, C., Antognazza, D., Marland, J. J., & Crescentini, A. (2017). A cross-cultural study of Italian and US children's perceptions of interethnic and interracial friendships in two urban schools. *Cogent Education, 4*(1), 1–12. https://doi.org/10.1080/2331186X.2017.1280255.
Piker, R. A. (2013). Understanding influences of play on second language learning: A microethnographic view in one Head Start preschool classroom. *Journal of Early Childhood Research, 11*(2), 184–200. https://doi.org/10.1177/1476718X12466219.
Prout, A., & James, A. (1997). A new paradigm for the sociology of childhood? Provenance, promise and problems. In A. James & A. Prout (Eds.), *Constructing and reconstructing childhood: Contemporary issues in the sociological study of childhood* (pp. 7–34). London: Falmer Press.
Rydland, V., Grøver, V., & Laurence, J. (2014). The potentials and challenges of learning words from peers in preschool: A longitudinal study of second language learners in Norway. In A. Cekaite, S. Blum-Kulka, V. Grøver, & E. Teubal (Eds.), *Children's peer talk: Learning from each other* (pp. 214–234). Cambridge: Cambridge University Press.
Scholtz, J., & Gilligan, R. (2017). Encountering difference: Young girls' perspectives on separateness and friendship in culturally diverse schools in Dublin. *Childhood, 24*(2), 168–182. https://doi.org/10.1177/0907568216648365.
Stafford, K., & Drury, R. (2013). The 'problem' of bilingual children in educational settings: Policy and research in England. *Language and Education., 27*(1), 70–81. https://doi.org/10.1080/09500782.2012.685177.
Theobald M. (2017a). Friendship and peer culture in multilingual settings: An introduction. In M.Theobald (Ed.) *Friendship and peer culture in multilingual settings* (pp. xvii–xxiv). London: Emerald.

Theobald, M. (2017b). The work of interpreters to gain children's perspectives within culturally and linguistically diverse classrooms. *International Journal of Early Years Education, 25*(3), 257–273. https://doi.org/10.1080/09669760.2017.1337565.

Theobald, M., Bateman, A., Busch, G., Laraghy, M., & Danby, S. J. (2017a). 'I'm your best friend': Peer interaction and friendship in a multilingual preschool. In M. Theobald (Ed.), *Friendship and peer culture in multilingual settings* (pp. 171–196). London: Emerald.

Theobald, M., Danby, S., & Ailwood, J. (2011). Child participation in the early years: Challenges for education. *Australasian Journal of Early Childhood, 36*(3), 19–26.

Theobald, M., Danby, S. J., Thompson, C., & Thorpe, K. J. (2017b). Friendships. In S. Garvis & D. Pendergast (Eds.), *Health and wellbeing in childhood* (2nd ed., pp. 114–132). Port Melbourne, Victoria: Cambridge University Press.

Watson, J., & Hua, H. (2017). Intercultural learning and friendship development in short-term intercultural education programmes. In M. Theobald (Ed.), *Friendship and peer culture in multilingual settings* (pp. 231–252). London: Emerald.

Wijesekera, H., & Alford, J. (2019). Bilingual Education classrooms in Sri Lankan schools: A social space for ethnolinguistic reconciliation. In I. Liyanage & T. Walker (Eds.), *Multilingual education yearbook 2019: Media of instruction & multilingual settings*. New York: Springer.

Maryanne Theobald is a Senior Lecturer in the School of Early Childhood and Inclusive Education and teaches in the undergraduate and Masters programs, at Queensland University of Technology (QUT). Her research investigates the social orders of children's talk-in-interaction in disputes and friendships in the home, school, playground and therapy, with digital technologies and in multilingual contexts. Maryanne's methodological expertise is in qualitative approaches including ethnomethodology and conversation analysis, and participatory research exploring video-stimulated accounts. She has expertise in participatory research with children and teachers, as well as working with teachers as teacher-researchers, facilitating professional learning and renewal. Maryanne has edited special volumes for the American Sociological Association's Childhood and Youth Section with Emerald, and is co-editor of Research on Children and Social Interaction (RCSI), Equinox.

Gillian Busch is the Head of Program, Early Childhood and a course coordinator of a number of courses in the Bachelor of Education, at Central Queensland University (CQU). She has over 25 years' experience in early childhood education having worked previously as an early childhood teacher and consultant. Gillian's Ph.D. (The Social Orders of Family Mealtime) was awarded the Early Childhood Australia Doctoral Thesis Award (2012). Gillian is currently involved in several research projects including young children and celebrations and how families use SKYPE or Facetime to support family interaction. She is a co-editor of Constructing Methodology for Qualitative Research: Researching Education and Social Practice.

Megan Laraghy has been an educator in the field of early childhood education for over 24 years. She is currently a teacher at Lady Gowrie Love Street Community Kindergarten. In 2014, the Queensland University of Technology acknowledged her for excellence in Mentoring Early Childhood Pre-service Teachers. As teacher-researcher, Megan takes on an active role in researching relationships, friendships and the role of the teacher in the kindergarten environment. She has presented at the Lady Gowrie Conference and was a key note speaker for the Jean Ferguson Memorial Lecture at Queensland University of Technology.

English in a Mongolian Ethnic Minority Primary School

Yayuan Yi and Bob Adamson

Abstract Primary schools in regional China with large ethnic minority populations are confronting the challenges of policies concerning multilingual education, comprising the minority language, Mandarin Chinese, and a foreign language, usually English from Year 3 (Adamson & Yi, China's English: A history of English in Chinese education, Hong Kong, Hong Kong University Press, 2015). English, which is selected for its significance as an international language, is different from both Chinese and Mongolian in its writing system as well as its linguistic features. This chapter analyses the role and nature of English in the curriculum of a Mongolian minority primary school in the Inner Mongolia Autonomous Region (IMAR). It focuses on three aspects: policy decisions at the state and provincial levels, the views and arrangements of the school leaders, and the pedagogical decisions made by teachers in the classroom, with a particular focus on the medium of instruction. In addition, the relationship between English and the other two languages is discussed in terms of models of trilingual education.

Keywords English as a foreign language · Trilingual education · Mongolian ethnic school · Chinese education

1 Introduction

English is the major foreign language taught in Chinese schools and, since 2002, it has been taught in many primary schools from Grade 3, subject to available resources. In some parts of the country, including areas inhabited by members of the 55 officially recognised ethnic minority groups, English is taught from Grade 2 or even the first year of primary school. Such moves have presented challenges to rural areas of the People's Republic of China (PRC), where resources are often scarce, and to

---

Y. Yi (✉) · B. Adamson
The Education University of Hong Kong, Tai Po, Hong Kong
e-mail: yiyayuan@gmail.com

B. Adamson
e-mail: badamson@eduhk.hk

ethnic minority regions of the country (affluent or otherwise) that are already trying to preserve the minority language in addition to teaching the national language (Mandarin Chinese). This study looks at English language teaching in a primary school in the Inner Mongolia Autonomous Region (IMAR) in northern China. The present situation regarding language curricula in the IMAR reflects three distinctive policy strands rather than a comprehensive, coordinated approach to multilingual education (Adamson & Feng, 2015). The three strands are intended to foster national unity through the promotion of Chinese, international engagement through English, and local preservation of Mongolian culture. These strands are the products of historical development that has followed a twisting path. A form of Mandarin Chinese ("*Putonghua*") was established as the national standard in 1956, and the government declared it should be used in all schools across the country. In recent decades, there has been particularly vigorous promotion of Putonghua, which, at times, has been to the detriment of minority languages in schools (Lam, 2005; Yi & Adamson, 2017). Meanwhile, English, which has a chequered history in the PRC because of concerns about its potential threats to national integrity (Adamson, 2004) and possible disruption to people's careers (Gil & Adamson, 2011), has come to occupy a major, if contested, space:

> A vast national appetite has elevated English to something more than a language: it is not simply a tool but a defining measure of life's potential. China today is divided by class, opportunity, and power, but one of its few unifying beliefs—something shared by waiters, politicians, intellectuals, tycoons—is the power of English… English has become an ideology, a force strong enough to remake your résumé, attract a spouse, or catapult you out of a village. (Osnos, 2008)

The power of English means that the language plays a significant role in tertiary education, where it is an important component in the highly competitive College Entrance Examinations, the medium of instruction (MOI) for some courses and a graduation requirement for many students, by passing the national College English Test. For ethnic minority students, competence in English offers a chance to improve their life chances in a competitive environment (Ma, 2019; Sunuodula, Feng & Adamson, 2015), which has ensured that the subject is taught where possible in IMAR schools.

Recent studies in ethnic regions of the PRC have identified different models of trilingual education (see, for example, the collection of papers in Feng & Adamson, 2015) and some of the facilitators and barriers that influence its effectiveness. A common finding is that ethnic minority languages are at a disadvantage compared to Chinese and English because of the lack of prestige and ethnolinguistic vitality, social and economic capital and the resources to teach them. Experiences to date suggest that including English in the curriculum in minority schools providing trilingual education can either boost the learning of the minority language if its ethnolinguistic vitality is strong or damage its sustainability if weak (Adamson & Yi, 2015).

The PRC has its own distinctive policies and practices related to minority language, culture, and rights (He, 2005; Kymlicka, 2005). Bilingual or trilingual education has been partly determined by the Constitution of the PRC through the Regional Autonomy Law for Minority Nationalities. A large share of the responsibility for policy making and implementation in respect of minority education falls to the State Council, which takes care of all aspects of education in the country. The Ministry of Education (MOE) is an agency of the State Council. Minority education has undergone frequent shifts in ideology, preference, and practice since the founding of the PRC in 1949. Lam (2005, p.124) identifies five distinct phases:

1. Egalitarian respect (1949–1956)
2. Unstable policy (1957–1965)
3. Suppression (1966–1976)
4. Restoration (1977–1990)
5. Bilingualism (1977 onwards).

There is, therefore, a degree of ambivalence historically towards minority education. The concept of *ronghe* (meaning fusion or amalgamation) is frequently used to refer to the long historical process of communication and cultural exchange between the minority groups and the majority Han, which has threatened minority languages, cultures, and knowledge (Mackerras, 1994). However, in some regions, schools have been set up by ethnic minority communities with strong ethnolinguistic vitality to work for the preservation of their language, culture, and traditions within the national context.

The language environment, demographic structures, and geopolitical characteristics render the IMAR an interesting case to examine the role and status of English. Mongolian-Chinese bilingual and multicultural environments are very common. Demographic changes, with the region attracting an influx of people from various parts of China since the 19th century, have led to the predominance of the majority Han, to the extent that, by 2010, the Mongolian population was 4,226,093 (17.11% of the total), and the Han population numbered 19,650,687 (79.54%) (National Bureau of Statistics of China, 2011). As Mongolian is a minority language in the IMAR, it is not universally taught, while the expectation that primary schools should also teach English (or other foreign language—Russian or Japanese can be found in a small number of schools) has resulted in different curricular solutions. Dong et al. (2015) identified a presence of four main models of trilingual education—Accretive, Balanced, Transitional, and Replacive (see the chapter by Ma Fu, this volume). Each model has different implications for the minority language (Accretive and Balanced Models are generally supportive of Mongolian or other minority language, while the Transitional and Replacive Models are potentially deleterious to sustainability). We have investigated these issues elsewhere (Yi & Adamson, 2017) and identified the ecological factors, such as geography, language characteristics, teaching methods, historical reasons, economic development and political circumstances, of the selection of a particular model of trilingual or multilingual education. There is a sensitivity surrounding the Mongolian language given the proximity of the country, Mongolia, which speaks a similar variety of the language, although it has adopted a Cyrillic script in contrast to the tradition vertical Uyghur script used in the IMAR. Chinese authorities are concerned to dampen transnational cultural identification while ensuring the benefits of cross-border trade.

The particular focus of this chapter is the role and nature of English in the curriculum in the IMAR, with reference to primary schools in which Mongolian is a significant local language. Some 325,443 primary school students in the IMAR are Mongolian (Inner Mongolia Autonomous Regional Bureau of Statistics, 2015) and, in some areas, primary schools with a distinctive Mongolian flavour have been set up in an attempt to promote the language and culture within the broader national context. This question is interesting given the various challenges associated with presence of the English language in the school curriculum in the PRC and the role and status of the language in the IMAR. The topic encompasses sociolinguistics, in the form of issues of globalisation (given the ascribed role of English as the major international language studied in contemporary China) and the nature of the presence of English in IMAR society. It also involves linguistic factors, as the oral and written forms of the language are very different (being Indo-European with an alphabetic writing system) from both Mongolian (a Mongolic language that uses a vertical script) and Mandarin Chinese (a Sino-Tibetan language that uses monosyllabic characters, many of which were simplified by the Chinese government in 1954). There are also related pedagogical issues at play, as views on language learning can vary according to the features and number of the languages being learnt and the educational traditions of a specific context. Of particular interest is the choice of language for the medium of instruction in classrooms, as decisions relating to this aspect reflect pedagogical, linguistic and socio-political factors.

2 The Study

This study is structured around the three inter-related domains of curricular innovation labelled by Tong (2005) as primary (issues relating to teaching and learning), secondary (how the school as an organisation handles a policy) and tertiary (system-level policy decisions). These domains will be presented in reverse order, with analysis of, first, policies towards English within the context of bilingual and trilingual education in the PRC, followed by curricular and resource decisions made by school leaders, and finally pedagogy and interactions observed in the classroom. The data comprise analysis of policy documents and secondary sources, interviews and questionnaire surveys with school leaders, teachers and students and observations from a field visit by the first author, Yi, a native of the IMAR who is trilingual in Mongolian, Putonghua, and English and who is a qualified language teacher. During her visits, she examined the linguistic landscape of the school and surrounding areas, as well as collecting data from the respondents using Mongolian (all quotations in this chapter are our translations). The questionnaire surveys asked students and teachers to respond to statements by using a Likert scale to indicate the degree of agreement or disagreement with statements about English and trilingual education. The choice of statements was based on similar research conducted with minority students in Yunnan Province, in southwest China, and Qinghai Province, in the west of the country.

The school was chosen for its geopolitical and demographic characteristics, being located in the town of Damaoqi, about 160 km from Baotou, the second biggest city in the IMAR, at the junction of the Bohai Economic Rim and the Upper Yellow River Natural Resources Enrichment Zone. Damaoqi has a population of around 17,000 Mongolians, while 120,000 Han have made it their home. There is a political dimension to the town's location, being in the vicinity of the border with the country of Mongolia: schools in the town are encouraged to promote patriotic education vigorously and strengthen the theme of national unity in the curriculum.

2.1 The National and Provincial Curriculum

English has not always been the main foreign language taught in Chinese schools—in the immediate aftermath of the establishment of the People's Republic of China in 1949, Russian was predominant in the curriculum because of the close relationship between China and the Union of Soviet Socialist Republics. After the schism between the two countries in the early 1960s, English became more important. Even during the turbulent anti-Western movements during the Cultural Revolution, there were still efforts to teach the language, and since 1978, interest in learning English has boomed (Tang, 1983; Adamson, 2004).

The presence of English in the curriculum at the present time is connected to globalization and the ideology of social and economic efficiency (Adamson, 2004; Hu, 2005; Hu & Adamson, 2012). Government officials have identified the needs for the education system to develop 'International Talents', multilingual individuals possessing specialist knowledge in a relevant field, global vision, an understanding of international laws and norms, and patriotic sentiments. These aspirations were embodied in the 'National Education Development Level Improvement Project' and 'National Education Talent Training Model Reform Pilot' initiated in 2014. Trade represents a major incentive for the IMAR to promote the learning of English, as, in addition to cross-border trade with Mongolia and Russia, it is strategically located to benefit from the opportunities afforded by the Belt and Road Initiative (BRI), which was established by President Xi Jinping to develop two major trade routes, one overland and one maritime, to connect China with Europe and countries in between. The economic dimension adds importance to the three languages: Mongolian facilitates cross-border trade with Mongolia; Chinese is a strong regional language; and English is acknowledged as the predominant international language. Well-educated people from the IMAR with trilingual competence in Mongolian, Chinese and English would be favourably positioned to contribute to, and benefit from, the BRI.

The national government decreed that English should be taught from Grade 3 in primary schools from 2003, albeit with fewer lessons than those allocated to the other core subjects, Chinese and mathematics (Qi, 2016). A curriculum, the first attempt at a unified framework covering primary and secondary schools (Zhang, 2012), was produced in 2003, with a revised version being published in 2011. The primary school section of the curriculum stressed literacy skills of reading and writing. By the end of primary school, students are expected to be able to read and understand simple instructions, information, stories, and essays, and to write simple greetings and short sentences (Zhang, 2012). In terms of listening and speaking, the standards specify the ability to participate in simple conversations (Zhang, 2005). To support the English curriculum, a textbook series, *Primary English*, was published by the People's Education Press, a division of the MOE in Beijing. These books were written in English, with some Chinese rubrics and translations of linguistic items. (Since 2004, the IMAR Education Bureau has provided enhanced Chinese translations for these textbooks.) In addition, the MOE encouraged schools to provide supplementary materials. In terms of pedagogy, the curriculum suggests that teachers should present the learners with appropriate materials and help them to develop their competence. Unlike previous curriculum innovations, this iteration is less prescriptive in terms of teaching methods, other than recommending a communicative orientation and task-based learning (Hu, 2005).

The policy of decentralisation from 1985 meant that different regions of China could develop their own textbook resources (Hu, 2005). A collaboration between the IMAR government and Beijing Normal University Press was undertaken to provide the students with more resources to help them in learning English. The book was called *Pan Deng Yingyu* ("Climbing English"). The content of these books is closely related to nomadic living habits of the Mongolians and the environment in which they live. For example, the topics include herders grazing in the mountains, the characteristics of the four seasons, the natural scenery such as the Gobi Desert, the traditional Mongolian diet, traditional festivals, and the techniques for constructing a yurt, the Mongolian traditional residence. The textbooks also include Inner Mongolian folk songs and traditional stories, as well as Chinese folk tales and an introduction to famous people overseas.

2.2 English in the School

This section is concerned with the linguistic environment of the school, how the school allocates time on the curriculum to English and other languages, and resource decisions. The specific school in this study was established in 1974, and the leadership sought to inculcate a strong sense of Mongolian culture alongside patriotism and love for the Chinese Communist Party and socialist theory and policy with Chinese characteristics.

Beyond the school gates, Mandarin Chinese dominates the linguistic landscape as the main language for daily interaction, business, mass media, and education. Mongolian is found on bilingual street signs and bilingual government documents. English is in the names of major corporations (such as the Bank of China) and some advertisements. One can hear international pop music booming from shops, and Hollywood movie trailers are displayed on public screens, alongside cultural festival advertisements, with Chinese subtitles. Satellite TV channels in English are available on subscription. Even in a small, remote town, English is becoming a part of the culture, and its importance is recognised by many parents, who send their children to private tuition centres after school.

Cooperation between the school, its stakeholders, the community supporters, and the local media ensure that Mongolian education remains strong in the area, despite the fact that the Han population far outnumbers Mongolians. With the majority of the staff being first language speakers of Mongolian (indeed, all of the 71 teachers in the primary school are Mongolian), the language is used for daily communication. It was also mandated as the medium of instruction. To boost students' exposure to Mongolian culture, each classroom had a framed portrait of Genghis Khan. Students learn traditional Mongolian arts and crafts, music and dance, and martial arts. As an acknowledgement of global dimensions, a few posters and signs in English were observed, depicting poems and popular sayings. Nationalism is represented by photographs on the school walls of the Chinese People's Liberation Army and some of their weapons.

Using the flexibility afforded by the devolution of curriculum decision-making, the school leadership decided that English should be introduced to the curriculum at the beginning of the first grade, with an allocation of one lesson a week, rising to two lessons in Grade Two, three in Grade Three, and four in Grade Four. It then drops to three in Grade Five and returns in four in Grade Six. This arrangement is the school's variant of the allocation in the National Primary School Curriculum Plan, which recommends three English lessons a week starting in Grade Three. The school wants the students to make an early start in learning the language but is cautious of overburdening them, given that they are also having lessons to improve their Mongolian and Chinese. Nonetheless, the importance of English is reflected in a further provision of extracurricular lessons, as suggested by the national curriculum:

> In fact, there is at least one extra class per week for English for English teachers to use independently. For example, we use an extracurricular textbook called "Hello, English Songs". In the process of teaching some songs and poems, we try to help students improve their sense of the English language and develop their interest in learning English. (English Teacher 1)

In the initial stage, the school syllabus is mainly concerned with enhancing the students' ability in listening and speaking in communicative situations. Attention is paid to vocabulary-building for every day contexts. In Grades Five and Six, the students are gradually introduced to written texts for reading comprehension.

The inclusion of English lessons in Grades One and Two, and the necessity (as well as the freedom) to prepare their own resources, all entailed extra work for these English teachers.

> Until last year, there was no textbook available ..., so the school gave us a lot of space to develop our own lesson content. We made up some simple conversations, and provided some words for the students to learn, but we avoided making a heavy demand on the students in terms of learning targets. We were simply laying the groundwork for students to learn English. So, first grade and second grade English teachers all had a lot of autonomy in selecting their course content. (English Teacher 2)

The situation improved with the publication of *Pan Deng Yingyu*. Feedback from students and teachers shows that the content of the books in this project is more interesting and more consistent with the modern digital age, making learning English more engaging and motivating for the students:

> *Pan Deng Yingyu* is good. Every day we can play short cartoon films for students. There are many video clips in this series. Starting this year, we will use this textbook in the 1st and 2nd grades. (English Teacher 1)
>
> This textbook is free. The Education Bureau said that it is not necessary for students to pay for it, provided that each school could ensure it employed enough English teachers. (English Teacher 2)

Although the school was generally well equipped, a number of teachers, when interviewed, expressed a view that it would be helpful for teaching and learning English if there was more investment in hardware such as computers, multimedia classrooms, and language training rooms. They felt that the government, rather than the school, should be responsible for supplying such facilities and equipment.

Teacher quality in the school is generally high. Some of these teachers have been teaching for more than 20 years. A few of them have participated in teaching competitions in and beyond the IMAR and have achieved excellent results. At the same time, however, there are also new teachers in their first teaching post. The school and the local education authority provide opportunities for teacher professional development, but the English teachers expressed their desire to receive short-term training in English-speaking countries; to date such opportunities had not been available due to limited funds.

> I hope that the government or the Education Bureau can contribute to the opportunity for us English teachers to go on exchange visits and study abroad. This is a meaningful activity. The process of receiving training in an English-speaking country will open people's eyes and even change our perspectives on the issues. English Teachers should go to English-speaking countries such as the United States or the United Kingdom to see how they teach English. Such an experience will help us. We would encounter the latest teaching methods and get to know the latest educational concepts. It is really necessary for us. We can also bear some of the expenses ourselves, such as 15,000 or 20,000 RMB. We can afford it. This represents six months' salary [*laughter*]. (English Teacher 3)

2.3 English in the Classroom

As the third language of the students, English was used quite sparingly in the observed lessons. The medium of instruction was Mongolian, and this language dominated the lesson. In one lesson, however, the teacher tried to use English for simple classroom management, rationalising that familiarity with set phrases could accustom the students to the language, and gradually prepare them for it being used as the medium of instruction. English classroom discourse analysis shows that teacher talk often accounts for 80% of the entire class. The teacher's contribution is mainly to provide guidance to students, assign tasks, and explain the content of the lesson. Out of 82 questions asked in one English class, the students only raised two of them. Even then, the substance of the students' questions (albeit posed in English) was "Can I try?" (It is worth noting that teacher questions also predominated in Chinese and Mongolian lessons.) The English teacher tried to encourage students to answer by simplifying the questions, repeating them and emphasising keywords. In an extracurricular lesson, the teacher was teaching a group of students the phrase, "how many". Her strategy was to repeat "how many" several times. To reinforce the meaning, she pointed to some farm animals that the students had drawn on the blackboard, and translated the main English vocabulary items and the question she was asking into spoken Mongolian, before writing them in Mongolian script next to the drawings. When the students translated the question (for example, "How many horses?") correctly into Chinese, the teacher was able to confirm that the students had understood the content of the new English words and sentences. Finally, the teacher emphasized that they needed to remember the phrases in English and explained the vocabulary and sentence patterns in Mongolian. This mode of teaching was interesting for the trilingual content. The interaction switched to Mongolian to ensure the students understood the meaning of the question and which of the animals the question referred to, as the Mongolian language would be the most familiar in this context. However, the students were required to translate the English question into Chinese, which was a more formal way of demonstrating their comprehension, in the sense that Chinese is the major academic language being taught in the school. On a few occasions, no reference to Mongolian would be made; English was taught solely through the medium of Chinese. Despite the linguistic frustrations, the students appeared to be much more active in the English class than, for example, in the Chinese class. This is consistent with the opinion expressed by teachers that students are motivated to learn English:

> Students are more interested in learning English than learning the other subjects. English is not taught every day, ... plus it is simple. If the students can memorize textbook articles and some vocabulary, they can get quite a high score. (English Teacher 2)
>
> Learning English seems like has become a social phenomenon. Compared with rural schools, the English level in this school has improved a lot. Mongolian students in this school can understand the teacher even if the teacher only speaks in English. Grade 6 can understand. Grade 1 can understand. (Chinese Teacher 1)

In the questionnaire survey that was distributed to the students (n = 120), the students were strongly receptive to the model of trilingual education offered by the school, with a mean of 4.47. There was a slight preference, registering a mean of 2.92 out of 5 ("strongly agree"), to learn English through the medium of English, believing that this would enhance their listening and speaking abilities. One question referred to an idea mooted in the school, of teaching Physical Education through the medium of English, because (as with classroom management) this could be carried out with a limited range of instructions and feedback. The students were lukewarm to this idea (with a mean of 2.29).

The overall average English scores of students in this Mongolian school are different from those of schools in the Banner (district) that cater more for the Han majority. In general, Han students perform better in English tests but the scores of some individual students in the Mongolian school are better than those of many

Han students, especially in spoken English. The students achieved good results in the English speech contest held in the Banner. Several teachers believe that Mongolian students who receive multilingual education at ethnic schools had the potential to learn English to a similar standard that Han students in bilingual schools might achieve:

> The average English standard of Mongolian students in our school is within the average range of all the students in the Banner, and it is almost the same as the English standard of Han students. We cannot compare with Han students in city-level schools in IMAR… but we only started to emphasize the importance of English over the past two years. The trend now is that our students' English proficiency is slowly improving and they are beginning to catch up with Han students locally. Maybe we will compare favourably in the future with those students in other schools in the IMAR who currently have better English proficiency. (English Teacher 3)

Students' assessments of their own English ability in the questionnaire shows that they are well satisfied with their spoken skills (mean = 4.52) by the time they finish primary school, more so than with their oral Chinese (3.76) and less so than with their spoken Mongolian (4.76). The reasons might lie in the exposure they have to Mongolian in their home lives, and its use in the school. Spoken English is a strong area of focus in the early years and the high levels of motivation and pleasure that teachers report in the students can help to explain the satisfaction rating. Oral Chinese receives less attention, as students are learning Chinese characters at this stage, and also they may be aware from their linguistic environment of the challenges they face in mastering spoken Chinese, so they may feel that they are making less progress. The students also seem to be confident in their ability to write English because they evaluate their satisfaction at 4.37, which is higher than their satisfaction levels in terms of written Chinese (3.56).

The survey also demonstrated agreement between students and teachers that the curriculum should focus on Mongolian before Chinese and English are introduced, on the grounds that competence in the first language affects the development of competence in the second and third language. Secondly, both students and teachers indicated that Mongolian teachers of English are best suited to teach the language because they can understand the needs of students better than Han Chinese teachers. The English teachers at this school also believe that if there were more opportunities to learn the latest Western teaching ideas and methods, it would improve the English learning of Mongolian students because they believed that these students had the potential to benefit from effective pedagogy.

In an interview, the Head of the English Department suggested that too much focus on English is not desirable, as it might be detrimental to the development of the students' competence in Mongolian:

> If their Mongolian is good, the students will do well in other subjects too. It is important that in the long term, Mongolian students should be trilingual. Living in a Chinese-dominated society, of course Chinese should be very good as well. English is not without value. Think of it this way: in time, of course it will be a plus to learn English. But it seems that in this environment; English is not so widely used. And yet society, the exam system and the exam policy are too crazy about English and have been ignoring mother language education. (English Teacher 4)

Several teachers expressed the opinion that it might be better to delay the introduction of English to secondary school, so that the students have the chance to establish their Mongolian and Chinese first. In some respects, English should be a lower priority, given the relative roles of the three languages in the students' daily life now and in the future:

> The most important language in the future will be Chinese. Mongolian will basically not be widely used in society, unless they do some work closely related with Mongolian culture or Mongolia. If the work is not related to Mongolian, then they would still use Chinese. All the documents are in Chinese, SMS is in Chinese, when we have meetings in the school, we also use Chinese. English may be forgotten in the future if their work is not in translation, or abroad or as a teacher. (Chinese Teacher 2)

3 Role and Nature of English in the IMAR

The snapshot of English in the IMAR in this chapter, presented within local, regional and national contexts, reveals a number of tensions around its position in the school curriculum. English is required to be taught in the primary school because of its alignment with the economic development policies of the PRC government. It is the main language of international trade for China and can facilitate the BRI that is the flagship of the current administration. At the regional level, English is also valued for its strategic importance. However, for the students at the school in Daomaqi, the language has little relevance in their daily lives and it does not have a strong ethnolinguistic vitality in the town or in the school. Nonetheless, the school faces the challenge by adopting a balanced view of English within the framework of trilingual education. The school leaders are juggling competing priorities: the *raison d'être* for the school is to conserve the Mongolian language and culture, while also attending to their needs as Chinese citizens living in an area where Mandarin Chinese is the predominant language. There is a danger that English, as a third language, might intrude on these goals. The solution is to allocate a relatively small amount of lesson time, with a view to meeting the standards set out in the national English curriculum. The school even feels comfortable enough to go beyond the requirements by starting English in Grade 1, albeit on a very small scale. The reason for this approach is that the leaders appreciate that trilingualism has positive benefits if carefully handled, as it can enhance the students' linguistic and general academic competence. The model selected is akin to the Accretive Model in that the languages are mutually supportive and presented in a coherent manner that reflects an appreciation of the interconnectedness of individual languages in multilingual education. The adaptations made by the school demonstrate a considered response to how the school can achieve its own mission while attending to the national and regional requirements.

Another reason for the school being well disposed towards the incorporation of English learning in the curriculum is the enthusiastic response of the students. They appear to be motivated and enjoying learning the language. Their pleasure in learning English could be attributable to the light touch in terms of lesson time and the way in which the language is presented. Although there was little evidence of the task-based approach (which involves active student participation, learner autonomy, and holistic communication) in the lessons observed, the topics were tailored to their daily life, with farm animals and local customs being presented. The freedom afforded by decentralisation enabled the IMAR to create special textbooks and the teachers to create their own resources, which added to the relevance of English to the students. Furthermore, the teachers chose to teach through the medium of Mongolian, rather than opting for an immersion, English-only, environment. The pedagogy was strongly teacher-controlled and the questioning quite closed (with few opportunities for creative language production) but these features offer a secure, risk-free environment for the young learners.

The preference for using Mongolian as MOI demonstrates the commitment of the school to preserving the local language. It also acknowledges that students learn well and teachers tend to feel more comfortable teaching through a familiar language. The occasional use of Chinese in English lessons can be seen as pragmatic for a variety of reasons. There may be occasions when the Chinese vocabulary or grammatical structures are closer to the English than the Mongolian equivalents; there may be some domains of language use in which Chinese is more familiar to the students than Mongolian; and, as students progress through the school, they need to be prepared for the possibility that their secondary education will be delivered through Chinese. The very restricted use of English as MOI indicates that the immersion approaches that are associated with a strong orientation towards communicative language teaching and learning do not have much traction in the school—at least in the early years of studying English. Instead, the teachers espouse the view that language learning should be structured to incorporate features of the linguistic environment in which the students find themselves and to draw upon their existing knowledge of languages and language systems. Thus, the choices appertaining to the MOI reflect the complexities of the sociocultural, linguistic and pedagogical contexts of the classroom, school, town and region.

Underpinning this appreciation of the potential benefits of trilingual education and the provision of a safe learning environment is the recruitment of suitable teachers. All the teachers in the school are Mongolian and many of them very experienced. The interviews with the teachers show that they are aware of the need for on-going professional development so they could improve the quality of the students' learning. They also called for greater investment in resources for the school. These attitudes bode well for the school, as they demonstrate the commitment of the teachers, who appear to have espoused the school goals and ethos, and who are prepared to use their professional skills to make English learning effective given the particular contextual features of the school. However, the teachers also recognize the pragmatic boundaries to the school's attitude towards English. For students who remain in the locality, the school is designed to bolster their sense of identity as Mongolians in the PRC. English will not play a major role in their lives unless they strive to enter university (for which English proficiency is a prerequisite), seek employment in international trade, or move abroad on a short- or long-term basis.

The outcome of these adaptations at the regional, school and classroom level shows that the education system in the PRC is capable of accommodating diversity. In this case, the powerful presence of English witnessed elsewhere in the country has been tempered to one that reflects its designation as a third language. School leaders and teachers have played a role in ensuring the relevance of the English curriculum to their students. However, many challenges remain. The Mongolian language is the weakest in terms of official standing in the curriculum—it is a school-based initiative that does not have systemic support in terms of recognised qualifications, for example. It is vulnerable to policy swings away from diversity towards suppression, to the possible demands that further promotion of Mandarin Chinese might make on curriculum time and MOI practices, and to parental pressure to concentrate more resources on English in line with the spirit of the times. At present, English is not a threat to the Mongolian language in the school: it has a complementary and symbiotic relationship. In terms of multilingual education, this is a healthy sign, but a not a cause for complacency.

References

Adamson, B. (2004). *China's English: A history of English in Chinese education*. Hong Kong: Hong Kong University Press.
Adamson, B., & Feng, A. W. (2015). Trilingualism in education: Models and challenges. In A. W. Feng & B. Adamson (Eds.), *Trilingualism in education in China: Models and challenges* (pp. 243–258). Dordrecht, The Netherlands: Springer.
Adamson, B., & Yi, Y. (2015). Trilingual education in Inner Mongolia—signposts for the future of English in Asia? In M. O'Sullivan, D. Huddart, & C. Lee (Eds.), *The future of English in Asia: Perspectives on language and literature* (pp. 193–206). Abingdon, UK: Routledge.
Dong, F., Narisu, Gou, Y. H., Wang, X. G., & Qiu, J. (2015). Four models of Mongolian nationality schools in the Inner Mongolia Autonomous Region. In A. W. Feng, & B. Adamson, (Eds.), Trilingualism in education in China: Models and challenges (pp. 25–45). Dordrecht: Springer.
Feng, A. W., & Adamson, B. (Eds.). (2015). *Trilingualism in education in China: Models and challenges*. Dordrecht: Springer.
Gil, J., & Adamson, B. (2011). The English language in China: A sociolinguistic profile. In A. W. Feng (Ed.), *English language education across Greater China* (pp. 23–45). Clevedon, UK: Multilingual Matters.
He, B. (2005). Minority rights with Chinese characteristics. In W. Kymlicka & B. He (Eds.), *Multiculturalism in Asia* (pp. 56–79). Oxford, UK: Oxford University Press.
Hu, G. W. (2005). English language education in China: Policies, progress, and problems. *Language Policy, 4*(1), 5–24.
Hu, R., & Adamson, B. (2012). Social ideologies and the English curriculum in China. In C. Leung & J. Ruan (Eds.), *Perspectives on teaching and learning English literacy in China* (pp. 1–17). Dordrecht, The Netherlands: Springer.
Inner Mongolia Autonomous Regional Bureau of Statistics. (2015). *Inner Mongolia statistical yearbook, 2015*. Beijing, China: China Statistics Press.
Kymlicka, W. (2005). Liberal multiculturalism: Western models, global trends, and Asian debates. In W. Kymlicka & B. He (Eds.), *Multiculturalism in Asia* (pp. 23–55). Oxford, UK: Oxford University Press.
Lam, A. S. L. (2005). *Language education in China: Policy and experience from 1949*. Hong Kong: Hong Kong University Press.

Ma, F. (2019). Trilingualism and medium of instruction models in minority schools in Qinghai Province, China. In I. Liyanage & T. Walker (Eds.), *Multilingual education yearbook 2019: Media of instruction & multilingual settings*. New York: Springer.

Mackerras, C. (1994). *China's minorities: Integration and modernisation in the twentieth century*. Hong Kong: Oxford University Press.

National Bureau of Statistics of China (2011). *Tabulation on the 2010 population census of the People's Republic of China*. http://www.stats.gov.cn/english/statisticaldata/censusdata/rkpc2010/indexce.htm.

Osnos, E. (2008, April 28). Crazy English: The national scramble to learn a new language before the Olympics. *New Yorker*. http://www.newyorker.com/reporting/2008/04/28/080428fa_fact_osnos?currentPage=all.

Qi, Y. G. (2016). The importance of English in primary school education in China: Perceptions of students. *Multilingual Education* 6(1. https://doi.org/10.1186/s13616-016-0026-0.

Sunuodula, M., Feng, A.W., & Adamson, B. (2015). Trilingualism and Uyghur identity in the People's Republic of China. In D Evans (Ed.) *Language and identity: Discourse in the world* (pp. 81–104). London: Continuum.

Tang, L. X. (1983). *TEFL in China: Methods and techniques*. Shanghai, China: Shanghai Foreign Languages Press.

Tong, S. Y. A. (2005). *Task-based learning in English language in Hong Kong secondary schools*. Unpublished Ph.D. dissertation, The University of Hong Kong.

Yi, Y., & Adamson, B. (2017). Trilingual education in the Inner Mongolia Autonomous Region: Challenges and threats for Mongolian identity. In C. Reid & J. Major (Eds.), *Global teaching: Southern perspectives on teachers working with diversity* (pp. 145–163). London & New York: Palgrave Macmillan.

Zhang, Y. F. E. (2005). *The implementation of the task-based approach in primary school English language teaching in mainland China*. Unpublished PhD dissertation, The University of Hong Kong.

Zhang, D. B. (2012). Chinese primary school English curriculum reform. In C. Leung & J. Ruan (Eds.), *Perspectives on teaching and learning English literacy in China* (pp. 67–83). Dordrecht, The Netherlands: Springer.

Yayuan Yi is currently a teacher of Chinese as a Foreign Language in Austria. She is an ethnic Mongolian and native speaker of the language. She holds an Ed. D. from the Education University of Hong Kong, specializing in trilingual education in the Inner Mongolian Autonomous Region, and an M. Ed in Educational Psychology from the Chinese University of Hong Kong. Her research interests include endangered languages and culture, minority identity, and multilingual education for ethnic minorities. She has published a number of research articles in these areas.

Bob Adamson is Chair Professor of Curriculum Reform at the Education University of Hong Kong. He publishes in the fields of language policy, teacher education, comparative education, and curriculum studies. He is a consultant to the People's Education Press in the Ministry of Education in China, Honorary Professor at a number of universities in China and, in 2013, was named "Kunlun Expert" by the Qinghai Provincial Government in recognition of his work in minority education.

Scrutinising Critical Thinking (CT) in Chinese Higher Education: Perceptions of Chinese Academics

Anhui Wang, Indika Liyanage and Tony Walker

Abstract Critical thinking (CT) has assumed the status of an obligatory graduate attribute in Western English-medium instruction higher education, with accompanying expectations that such thinking be evident in students' academic literacy practices. These literacies are presented to students from outside English-dominant settings as higher-order language skills, as evident in, for example, English-for-Academic-Purposes programs, reflecting widely-held assumptions that CT is not a dimension of academic literacy practices of many non-English dominant education systems, particularly those reductively categorized as 'Asian'. In this chapter, we use interview data from multilingual Chinese academics of diverse ethnolinguistic backgrounds to scrutinise assumptions that CT is not recognised nor encouraged in Chinese HE. Drawing on the responses of these academics, we also contest essentialization of the character of Chinese HE as bounded by inflexible traditional knowledge practices, and point to the experiences of these academics of English-medium education and collaboration as a source of dynamism in Chinese HE. Given the impetus for education institutions outside the EMI sphere to build international reputations and to prepare graduates for international postgraduate study and competition in global employment markets by adopting English-dominant academic literacy practices, we conclude by reflecting on the question of whether these institutions, in the context of rapid change, are gradually embracing a critical approach to the practices of CT.

Keywords Critical thinking · Academic literacy · Chinese higher education · English medium instruction · International students · Chinese academics

---

A. Wang (✉)
Sichuan Normal University, Chengdu, China
e-mail: 277106581@qq.com

I. Liyanage · T. Walker
School of Education, Deakin University, Geelong, Australia

1 Background

It is unsurprising that 'Asian' students, and especially those from China, and 'Asian' practices of thinking have come under the critical thinking (CT) spotlight. The capacities, in particular, of students grouped generically as of 'Asian' origins to satisfy the expectation of CT in their written work and in their participation in classroom discourse have provoked much discussion among teaching academics and observers of shortcomings, cultural dispositions, and linguistic inadequacies. The premise that underpins the orientation of this chapter is that there is no disagreement about the centrality of the idea of CT in what is reductively imagined as an English medium 'Western education' (Barnett, 1997; Wilson, 2016), and that this has some significance in the context of internationalization. Multilingualism is indispensable to the enterprise of 'internationalized' HE (Liyanage, 2018), but the ubiquity of EMI means that not only must it be a "multilingualism with English" (Hoffmann, 2000, p. 3), but a multilingualism with *academic* English. Success for international students in programs in Anglophone universities, and in EMI programs introduced in locations across Asia, demands high levels of proficiency in a prestige variety of English, realized in spoken and written texts that embody "particular cultural norms and expectations" (Hughes, 2008, p. 113) of forms of knowledge and ways of knowing. Central among these is critical thinking (CT), which has assumed the status of an obligatory graduate attribute in Western EMI higher education, with accompanying expectations that such thinking be evident in students' oral and written academic literacy practices; "language, and especially written language, has a privileged position in an academic context, which in turn means that critical thinking is closely linked to academic literacy in the traditional sense of the word" (Chirgwin & Huijser, 2015, p. 340). Agreement on any precise conceptualization of CT remains elusive (Moore, 2013)—indeed, the idea as variously proposed has evoked considerable critical attention—and the 'teachability' and transferability of CT continues to be argued. We do not intend to dwell here on what is meant by CT in EMI settings, something extensively discussed in existing literature. Davies (2015), for example, provides an excellent discussion of the tensions between various approaches to CT in EMI education.

Many millions of students of diverse linguistic backgrounds participate physically and/or virtually in programs offered by foreign institutions in pursuit of quality and advantage associated with highly-ranked universities. Many governments and institutions outside the Anglosphere have responded by pursuing their own internationalization agendas. These are frequently equated with introduction of English-medium instruction (EMI) and borrowing of foreign programs (Tran & Nguyen, 2018) with the aim of joining the ranks of 'world class' universities, not only to expedite participation in the global knowledge economy, but also to attract some of the international trade in education. Indeed, encouraging a flow of international students—and academic staff—is frequently adopted as a strategy on the assumption that global recognition and ranking will follow (see, e.g., Byun & Kim, 2011; Chan & Lo, 2008; Hou, Morse, Chiang, & Chen, 2013; Lassegard, 2016; Mok, 2007).

Underlying the attractions of HE programs in English-dominant settings, and the pervasiveness of EMI in the various models of 'internationalized' programs outside these, are a complex suite of discursively constructed perceptions. For example, to name a few, these include superiority of English-dominant universities on the basis of various international rankings systems, English as the language of scientific and technological advance and innovation, English as the gatekeeper of advancement through economic globalization, and English as the means to satisfy individual desires for prosperity, cosmopolitanism, and identity. The upshot is, as is often observed (e.g., Díaz, 2018), the ostensible internationalization of higher education (HE) is dominated by a "monolingual ethos and ideology" (Preece, 2011, p. 122) that privileges English-language medium instruction (EMI) and Anglophone academic literacy and knowledge practices. Many agree that internationalization of HE outside the English-dominant nations might more correctly be considered Westernization (Mok, 2007; Ng, 2012), or even more accurately, Englishization (Kirkpatrick, 2011).

The spread of English as academic lingua franca and MOI, and, in a variety of modes, of universities based in nations such as Australia, the USA, and the UK to other linguistic settings, has transplanted academic practices, conventions and expectations centred upon CT into HE settings across the globe. Success in Western or Western-style English language higher education is predicated upon the capacity for and development of CT. In this context, the literacies presented to students from outside English-dominant settings as higher-order language skills, as evident in, for example, English-for-Academic-Purposes (EAP) programs, reflect widely-held assumptions that problematize these students—that CT is not a dimension of academic literacy practices of many non-English dominant education systems, and, particularly those reductively categorized as Asian. In Australia, for instance, growth in enrolments of students from nations in the Asian region since the 1980s generated a parallel burgeoning of studies of the experiences and academic performance of 'Asian' learners that documented difficulties from the perspectives of both students and their teachers (e.g., Ballard, 1981, 1987, 1989; Novera, 2004; Samuelowicz, 1987, to identify just a few), and proposed responses to these difficulties (e.g., Anderson & Moore, 1998; Dawson & Conti-Bekkers, 2002). An implicit assumption in much of that literature has been an "idealised version of the 'Western student'" (Doherty & Singh, 2005, p. 53), 'native speakers' of English who are "somehow inherently superior in their knowledge of academic discourse and their ability to engage effectively in sophisticated language/literacy practices" (Duff, 2007, p. 01.06). Requirements that prospective international students—those whose language repertoire can be characterized as multilingualism with English as an additional language—demonstrate control of English academic language and literacies perpetuate ideologies of 'native speaker' ownership of academic literacies and language practices such as CT. This situation has turned attention to the sociocultural and educational backgrounds of students from the Asian region, and thus to more broadly-based cultural practices of academic literacies such as CT. In turn, as internationalization progressively transplants EMI higher education and its practices to universities across the Asian region, academics in those institutions have found themselves at the interface of local ways of thinking and academically literate ways of expressing that thinking, and the practices and expectations of a globally dominant and powerful English-language academy.

Underpinning discussions of 'Asian' and 'Chinese' learners, and ways of thinking, teaching and learning, is not just essentialization, but assumptions that practices in countries like China are unchanging, that tradition overpowers innovation or momentum for change. To even the casual observer, the transformation of many dimensions of life in China, and the global engagement of the nation and its people, is difficult to ignore. This provokes an obvious question about current practices of CT in China's education system: what has been the impact on Chinese HE of the consumption of EMI education by international students, of introduction and importation of EMI programs and academic literacies (Huang, 2003), of collaboration with many of the powerful Anglophone universities that dominate global research, of the presence of local campuses of some of these institutions (Ennew & Fujia, 2009; Li & Roberts, 2012), and of the Chinese government's policy imperatives to introduce EMI (Zhang, 2018) and to develop competitive world-class HE (Kim, Song, Liu, Liu, & Grimm, 2018; Mok, 2007)? English is perceived as "a necessary means to internationalise" (Yang & Welch, 2001, p. 43), policy initiatives have prompted the growth of EMI in disciplines such as medicine and engineering (Botha, 2016) aimed at local and international students, and the long-term policy objective is EMI in 10–20% of all undergraduate programs (Hughes, 2008). Importation of programs, joint campus ventures, and the objective of international competitiveness all suggest one of the core principles of EMI higher education, development and demonstration of (Western-style) CT, must be visible in the Chinese academic landscape.

We note several points to contextualize perceptions of CT in students from nations such as China. First, essentializing the inhabitants of an entire region or nation is unproductive and misleading. For example, even if we accept the idea of difference, there is evidence of diversity of academic behaviours and participation of 'Asian' international students within difference (Kettle, 2007; Koehne, 2005). Second, within the English MOI academy, CT is a "contested notion" (Moore, 2013, p. 519). While academics have clear ideas about CT, their agreements differ across disciplines as they look for behaviours as evidence of CT. This in itself suggests existing CT capacities or potentials in students might not align with expectations, might not be recognised, and that perceptions of any ostensible 'deficit' might vary across disciplines and between the academics teaching these students. Third, the privileging of spoken participation by students in EMI classrooms, and assumptions about the capacities and performance of those who satisfy expectations of speaking, has arguably underpinned problematisation of international students (Kubota, 2001). Beliefs and values to do with meanings of talk relate directly to privileging of talk in EMI classrooms, at all levels of education, to the extent that in university classrooms "expectation for speech is clearly a norm of academic culture" (Ellwood & Nakane, 2009, p. 205). Whether or not we accept that actual modes or processes of thinking are culturally variable, practices and conventions to do with organization, expression, and communication of thinking and knowledge are considered to be socio-culturally specific (Kim & Markus, 2002; Smith & Bond, 1999), including, of course, those identified with EMI settings. Fourth, observed or perceived differences in capacities for CT of students from Asian nations such as China are frequently attributed in the literature solely to sociocultural, educational and linguistic backgrounds of the students, but, as Hellstén and Prescott (2004) point out, the roles of participants in classrooms are jointly constituted and the risk of imposition of reductive identities on 'Asian' students by teachers complicates perceptions and appreciation of CT. Given these caveats, what then can be gleaned from the literature about CT and students from places such as China, and more specifically, is the multilingual EMI setting of significance?

In the rest of this chapter, we consider the apparent ascendancy of CT models associated with 'Western' EMI education through the self-reported thinking, experiences, and practices of a group of seven academics (hereafter, P-1 to P-7), Chinese nationals of diverse ethnolinguistic backgrounds, who teach in a provincial university in western China. We captured these using semi-structured interviews to allow exploration of the unique experiences of each participant. Interviewees were purposively selected with the intention of assembling a group representative of diverse ethnolinguistic backgrounds, personal educational pathways as multilingual students and researchers, and experiences teaching in multilingual settings. All possess varying degrees of multilingual communicative proficiencies that can be characterized as multilingualism with English, although English communicative proficiency differs across the group. Some completed their own school and under- and post-graduate higher education in an additional language, Mandarin, and most have pursued postgraduate studies, attended conferences, or participated in academic collaboration in English-dominant settings outside China. While the teaching activities of the group are conducted primarily using Mandarin as MOI, they referred to instances and circumstances in which English is introduced.

We use their perceptions and experiences to scrutinise assumptions that the broad notion and practice of thinking critically is not recognised nor encouraged in higher education in 'Asian' non-EMI settings, and to foreground the responses to and experiences of CT of academics in non-English dominant settings in order to focus upon possible relations between multilingual education and CT in what is a rapidly changing culture of higher education in China. In doing so, we attempt to provoke reassessment of the ostensible superiority of what amounts to a 'monolingual' CT that goes hand-in-hand with EMI, offering instead the suggestion that thinking critically for multilingual students and academics may parallel notions such as multicompetence (Cook, 1992; Hall, Cheng, & Carlson, 2006) and translanguaging (Canagarajah, 2011, 2013; García, 2009), in which academic literacies developed in linguistically diverse educational settings are best considered as a unified repertoire of resources. We conclude with the implications of these for participants' immediate context of work and similar multilingual settings elsewhere.

2 Scrutinising Assumptions of CT in Chinese HE

Suggestions that CT is not cultivated by Chinese HE ignores both the dynamic for change and the evidence. Chinese culture can be considered as unified, historical, and traditional, but more usefully as diverse, dynamic and contemporary, open to influence and change like any other; "what is needed is more research, context-sensitive research, and ongoing research, inasmuch as Chinese culture and educational culture show marked diversity and are changing rapidly from year to year" (Tian & Low, 2011, p. 73). Reflecting this more organic perspective of education culture as contingent upon temporal relations of national, international and local circumstances, our participants emphasised that the environment in which they work is changing rapidly. They acknowledged the significance and influence of ideas originating outside China in their own development, including their experiences of new and different media of instruction and of interpersonal communication, because 'it is helpful to your critical thinking that you are more exposed to different languages, different nationalities, and different cultures' (P-3, 88–90). Increasing numbers of Chinese academics are exposed to the academic literacies of the English-language academy—through English-language academic literature, participation in overseas study, and collaboration with English-dominant peers. In the context of reform and openness, government has not obstructed the continual publication of textbooks, translations, and articles (Dong, 2015). Although the capacity of individuals to influence any transformation of the academic literacies and conventions of the HE sector as a whole is arguably, as in most instances, institutionally and structurally constrained, when positioned within a much larger phenomenon of national objectives of absorbing and appropriating knowledge in order to be globally competitive and to generate prosperity, the thinking and actions of individuals become a vital component of broader change. Participant 5 provided an explicit commentary, not only on changes in Chinese HE approaches to thinking, but on the openness to influences on that thinking:

> these achievements in science and technology are closely related to western critical thinking. … Chinese scholars have seen a lot of foreign literature. They have a broader view of knowledge than their predecessors. They can see more information and can stand on the shoulders of their predecessors. … Many technologies are imported from abroad. For example, computers, all our achievements occurred after the first computer abroad was invented. And AI too. We created it on the basis of civilized achievements, mainly from westerners. In addition, we can read many foreign articles about thinking, and critical thinking has also been affected. (P-6, 149–159)

As Participant 6 notes, the changes taking place have been influenced by opportunities for multilingual Chinese academics to read foreign (English) literature and articles, including those about CT, but the spread of the practices of EMI academic literacies such as CT among both academics and students has also occurred through local Mandarin-medium programs and via the practices of introduced EMI programs from foreign universities. In 2018 there were seventeen branch campuses of foreign universities operating in China (Top Universities, 2018), such as the University of Nottingham Ningbo, where all teaching is conducted using EMI by staff seconded from the UK (or appointed using Nottingham's UK standards), "firmly rooted in all that is distinctive about UK education and ... (using) innovative teaching and assessment methods that encourage *independent and creative thinking* among students" (University of Nottingham, 2018, emphasis added).

Apart from encouraging local campuses of prestigious foreign universities, the drive to make China's education system internationally competitive has prompted institutions and individual academics to turn to Western teaching and learning practices, predominantly those associated with EMI. 'Western' models of CT have been gradually introduced to local courses since the ideas began to circulate in the 1980s (Dong, 2015). Courses explicitly focused on cultivating CT through Mandarin-medium instruction appeared in locally prestigious universities in the 1990s, and by the early 2000s local Mandarin-language textbooks, borrowing heavily from those in use in the USA, were available. Significantly, influential exemplars (see Dong, 2015) also borrowed pedagogic practices that embedded EMI written and spoken academic literacies in both teaching and assessment. In the last decade dedicated CT courses of this type are beginning to be mandated as a compulsory element of first-year undergraduate courses at some leading universities (Dong, 2015). Despite this, Dong (2015, p. 354) laments the failure of Chinese HE to embrace CT, asserting that "something unexpected has taken place in most educational institutions: nothing." While he is primarily concerned with the introduction of courses dedicated explicitly to teaching CT, he apportions responsibility for this 'nothing' to the cognitive orientation of academics who, he argues, are unwilling to risk challenges, not to any culturally perpetuated social authority, but to their own cognitive authority embedded in teaching practices that exclude open-mindedness or self-criticism. The reflections of our participants, although none are involved in teaching stand-alone CT courses, challenge this view of teaching academics. The reader can judge the readiness of Participant 6 to engage in open-minded self-criticism and articulate recognition of the risk posed to CT by determination to preserve cognitive authority: 'Chinese are the most intolerant of mistakes. It completely strangles critical thinking. ... To become a heretic, not only does the teacher say he is wrong, he is afraid of the students saying he is very foolish' (P-6, 170–174). Participant 2 describes an experience of learning from his students who, when he posed a question, offered ideas 'from many angles I didn't even think about ... If I were asked to do this topic, I could only think of seven or eight angles. I did not think of many of the points they raised' (P-2, 87–94). He identified this as an advantage of teaching, as an opportunity to 'cultivate' his own thinking. It is enlightening to compare Dong's (2015, p. 353) description of an example of "exceptional" teaching with the practices of Participant 4 in an undergraduate classroom:

> Another exceptional aspect of this course was its interactive and practical style of teaching and testing. The teachers encouraged students to engage in active, reasonable, open-minded, and practical thinking exercises. ... Socratic questioning, just-in-time teaching, problem-based learning, cooperation learning, peer teaching, group projects, guided practice, and scenario-based exercises and tests. The students' final marks were based on a combination of participation in learning, a group project on analyses of real-life examples, critical writing, and a classroom presentation by each group. (Dong, 2015, p. 353)

> The method we have is to let the study group hold internal discussions and record that. In the course of their discussions, they will find that they originally had different viewpoints. In the face of different problems, how to convince each other and how to find more reliable evidence to show that their method is feasible, and that other methods are flawed, they will start to actively search for information to identify. This is what kind of problems are encountered in the process of using the method and how to solve this problem. After the discussion in the group is finished, there will be communication between the groups. They will communicate with each other in the form of e-mail or in that class group. There will also be other forms of presentation in the class. After the presentation is finished, fellow students of other groups will ask questions about the report of this group. They must answer the questions on the spot. (P-4, 96–107)

The repertoire of classroom learning activities Participant 4 describes as part of her practice could equally be those of a teaching academic in a Western university aiming to embed CT in the learning activities enjoyed by students. The visibility of these practices in a Chinese Mandarin-medium classroom not only gives us pause to ponder Dong's claim that Chinese academics shun change, it provokes at least two questions: Have our participants been influenced by EMI academic literacy practices such as CT? Do these practices really differ significantly from any CT that has been encouraged in what has been portrayed as passive, unquestioning, rote learning of Confucian influenced education.

We turn to the experiences of our participants to explore the first question. What does seem to play a role in how CT is made visible is background, not only more general cultural practices and conventions, but educational background and prior training (Manalo, Kusumi, Koyasu, Michita, & Tanaka, 2015; Tian & Low, 2011). Academic experiences in English-dominant settings, such as study abroad, participation in international conferences, academic exchanges, and international collaboration have exposed our participants to difference, to opportunities to reflect critically on their pre-existing practices and attitudes. What has been until then regarded as unacceptable, has assumed new dimensions, as 'a little more diversity abroad can allow different things to exist. It is uncivilized when we saw other people quarrelling in Chinese opinion. In fact, quarrelling is civilized. Quarrels are conflicts of thinking' (P-3, 157–159). Exposure to other ways of realizing academic literacies in their own work, and in their teaching and evaluation of students aside, there is an agreement among these academics that their experiences of different practices provoked some restructuring of their personal knowledge systems, and prompted CT that led them to new insights, neatly summed up by Participant 5 who described her interactions in EMI settings as 'definitely a promotion for me personally. The growth of my thinking often touches on value and makes me change' (P-5, 235–236). Yet there was also a perception that such experiences harmonized with traditional ideas about thinking and learning:

> Subtle influences on you can be said to be all around. Therefore, the ancients actually said that you only have this kind of communication with others when you read thousands of books and travel thousands of miles. Only during observation and study can you find open-mindedness. So the whole process of a person, as long as you open your mind will have a lot of gains. (P-2, 162–166)

As mediators of change in Chinese HE, it was exposure of our participants to the practices and approaches of their colleagues in EMI environments that is significant. They speak of a powerful awareness of a different cultural environment, of being impressed with the active and strong thinking of their English-dominant peers, and enlightened by the processes of various forums that encouraged the sharing of and critical engagement with diverse ideas, of students' freedom to speak directly to their teachers:

> When I went to graduate school, I found that there were very few desks in the classroom. During the week, there were many reading papers. It must also be seen that the teacher in class speaks very little. According to my observation, among the three classes in the afternoon of graduate students, only half were taught by the most teachers and the other half were discussions. The teacher is the lead, the guide, and most of the time it is for the students to discuss themselves. Then you put forward your own opinions and make a summary, no matter what method you adopt. To sum up. You have to make comments and express your thoughts. (P-2, 204–212)

A theme echoed by most participants was that in the new and different EMI environments 'we do not have the constraints of the original culture and environment. We are freer and more open. Thinking becomes more active' (P-7, 178–179). Yet although there was agreement that development in China of a kind of teaching 'that allows different voices to be made' (P-2, 236–237) was desirable, participants' reflections also revealed that, while ready to entertain the new, they continue to advocate academic literacies that have been at the core of Chinese education for much longer. Thus, their advocacy of change is best seen in terms of development or reform rather than rejection or overturning. This is not suggested as some kind of acknowledgement that the urge for change dissipates in the face of the constraints of the capacities, inclinations and expectations of many of their students or of institutional demands. There was clearly stated recognition of the differences between the CT practices of EMI settings and those of Chinese education, but also an evident sense of the value of a blended or additive both/and approach to EMI and local academic literacies, rather than an exclusionary either/or position. This leads us the second question we posed earlier in response to Dong's critique of CT in China: Do EMI CT practices differ significantly from any CT that has been encouraged in what has been portrayed as passive, unquestioning, rote learning of Confucian influenced education?

2.1 CT in China and Language Practices

If our participants' experiences, which include some as international students, are typical then the academic literacies that are commonly considered to characterize CT in EMI classrooms do not go unnoticed by Chinese students. In fact, they acknowledged the many differences they observed, not just in the norms of academic literacies and behaviours, as stimulants of their own critical thinking. Not only did they observe CT as a social practice, but they also engaged in CT as they processed their responses to what they encountered. Some identified their multilingual capacities as key to participation in social and professional interactions that brought to the fore assumptions and normative practices that would otherwise have gone unquestioned in their home setting. For one participant, it resonated with her experience as member of an ethnic minority because, unlike the majority of Chinese students who 'grow up in a relatively single cultural environment' (P-1, 83), her heritage meant learning an additional language and questioning what is 'normal (and) reasonable' (P-1, 79) was already integral to her lived experiences in Chinese academic settings. What we wish to focus on here is the contrast between these self-reported impacts on thinking, and the observed behaviour of Chinese students that leads many of their teachers to make assumptions about thinking capacities and dispositions. Some reference to socio-culturally specific practices and conventions to do with organization, expression, and communication of thinking and knowledge was made earlier in this chapter. The ramifications for multilingual students of, for example, the cultural privileging of speech and devaluing of silence in EMI classrooms is documented (e.g., Ellwood & Nakane, 2009; Nakane, 2006, 2007). Other observers have pointed to the behaviours of Chinese students in EMI classrooms in their home settings as evidence that relationships between operating in an additional language, language proficiency, behaviours in classrooms, and the variables of linguistic settings of MOI are complicated:

> back home in their respective countries, these students are not as quiet and passive as they are here. Hands come up more often and responses are shot out more readily. When surrounded by their own countrymen, they are more confident and less shy of making mistakes when speaking in English. (Chuah, 2010, para 4)

To begin, language proficiency of multilingual students with English must be considered a crucial variable in control of academic literacies scrutinized for demonstration of CT (Manalo et al., 2015; Paton, 2005; Rear, 2017), given "it is almost impossible to avoid the use of language in critical thinking" (Lun, Fischer, & Ward, 2010, p. 614). The emphasis on behavioural expression of CT in academic settings (Lun et al., 2010) assumes students who do not demonstrate CT are deficient in disposition and/or skills. Participation, or lack of it, in classroom argumentation and debate is frequently cited as an observable indicator of CT, but there exists considerable evidence that using an additional language for such cognitively demanding tasks impacts negatively on performance (Lun et al., 2010; Rear, 2017). That is, demonstrable capacities for CT in a first language are constrained by cognitive demands of using the additional language, complicated by level of proficiency. Verbal expression of CT, especially realized as disputation or adversarial debate, is additionally complicated by cultural differences, not necessarily in thinking, but in attitudes to talk. For Chinese students, listening is important (Smith & Bond, 1999), indirect and inferential speaking is socially valued (Gao, 1998a, 1998b), and "what appears as passivity … (has) highly positive associations, including intelligence, flexibility, managing face, cooperativeness, caring, and maturity" (Kim & Markus, 2002, p. 440). Also, as Rear (2017, p. 23) reminds us, CT "does not need to take place in an atmosphere of heated discussion and debate." Empirical studies using testing instruments or tasks (Floyd, 2011; Lun et al., 2010; Manalo, Watanabe, & Sheppard, 2013) concluded English as additional language proficiency accounted for any variations in CT performance between Chinese background students and English-dominant students.

While accepting the case made above, we suggest an additional dimension to be interrogated. The emphasis on language proficiency is grounded in the assumption that CT is behaviourally evident in talk and action, expectations that originate in currently popular (Western) constructivist and social constructivist theories of learning (Li & Wegerif, 2014). The proficiency explanation assumes that, given the necessary proficiency, (more) Chinese students would behave as do (some of) their English-dominant peers in EMI settings. In this view, MOI is positioned as the mitigating variable in the critical thinking of 'Asian'/Chinese multilingual students with English, rather than any existing predispositions related to *how* and *when* one engages in thinking critically. As regards *when*, while the practice in EMI settings promotes CT as a learning process, in more conventional Chinese practice, learning must precede CT because 'everything is made on the basis of predecessors' (P-1, 104–105), and only after there is understanding of current thinking can deficiencies be identified, alternatives proposed, and (any) improvement achieved. Questioning current thinking is considered essential for human progress, but a privilege of those who have made the effort to achieve a position from which to do so. The path to this position is the training to think:

> I often tell graduate students that there are several stages in studying. The first is kneeling to read. This is when everything is absorbed. Everything is very devout and fully accepted. In the second stage, if the graduate students continue to do this, it will not be very rewarding. At this stage, you will sit and read. That is, to hold your peace of mind. Use one's own thinking and one's own judgment to examine all this. The discovery and progress of all human beings began with questioning. That is, if there is no question about this thing there is no progress. This stage of graduate students' sitting study is to resolve sceptical comment. Our CT was generated during this process. The third stage is standing and reading. For example, a doctoral student cannot tell me what this is. He should look at the logical connection between thousands of things from a higher perspective, or he should give something with explanatory power. If your thinking has reached that stage, it can be said that on the basis of the predecessors, you have further advanced it and can even come up with your own new idea or theory and learn from it in an opinionated way. Therefore, if you don't go through the process of CT training, you will not make any progress at the stage of kneeling there all the time. (P-2, 96–111)

The goal of effective teaching is 'not to pass on, or students obtain a large number of existing facts and existing research conclusions and information. … the ultimate goal of our teaching is actually to know how to solve problems when facing various new problems in the future' (P-4, 40–46); to engage in the re-examination of the basis of existing knowledge, it is necessary first to learn. However, in the undergraduate classroom learning activities recounted by Participant 4, included earlier in the chapter for comparison with Dong's (2015) example of exceptional teaching, we find an example of blending of local and EMI CT thinking, but through a process including drawing on earlier learning.

The questions of *when* and *how* CT is expressed are both fundamental issues for Chinese students and their teachers in EMI settings. In past considerations of both questions, much has been made of Confucian models and differing culturally-based conceptions of what constitutes effective learning, of learning styles and preferences (Biggs, 1994; Watkins & Biggs, 2001). Claims Confucian cultural thinking does not value or foster CT, and popular perceptions of it as promoting a passive reproductive and unquestioning mode of learning and thinking have been contrasted, pejoratively, with 'Western' self-conceptions of individualism and free expression (Floyd, 2011). This continues regardless of contestation of proposals that critical thought is radically different in 'western' and 'eastern' cultures, that Confucianism does not value or encourage critical thought, or that CT is the outcome solely of a 'Western' philosophical tradition (see Chan & Yan, 2007; Floyd, 2011; Kim, 2003; Li & Wegerif, 2014; Paton, 2005, 2011; Rear, 2017). Despite evidence that, irrespective of linguistic and cultural background, both English-dominant and multilingual (with English) students experience "similar developments in slow transformation of beliefs and concepts about the nature of knowledge and the process of teaching and learning" (Durkin, 2008, p. 18) as they transition from school to HE (Paton, 2005), a discourse of the 'Asian learner' has shaped both thinking and talking about students and pedagogic responses (Doherty & Singh, 2007; Rear, 2017). EAP programs, for example, tend to be developed on (culturally-based) assumptions of deficit in product-oriented critical reading and writing processes (Rear, 2017; Wilson, 2016). Yet the limited research that compares how English-dominant and 'Asian' students conceptualize CT suggests some understanding and some confusion, but little difference that can be attributed to cultural background more broadly (Manalo et al., 2015; O'Sullivan & Guo, 2011). Based on his personal experience, Participant 2 compares the capacities of locals with those of students in EMI settings, ultimately with a focus on differences rather than inherent superiority or inferiority, and prepared to acknowledge the respective strengths of different ways of thinking:

> There are some things that we can think of that are very smart, but they are not necessarily thought of abroad. I think one of the interesting things is that we are going to America. In the class, I took a notebook computer and took notes there. Chinese people would surpass American in some aspects of thinking, such as calculation and mathematics. I think the Chinese people are very capable of thinking about these big issues in philosophy and mathematics. Foreign students are not so good at torturing themselves. Most American children have less computing power in elementary school and in universities than we Chinese. I just think that our ability is no worse than others, sometimes even better than others. But the key is that there are differences. Maybe there are some aspects of foreign children who are very capable. We are different in some ways and paths for you to ask questions. We can't compete. We can only talk about differences. (P-2, 223–235)

If anything, it is arguably not the capacity or inclination to think critically that sets Chinese students apart, but differing literacies that distinguishes them in EMI classrooms. The 'traditional Chinese culture does not emphasize a kind of argument, and western culture is argued out. The west is the culture of debating, however China is the culture of writing, and does not like debates' (P-7, 185–187). This more reflective approach emphasizes listening as an academic literacy integral to CT; a student must first listen 'when others say something, you must think about whether it is true or false. You must have such a judgment. Then the other is to dare to question some things that everyone thinks are reasonable' (P-1, 65–67). Li and Wegerif (2014), drawing on Confucian texts and the work of Bakhtin, argue for recognition of a CT that takes the form of an internal dialogue. Bakhtin (1986) posited that many responses to speech are not always immediate, that these can be characterised as silent responsive understanding, and that "sooner or later what is heard and actively understood will find its response in the subsequent speech or behaviour of the listener" (Bakhtin, 1986, p. 69). Instances have been identified in an Australian HE setting of Chinese students' verbal critical responses to classroom discourse (two weeks) 'later', rather than immediately (Walker, 2010). Similarly, Participant 6 provides a thoughtfully considered response to his daughter's experiences of learning in an EMI classroom in the USA and the relation to CT:

> My daughter came back and said to me, when the teacher asked me a question, everyone did not think it over and began to say it out. This kind of atmosphere is really a good atmosphere for CT. The chaos I am talking about is aimed at this problem and I have thought about it. Absurdity is okay, because many scientific inventions were absurd at first. Those burned to death by religion were initially absurd. (P-6, 164–169)

Li and Wegerif (2014, p. 28) argue that, broadly speaking, any Confucian influence on ways to 'do' thinking in Chinese education might mean that "teaching thinking has not been visible as 'teaching thinking' from a Western perspective because it is neither individualistic nor is it noisy and it assumes a somewhat different understanding of what reflection is." The idea of reflective internal dialogue aligns with dialogical conceptions of learning, the development in individuals of ideas and views of the world, as a social phenomenon. When students are exposed to the voices of 'others' in authoritative discourse (Morson, 2004), appropriation of these voices emerges as internally persuasive discourse, "what each person thinks for him- or herself, what ultimately is persuasive to the individual" (Freedman & Ball, 2004, p. 8). In this scenario, then, MOI and language proficiency can influence CT in 'Asian'/Chinese students in EMI settings, although not just for participation through spoken and written literacies, but also in terms of receptive language proficiency that mediates students' capacity to engage in inner dialogue.

3 Conclusion

We have used the reflections of some Chinese academics to scrutinize critical thinking skills of Chinese students from the perspective of a dynamic relation between the conventions and practices of academic literacies in two different MOIs mediated by global mobility and communication. This relation encompasses matters of language and language proficiency, educational background and experiences, and the interactions of individuals in and with social contexts of media of instruction in the (re)constitution of ways of academic thinking and acting. We have suggested that multilingual academics' experiences of English-medium education contexts are playing a significant, perhaps essential, role in the processes of changes in Chinese HE, insofar as recognising, developing, and making visible practices of CT are concerned. An inclination for change and openness is present at both the highest levels and, based on the findings presented here, at the classroom level, but this does not mean wholesale, and uncritical, adoption by Chinese HE of the model of CT vaunted in English-medium academia.

Given our findings, some of the criticisms of efforts to 'introduce' CT in Chinese HE need interrogating. Dong (2015, p. 356) identifies what he considers shortcomings, including examination-oriented goals, insufficient content, irrelevance to practice, and rote-learning pedagogy. We suggest alternative interpretations. Our participants have identified opportunities to refine their practices through attempts to introduce academic literacies they see as advantageous to learning and to the outcomes for their students, but classrooms are constituted mutually, and organizational and institutional imperatives often mean compromise is inevitable. All universities evaluate and assess students, students and teachers are oriented to examinations, but what is examined and assessed can be open to change. The relation between theory and practice in HE is an ongoing challenge in the context of rapid change, regardless of setting; some would argue that introduction of generic CT courses elevates theory, pointing to variations in practice between disciplines and questions of transferability of generic CT models. Such models, arguably, encourage rote learning, or routinization that in itself can be construed as a failure of CT. In sum, these "Chinese characteristics" (Dong, 2015, p. 356) are not the preserve of Chinese HE, of Chinese students, or of academic literacy practices associated with the medium of Mandarin. During their education experiences English-dominant students, like multilingual students with English, learn to demonstrate their thinking through modes and instantiations of academic literacy they believe their teachers expect (Paton, 2011). In the midst of these debates about 'introduction' of CT in China, the experiences of our participants suggest that it is individual and authentic learning through lived experiences in EMI settings that will sustain any transformation of CT in Chinese higher education. Their responses suggest that learning through the medium of additional language/s can nurture authentic development of a richer, more cognitively complex, and comprehensive CT. Even in an education system on the scale of China's, the experiences of individuals are significant in the ongoing dialogical (re)constitution of the social world because, as Bakhtin emphasises, "the individual influences the social world, just as the social world influences the individual" (Freedman & Ball, 2004, p. 5). Although it is often convenient to position the individual as powerless in a context of rigid social and cultural macro-structures, the personal, and ultimately subjective, responses of individuals, "sometimes considered mundane, ineffable, private, and trivial, nonetheless produces important consequences for cultural and social formations and distinctions" (Park, 2015, p. 59).

In contrast to the "simple binary of critical and non-critical educational cultures" (Moore, 2011b, p. 12) still prevalent in Anglophone HE, Chinese academics seem to be open to new ideas and new practices in their classrooms, to "understand and value the new practices, seeing them as opportunities for growth and development, without becoming fully acculturated" (Durkin, 2008, p. 24); they critique them from their extant knowledge perspective, to find and pursue a 'middle way'. In the end, they seem perhaps more flexible than western counterparts who generally are yet to entertain ascription of value to any alternative ways of approaching thinking and learning exemplified in other academic literacies. We need to remember that "English became the global language not because of its linguistic features, but because of the power of the people who speak the language" (Cheng, 2012, p. 327), and that power persists in discourses that elevate Anglophone academic literacies and ways of thinking to positions of dominance; "the use of English establishes a certain methodology of expression of critical thinking, but this is only a methodology, not the critical thought per se" (Paton, 2011, p. 37).

Positioning the literacies of EMI CT as "an intrinsic good and that it is this, perhaps more than anything else, that should be the goal of a higher education" (Moore, 2011a, p. 261) is a preoccupation of Western, Anglophone HE. While something akin to this form of CT is arguably recognized and practised in universities in places such as Western China, it is not regarded as pre-eminent, but more as one approach among many. Ironically, instead of any sense of the mode of thinking identified as essential in EMI as some kind of non-negotiable and universally necessary attribute of rational, higher order thinking characteristic of an educated individual, a more open attitude prevails. It is perhaps inevitable that, as multilingual diversity becomes ever more visible and characteristic of the global HE community, recognition and advocacy of thinking that differs from the orthodoxy of Anglophone HE and research practices emerges (Li & Exley, 2019; Singh & Han, 2017; Wisker & Robinson, 2014), with recognition of the opportunities of a "post-monolingual era in knowledge production" (Díaz, 2018, p. 27). Providing spaces for the voices of multilingual academics working in multilingual settings outside the Anglosphere, such as those heard in this chapter, can contribute to embracing a critical approach to the practices of CT to explore 'middle ways' (Durkin, 2008) that are also slowly beginning to find a place in globally prestigious EMI institutions.

References

Anderson, M., & Moore, D. (1998). *Classroom globalization: An investigation of teaching methods to address the phenomenon of students from multiple national cultures in business school classrooms*. Melbourne: Monash University Faculty of Business and Economics.
Bakhtin, M. M. (1986). *Speech genres and other late essays* (V. W. McGee, Trans.). Austin, TX: University of Texas Press.
Ballard, B. (1981). *Language is not enough—Responses to the academic difficulties of overseas students*. Paper presented at the Communication at University: Purpose, Process and Product Conference, Latrobe University, 1981.
Ballard, B. (1987). Academic adjustment: The other side of the export dollar. *Higher Education Research and Development, 6*(2), 109–119.
Ballard, B. (1989). Overseas students and Australian academics: Learning and teaching styles. In B. Williams (Ed.), *Overseas students in Australia: Policy and practice* (pp. 87–98). Canberra: International Development Program of Australian Universities and Colleges.
Barnett, R. (1997). *Higher education: A critical business*. Buckingham, UK: Society for Research into Higher Education & Open University Press.
Biggs, J. B. (1994). Asian learners through Western eyes: An astigmatic paradox. *Australian and New Zealand Journal of Vocational Education Research, 2*(2), 40–63.

Botha, W. (2016). English and international students in China today: A sociolinguistic study of English-medium degree programs at a major Chinese university. *English Today, 32*(1), 41–47. https://doi.org/10.1017/S0266078415000449.

Byun, K., & Kim, M. (2011). Shifting patterns of the government's policies for the internationalization of Korean higher education. *Journal of Studies in International Education, 15*(5), 467–486. https://doi.org/10.1177/1028315310375307.

Canagarajah, A. S. (2011). Translanguaging in the classroom: Emerging issues for research and pedagogy. *Applied Linguistics Review, 2*(1), 1–28. https://doi.org/10.1515/9783110239331.1.

Canagarajah, A. S. (2013). Introduction. In A. S. Canagarajah (Ed.), *Literacy as translingual practice: Between communities and classrooms* (pp. 1–10). New York & London: Routledge.

Chan, D., & Lo, W. (2008). University restructuring in East Asia: Trends, challenges and prospects. *Policy Futures in Education, 6*(5), 641–652. https://doi.org/10.2304/pfie.2008.6.5.641.

Chan, H. M., & Yan, H. K. (2007). Is there a geography of thought for East-West differences? Why or why not? *Educational Philosophy and Theory, 39*(4), 383–403.

Cheng, L. (2012). The power of English and the power of Asia: English as lingua franca and in bilingual and multilingual education. *Journal of Multilingual and Multicultural Development, 33*(4), 327–330. https://doi.org/10.1080/01434632.2012.661432.

Chirgwin, S. K., & Huijser, H. (2015). Cultural variance, critical thinking, and indigenous knowledges: Exploring a both-ways approach. In M. Davies & R. Barnett (Eds.), *The Palgrave handbook of critical thinking in higher education* (pp. 351–368). New York: Palgrave Macmillan.

Chuah, S.-H. (2010). Teaching East-Asian students: Some observations. Retrieved from https://www.economicsnetwork.ac.uk/showcase/chuah_international.

Cook, V. J. (1992). Evidence for multicompetence. *Language Learning, 42,* 557–591. https://doi.org/10.1111/j.1467-1770.1992.tb01044.x.

Davies, M. (2015). A model of critical thinking in higher education. In M. B. Paulsen (Ed.), *Higher education: Handbook of theory and research* (Vol. 30, pp. 41–92). Cham: Springer International Publishing.

Dawson, J., & Conti-Bekkers, G. (2002). Supporting international students' transition to university. In A. Bunker & G. Swan (Eds.), *Proceedings of the Focussing on the Student: 11th Annual Teaching and Learning Forum for Western Australian Universities, Edith Cowan University, 5–6 February, 2002* (pp. 87–94). Retrieved Feburary 6, 2006 from http://www.ecu.edu.au/conferences/tlf/2002/pub/docs/Dawson.pdf.

Díaz, A. (2018). Challenging dominant epistemologies in higher education: The role of language in the geopolitics of knowledge (re)production. In I. Liyanage (Ed.), *Multilingual education yearbook 2018: Internationalization, stakeholders & multilingual education contexts* (pp. 21–36). New York: Springer.

Doherty, C., & Singh, P. (2005). How the west is done: Simulating western pedagogy in a curriculum for Asian international students. In P. Ninnes & M. Hellsten (Eds.), *Internationalising higher education: Critical explorations of pedagogy and policy* (pp. 53–74). Dordrecht: Springer.

Doherty, C., & Singh, P. (2007). Mobile students, flexible identities and liquid modernity: Disrupting Western teachers' assumptions of 'The Asian Learner". In D. Palfreyman & D. McBride (Eds.), *Learning and teaching across cultures in higher education* (pp. 114–132). London, New York: Palgrave Macmillan.

Dong, Y. (2015). Critical thinking education with Chinese characteristics. In M. Davies & R. Barnett (Eds.), *The Palgrave handbook of critical thinking in higher education* (pp. 351–368). New York: Palgrave Macmillan.

Duff, P. A. (2007). Problematising academic discourse socialisation. In H. Marriot, T. Moore, & R. Spence-Brown (Eds.), *Learning discourses and the discourse of learning* (pp. 01.01–01.18). Clayton, VIC: Monash University ePress.

Durkin, K. (2008). The adaptation of East Asian masters students to Western norms of critical thinking and argumentation in the UK. *Intercultural Education, 19*(1), 15–27. https://doi.org/10.1080/14675980701852228.

Ellwood, C., & Nakane, I. (2009). Privileging of speech in EAP and mainstream university classrooms: A critical evaluation of participation. *TESOL Quarterly, 43*(2), 203–230. https://doi.org/10.1002/j.1545-7249.2009.tb00165.x.

Ennew, C. T., & Fujia, Y. (2009). Foreign Universities in China: A case study. *European Journal of Education, 44*(1), 21–36. https://doi.org/10.1111/j.1465-3435.2008.01368.x.

Floyd, C. B. (2011). Critical thinking in a second language. *Higher Education Research & Development, 30*(3), 289–302. https://doi.org/10.1080/07294360.2010.501076.

Freedman, S. W., & Ball, A. F. (2004). Ideological becoming: Bakhtinian concepts to guide the study of language, literacy, and learning. In A. F. Ball, S. W. Freedman, R. Pea, J. S. Brown, & C. Heath (Eds.), *Bakhtinian perspectives on language, literacy, and learning* (pp. 3–33). Cambridge: Cambridge University Press.

Gao, G. (1998a). "Don't take my word for it."—Understanding Chinese speaking practices. *International Journal of Intercultural Relations, 22*(2), 163–186. https://doi.org/10.1016/s0147-1767(98)00003-0.

Gao, G. (1998b). An initial analysis of the effects of face and concern for "other" in Chinese interpersonal communication. *International Journal of Intercultural Relations, 22*(4), 467–482. https://doi.org/10.1016/S0147-1767(98)00019-4.

García, O. (2009). *Bilingual education in the 21st century*. Oxford: Blackwell.

Hall, J. K., Cheng, A., & Carlson, M. T. (2006). Reconceptualizing multicompetence as a theory of language knowledge. *Applied Linguistics, 27*(2), 220–240. https://doi.org/10.1093/applin/aml013.

Hellstén, M., & Prescott, A. (2004). Learning at university: The international student experience. *International Education Journal, 5*(3), 344–351.

Hoffmann, C. (2000). The spread of English and the growth of mulitlingualism with English in Europe. In J. Cenoz & U. Jessner (Eds.), *English in Europe: The acquisition of a third language* (pp. 1–21). Clevedon, UK: Multilingual Matters.

Hou, A. Y. C., Morse, R., Chiang, C. L., & Chen, H. J. (2013). Challenges to quality of English medium instruction degree programs in Taiwanese universities and the role of local accreditors: A perspective of non-English-speaking Asian country. *Asia Pacific Education Review, 14*(3), 359–370. https://doi.org/10.1007/s12564-013-9267-8.

Huang, F. (2003). Policy and practice of the internationalization of higher education in China. *Journal of Studies in International Education, 7*(3), 225–240. https://doi.org/10.1177/1028315303254430.

Hughes, R. (2008). Internationalisation of higher education and language policy. *Higher Education Management and Policy, 20*(1), 111–128. https://doi.org/10.1787/17269822.

Kettle, M. A. (2007). *Agency, discourse and academic practice: Reconceptualising international students in an Australian university* (Ph.D. thesis). University of Queensland, Brisbane.

Kim, D., Song, Q., Liu, J., Liu, Q., & Grimm, A. (2018). Building world class universities in China: Exploring faculty's perceptions, interpretations of and struggles with global forces in higher education. *Compare: A Journal of Comparative and International Education, 48*(1), 92–109. https://doi.org/10.1080/03057925.2017.1292846.

Kim, H.-K. (2003). Critical thinking, learning and Confucius: A positive assessment. *Journal of Philosophy of Education, 37*(1), 71–87. https://doi.org/10.1111/1467-9752.3701005.

Kim, H. S., & Markus, H. R. (2002). Freedom of speech and freedom of silence: An analysis of talking as a cultural practice. In R. Schweder, M. Minow, & H. R. Markus (Eds.), *Engaging cultural differences: The multicultural challenge in liberal democracies* (pp. 432–452). New York: Russell Sage Foundation.

Kirkpatrick, A. (2011). Internationalization or Englishization: Medium of instruction in today's universities. Retrieved from repository.lib.ied.edu.hk.

Koehne, N. (2005). (Re)construction: Ways international students talk about their identity. *Australian Journal of Education, 49*(1), 104–119.

Lassegard, J. P. (2016). Educational diversification strategies: Japanese universities' efforts to attract international students. In C.-h. C. Ng, R. Fox, & M. Nakano (Eds.), *Reforming learning and* teaching in Asia-Pacific universities: Influences of globalised processes in Japan, Hong Kong and Australia (pp. 47–75). Singapore: Springer.

Li, L., & Wegerif, R. (2014). What does it mean to teach thinking in China? Challenging and developing notions of 'Confucian education'. *Thinking Skills and Creativity, 11,* 22–32. https://doi.org/10.1016/j.tsc.2013.09.003.

Li, M., & Exley, B. (2019). Benefits of translanguaging and transculturation exchanges between international higher degree research students and English medium research supervisors. In I. Liyanage & T. Walker (Eds.), *Multilingual education yearbook 2019: Media of instruction & multilingual settings* (pp. 121–135). New York: Springer.

Li, X., & Roberts, J. (2012). A stages approach to the internationalization of higher education? The entry of UK universities into China. *The Service Industries Journal, 32*(7), 1011–1038. https://doi.org/10.1080/02642069.2012.662495.

Liyanage, I. (2018). Internationalization of higher education, mobility, and multilingualism. In I. Liyanage (Ed.), *Multilingual education yearbook 2018: Internationalization, stakeholders & multilingual education contexts* (pp. 1–20). New York: Springer.

Lun, V. M.-C., Fischer, R., & Ward, C. (2010). Exploring cultural differences in critical thinking: Is it about my thinking style or the language I speak? *Learning and Individual Differences, 20*(6), 604–616. https://doi.org/10.1016/j.lindif.2010.07.001.

Manalo, E., Kusumi, T., Koyasu, M., Michita, Y., & Tanaka, Y. (2015). Do students from different cultures think differently about critical and other thinking skills? In M. Davies & R. Barnett (Eds.), *The Palgrave handbook of critical thinking in higher education* (pp. 299–316). New York: Palgrave Macmillan.

Manalo, E., Watanabe, K., & Sheppard, C. (2013). Do language structure or language proficiency affect critical evaluation? *Proceedings of the Annual Meeting of the Cognitive Science Society, 35.* https://cloudfront.escholarship.org/dist/prd/content/qt4956v4906d/qt4956v4906d.pdf.

Mok, K. H. (2007). Questing for internationalization of universities in Asia: Critical reflections. *Journal of Studies in International Education, 11*(3–4), 433–454. https://doi.org/10.1177/1028315306291945.

Moore, T. (2011a). Critical thinking and disciplinary thinking: A continuing debate. *Higher Education Research and Development, 30*(3), 261–274. https://doi.org/10.1080/07294360.2010.501328.

Moore, T. (2011b). *Critical thinking and language: The challenge of generic skills and disciplinary discourse.* London: Bloomsbury.

Moore, T. (2013). Critical thinking: Seven definitions in search of a concept. *Studies in Higher Education, 38*(4), 506–522. https://doi.org/10.1080/03075079.2011.586995.

Morson, G. S. (2004). The process of ideological becoming. In A. F. Ball, S. W. Freedman, R. Pea, J. S. Brown, & C. Heath (Eds.), *Bakhtinian perspectives on language, literacy, and learning* (pp. 317–331). Cambridge: Cambridge University Press.

Nakane, I. (2006). Silence and politeness in intercultural communication in university seminars. *Journal of Pragmatics, 38*(11), 1811–1835.

Nakane, I. (2007). *Silence in intercultural communication.* Amsterdam, The Netherlands: John Benjamins.

Ng, S. W. (2012). Rethinking the mission of internationalization of higher education in the Asia-Pacific region. *Compare: A Journal of Comparative and International Education, 42*(3), 439–459. https://doi.org/10.1080/03057925.2011.652815.

Novera, I. A. (2004). Indonesian postgraduate students studying in Australia: An examination of their academic, social and cultural experiences. *International Education Journal, 5*(4), 475–487.

O'Sullivan, M. W., & Guo, L. (2011). Critical thinking and Chinese international students: An East-West dialogue. *Journal of Contemporary Issues in Education, 5*(2), 53–73. https://doi.org/10.20355/C5NK5Z.

Park, J. S.-Y. (2015). Structures of feeling in unequal Englishes. In R. Tupas (Ed.), *Unequal Englishes: The politics of English today* (pp. 59–73). Basingstoke, UK: Palgrave Macmillan.

Paton, M. (2005). Is critical analysis foreign to Chinese students. In E. Manalo & G. Wong-To (Eds.), *Communication skills in university education: The international dimension* (pp. 1–11). Auckland, New Zealand: Pearson Education.

Paton, M. (2011). Asian students, critical thinking and English as an academic lingua franca. *Analytic Teaching and Philosophical Praxis, 32*(1), 27–39.

Preece, S. (2011). Universities in the Anglophone centre: Sites of multilingualism. *Applied Linguistics Review, 2,* 121–146. https://doi.org/10.1515/9783110239331.121.

Rear, D. (2017). Reframing the debate on Asian students and critical thinking: Implications for Western universities. *Journal of Contemporary Issues in Education, 12*(2), 18–33. https://doi.org/10.20355/C5P35F.

Samuelowicz, K. (1987). Learning problems of overseas students: Two sides of a story. *Higher Education Research and Development, 6*(2), 121–133.

Singh, M., & Han, J. (2017). Post-monolingual education. In M. Singh & J. Han (Eds.), *Pedagogies for internationalising research education* (pp. 195–231). Singapore: Springer.

Smith, P. B., & Bond, M. H. (1999). *Social psychology across cultures* (2nd ed.). Boston: Allyn and Bacon.

Tian, J., & Low, G. D. (2011). Critical thinking and Chinese university students: A review of the evidence. *Language, Culture and Curriculum, 24*(1), 61–76.

Top Universities. (2018). University branch campuses. Retrieved from https://www.topuniversities.com/student-info/choosing-university/university-branch-campuses.

Tran, L. T., & Nguyen, H. T. (2018). Internationalisation of higher education in Vietnam through English Medium Instruction (EMI): Practices, tensions and implications for local language policies. In I. Liyanage (Ed.), *Multilingual education yearbook 2018: Internationalization, stakeholders & multilingual education contexts* (pp. 91–106). New York: Springer.

University of Nottingham. (2018). The University of Nottingham Ningbo China: Study with us. Retrieved from https://www.nottingham.edu.cn/en/study/.

Walker, A. W. (2010). *Language diversity and classroom dialogue: Negotiation of meaning by students in an internationalised postgraduate classroom.* (Doctoral Thesis). Griffith University, Brisbane. Retrieved from https://research-repository.griffith.edu.au/bitstream/handle/10072/367748/WalkerA_2010_02Thesis.pdf?sequence=1.

Watkins, D. A., & Biggs, J. B. (Eds.). (2001). *Teaching the Chinese learner: Psychological and pedagogical perspectives*. Hong Kong: CERC/ACER.

Wilson, K. (2016). Critical reading, critical thinking: Delicate scaffolding in English for Academic Purposes (EAP). *Thinking Skills and Creativity, 22,* 256–265.

Wisker, G., & Robinson, G. (2014). Examiner practices and culturally inflected doctoral theses. *Discourse: Studies in the Cultural Politics of Education, 35*(2), 190–205. https://doi.org/10.1080/01596306.2012.745730.

Yang, R., & Welch, A. (2001). Internationalising Chinese universities: A study of Guangzhou. *World Studies in Education, 2*(1), 21–51. https://doi.org/10.7459/wse/02.1.03.

Zhang, Z. (2018). English-medium instruction policies in China: Internationalisation of higher education. *Journal of Multilingual and Multicultural Development, 39*(6), 542–555. https://doi.org/10.1080/01434632.2017.1404070.

Anhui Wang is a lecturer in the Faculty of Education of Sichuan Normal University, China. She has been an investigator of a number of international collaborative research projects. Anhui is currently an International visiting Scholar at the School of Education Deakin University, Australia.

Indika Liyanage (Ph.D.) is Associate Professor in TESOL and Discipline Leader (TESOL/LOTE) at Deakin University, Australia. He is also an Honorary Professor at the Faculty of Education, Sichuan Normal University, and Researcher at the Research Centre for Multi-culture, Sichuan Province, People's Republic of China. He has been an English language teacher educator and doctoral supervisor for many years. He has published widely and worked as an international consultant on TESOL in the Pacific.

Tony Walker (Ph.D.) is a Research Fellow in TESOL and LOTE in the School of Education, Deakin University, Australia. He worked in Australia as an English teacher and language teacher educator for many years, and continues to publish in the field and to work with teacher educators in Asia as an international consultant on academic writing.

Media of Instruction in Indonesia: Implications for Bi/Multilingual Education

Tony Walker, Indika Liyanage, Suwarsih Madya and Sari Hidayati

Abstract Indonesia is among the world's most linguistically diverse nations. Consequently, inherent issues of language of instruction and of language in-education policies more generally have been unavoidable for policy-makers and of great significance to the people of Indonesia. Ideally, policies would balance several needs: continued development of a cohesive national identity; provision of high-quality education that is equitable and accessible; and, positioning the nation and its people for participation in the global knowledge economy. From the perspective of local languages, medium of instruction (MOI) policy in the school-level education system for the past seventy years has followed a monolingually-oriented path. Local languages, some of which continue to have tens of millions of users, have been slowly replaced by the national language, *Bahasa Indonesia*. Since 2013, local languages exist at the margins of the national school curriculum, without status or official use as MOI. English MOI has become the focus of controversy and legal intervention in the national school system, and the use of English MOI in school education is now ostensibly restricted to a thriving private school sector. However, government policy has encouraged the use of English MOI in internationally-oriented bilingual programs in higher education, and in 2015 a plan was announced to begin development of an Indonesian/English bilingual curriculum to be implemented across all universities in Indonesia (Dewi in English medium instruction in higher education in Asia-Pacific, pp. 241–258. Cham, Springer, 2017). In the current circumstances, enactment of this MOI policy means higher education is the site of attempts at transformation and innovation in bilingual education. This chapter offers an overview of the current MOI policy situation and its background, identifies and discusses issues that have shaped the outcomes and prospects of bi/multilingual education under current MOI policy, and considers implications for bi/multilingual education in Indonesia going forward.

T. Walker (✉) · I. Liyanage
Deakin University, Geelong, Australia
e-mail: t.walker@deakin.edu.au

S. Madya · S. Hidayati
Yogyakarta State University, Yogyakarta, Indonesia

Keywords Langue education policies · Media of instruction policies · Bi/multilingual education · National identity · Teacher quality

In an era of increasing acknowledgement of multilingualism as an educational resource (Catalano & Hamann, 2016) and in the context of a shift towards multilingual education in the south-east Asian region more generally (Kosonen, 2017a), Indonesia appears to stand out in many ways as an exception. Despite, or indeed perhaps because of, the people of Indonesia being the second most linguistically diverse national group on Earth (Hadisantosa, 2010), the mother tongue of less than ten per cent of the population (Fillmore & Handayani, 2018), *Bahasa Indonesia* (hereafter Indonesian) is mandated by the nation's constitution as the sole medium of instruction (MOI) in all Indonesian schools from Grade One (Coleman, 2016). From the local linguistic perspective, the trend since independence was declared in 1945 has been language-in-education and language-of-education policies of slow but persistent official marginalization of the multitude of local languages, both as MOI and subject of study, in favour of the national language, a not uncommon—although not universal—strategy of statist development in circumstances of diversity. The situation for multilingual education through foreign/additional languages teaching and/or use as MOI—effectively, for our purposes here, English—has followed a somewhat different trajectory. Teaching of English has been a feature of Indonesian public secondary education since 1945, was extended into the primary sector in 1993, and for a period between 2003 and 2013 English received official imprimatur for use as MOI in the introduction of closely regulated Indonesian/English bilingual education at both primary and secondary levels (Hadisantosa, 2010).

In 2013, however, both the practice of using English as MOI in Indonesian/English bilingual schools and the option of teaching of English as a designated curriculum element in primary schools ceased (Coleman, 2016; de Lotbinière, 2013). At the same time the hours devoted to English in the secondary curriculum were reduced (Coleman, 2016). Indonesia offers, in fact, yet another example of the impact of national language policies driven by larger ideological and political agendas on the practices of educators at all levels (Widodo, 2016). Policies dictating MOI have been formulated at a distance from the practicalities of expert knowledge of language and learning, and of language teaching and learning. There are examples of policy determined through processes that involve little or no negotiation or consultation with teachers or developers of curriculum, of others without adequate attention to structural constraints, or to consideration of the interplay of objectives and competencies with the needs and demands of the multitude of contexts of language use. The current situation appears to be confusingly inconsistent and paradoxical, one that both discourages and encourages the use of MOI other than the dominant local language. In such a context, teaching practitioners bear a significant responsibility for policy enactment and innovation, and a number of such examples are included in the discussion that follows. This chapter offers a brief overview of the current MOI policy situation and its background, identifies and discusses issues that shape the outcomes and prospects of bi/multilingual education under current MOI policy, and considers implications for bi/multilingual education in Indonesia going forward.

1 Local Languages and Medium of Instruction

Striking contrasts characterize Indonesia's multilinguality and policies stipulating the MOI to be used in education. Although estimates vary, there seems to be agreement that in excess of 700 languages are in use by the people of Indonesia (Hadisantosa, 2010; Simons & Fennig, 2018; Widodo, 2016). At least thirteen of these are each used by more than two million speakers. Some, for example, Javanese and Sundanese are used by many tens of millions (Coleman, 2016), and from an education perspective, these have extensive histories of writing and literature. Many of the minority languages are considered threatened by development and globalization (Hadisantosa, 2010), but among the hundreds that retain their vitality (Simons & Fennig, 2018) many have an oral tradition only. In practice, a focus on individual languages ignores the fluidity of multilingual practices. Many of the majority local languages have dialects across the range of "distinct linguistic levels: phonetic, phonological, lexical, syntactic, and pragmatic and cultural" (Widodo, 2016, p. 130) and daily life for most Indonesians involves bi/multilinguality, regularly switching or mixing languages as required and appropriate (Wright, 2016). Indonesian occupies a unique place in this multilingual environment, in the sense that it belongs to no-one and to everyone; originating from Malay (see Wright, 2016, pp. 95–98 for more detailed background), it had served historically as a trading *lingua franca* (Coleman, 2016) until it was adopted in 1928 as national *lingua franca* expressly because it was not identified with any of the nation's diverse ethnolinguistic groups. The decision was made "on a supra-ethnic basis where all ethnic groups accepted the decision" (Widodo, 2016, p. 131), the objective being to forge a new national identity, and then formalized in the 1945 Constitution of the Republic of Indonesia, which stipulated Indonesian as the official language of government administration and, among other functions, of education. Seventy years later, it is estimated that somewhere between 10 and 20% of the population use Indonesian as their first language in the home, although the ubiquitous presence of the language across public domains means about 70% of Indonesians use it as a second/additional language (Kosonen, 2017b).

Whilst the adoption of Indonesian avoided overt conflict over linguistic equality and rights (Wright, 2016), its imposition as the MOI for education and the language of academic literacy in the context of such enormous language diversity has had significant consequences. To begin, Indonesian is far from a unified code, but has both standard, 'educated' versions, and vernacular varieties grouped under the term Bazaar Malay (Wright, 2016). The official attitude to local languages, even those with many millions of users, has arguably been ambivalent, given that a supplement to the Constitution (Asshiddiqie, 2008) guaranteed that "local languages which are cared for by their speakers ... will also be respected and cared for by the State. ... (as) part of Indonesia's living culture" (Coleman, 2016, p. 43). Any evidence of this in the form of the presence of local languages in schools, both as MOI and as subjects for study, has gradually disappeared. Initially, until the mid-1970s, primary schools had the option of either using Indonesian MOI from the outset, or using a local language as MOI until Grade 3 when Indonesian language was introduced for use as MOI from Grade 4 onwards, whilst instruction and development of literacy in the local language continued until the end of primary school (Coleman, 2016; Wright, 2016). Since that early period, Indonesian has become entrenched as the prescribed MOI from Grade 1 in all schools. Although use of a local language as MOI in initial schooling continued to be accepted if required, curriculum reforms in 2013 left only a provision for a local language to be used as MOI "in an auxiliary function during the early years" (Fillmore & Handayani, 2018), if required. Apart from being displaced as MOI, local languages were progressively marginalized as subjects of study (see Djojonegoro, 1996), their only place in the curriculum throughout primary and secondary schooling now restricted to local decisions to include it in Art and Culture classes (Paku Alam IX, 2008) or in school-funded extra-curricular offerings, while in senior secondary classes "local content [i.e. any subject of particular local relevance] may include the local language" (Republik Indonesia, 2013, cited in Coleman, 2016, p. 43; see also Sugito, 2008).

In practice, although few instances of schools exercising their options to use or include local languages in classrooms are reported, it is difficult to judge the true situation. Although outside observers such as Kosonen (2017a), reporting to UNESCO on language of instruction in Indonesia, claim a clear majority (approaching 90 percent) of children in primary schools do not receive education using their first language, local authorities disagree, arguing that the 2015–2019 National Medium Term Development Plan was "extremely explicit in that it stipulated that the native tongue should be used as the primary language in class until the third grade" (The Jakarta Post, 2015, p. 4). This latter view is difficult to reconcile with repeated calls from local educators for just such a policy to be introduced (Kompas, 2016; Suara Pembaruan, 2014; The Jakarta Post, 2014). Even this type of early-exit transitional model is considered inadequate for development of the language and literacy needed to effectively transition to another MOI, which researchers have recommended be between five to seven years in optimum circumstances (Benson, 2016); continued learning of the L1 until at least the end of primary school can alleviate the difficulties experienced by learners (Benson, 2016), but in Indonesia this practice has effectively ceased as well. Perversely, even during the period prior to 2013 when teaching local languages was required as part of local content in primary schools, prompted by "the emerging and mushrooming demand for English, schools then drop the local language in order to give more time to the English teaching" (Hadisantosa, 2010, p. 31). Since the introduction of the 2103 curriculum, regulations that guide development of local content refer to local languages, English, traditional arts, traditional handicrafts, knowledge on regional natural resources, and information that is considered beneficial to develop the regions (Ministry of Education and Culture, 2013). English is considered as local content as it is considered beneficial to enhance the capacity of human resources in particular regions, for example, areas that have many tourism destinations. Kosonen (2017a, p. 6) refers to "a few pilot projects of mother tongue-based multilingual education (that) have begun in Eastern Indonesia," (e.g., see below) and Fillmore and Handayani (2018), in their description of an Australian Government sponsored project in primary schools in Bima province in the island of Sumbawa, provide some insight into what might be happening more widely in areas where, like Bima, the local language has no standardized alphabet, and learning materials using the language are non-existent:

> ... we found a significant gap between teaching practice, materials, and the first languages of students. Around 90 per cent of teachers in target Bima schools were using local languages as an oral instructional language in the classroom, while the supporting materials and assessment tools were in Bahasa Indonesia. ... The default strategy we observed teachers using in Bima when students didn't understand the message in Bahasa Indonesia or materials, was to directly translate or code switch – an unsustainable strategy long-term as local languages are no longer permitted beyond early grades. (Fillmore & Handayani, 2018)

Thus, it is difficult to ascertain the day-to-day, moment-by-moment MOI practices that teachers across Indonesia adopt when the best estimates are that between 75 and 90% of Indonesian children begin their education in a language other than their own (Kosonen, 2017a). Given that the project described by Fillmore and Handayani (2018) was prompted by extremely low student learning outcomes, the consequences of Indonesia's MOI policy in such a multilingual setting are profound for many students, their families, and their teachers.

The challenges of developing a MOI policy that balances the need for academic literacy in a language that offers pathways to educational opportunities with the needs of a multilingual population cannot be dismissed, and nor can the structural impediments of resourcing and staffing schools that implementation of bi/multilingual MOI would involve. A further impediment to a more multilingual approach and the use of local languages as MOI has ensued from internal migration which complicates local language ecologies (Sukamdi & Mujahid, 2015). Persistence with the current approach, however, seems in part to rely on a gradual intergenerational spread of bi/multilingualism with Indonesian into the homes of local language users, or even the abandonment of local languages in favour of the national language, although there is no evidence of any such shifts simply because data on bi/multilingualism is not collected in the Indonesian census (Kosonen, 2017a). In the interim there continue to be regular public calls from academics and educators (Kompas, 2016; Suara Pembaruan, 2014; The Jakarta Post, 2014) to address the needs of students who "begin their schooling in an education system that they cannot fully understand or participate in" (Fillmore & Handayani, 2018). Use of local languages as MOI at least for the initial two or three years, it is argued, would improve learning outcomes, not only across the curriculum but also in later learning of the national language, and address the problem of participation and retention rates which are very low in rural and more remote areas (Media Indonesia, 2015). Others have suggested the option of bilingual instruction in the early years of education could achieve similar results (The Jakarta Post, 2015). In some parts of the country, arguably where the need from an educational perspective is probably the greatest, isolated projects to demonstrate a place for instruction using the first/local language have been undertaken. In a district of West Papua, where at least 300 languages are in use, Analytical and Capacity Development Partnership (ACDP) Indonesia, Papua administration, and Summer Institute of Linguistics (SIL), conducted a two-year project during 2015–2017 in a small number of pre- and elementary schools in which the curriculum, including literacy development, was provided to students in their local Lani language (Somba, 2017) prior to introduction of Indonesian in Grade Three. Despite the short duration of the pilot phase of the project, those responsible claim to have increased retention, improved linguistic skills and learning in all subjects, and encouraged students' critical thinking. This project, and that described by Fillmore and Handayani (2018), which aim for a structured transition to the national language MOI through parallel development of first language oral fluency and second language acquisition, offer some promise, as well as models, to address those needs, and to encourage development of others. At the moment, however, there seems to be little evidence to refute the assertion that local languages "play only a peripheral role in education, and in most schools they have disappeared completely" (Coleman, 2016, p. 43), with isolated projects the exceptions to the universal use of Indonesian as MOI. Kosonen (2017a, p. 13) suggests a link between low learning achievements of many students in Indonesia and the "clear majority" denied any instruction in their first language, concluding that more research on MOI practices in Indonesia's schools is "urgently needed."

2 English Medium Instruction in Indonesian Education

While there is much evidence across many domains of a steady increase in the position and visibility of English in Indonesia (Coleman, 2016), as a target of teaching and learning, and as MOI, the status of English has fluctuated. Considered obligatory for study by junior and senior secondary school students (Coleman, 2016; Sukyadi, 2015), English is not the only foreign language studied, but is unquestionably the "the first foreign language" (Komaria, 1998, cited in Sukyadi, 2015, p. 124) in Indonesia's national education system. Although, as we shall see, Indonesia has a distinct and arguably atypical history and current stance regarding English education and English MOI, the essential rationale for teaching and learning the language echoes that of any post-colonial nation pursuing development, prosperity, and participation in global commercial and knowledge economies (Huda, 1997; Lauder, 2008). Policy as realized in curriculum documents champions English as the unchallenged pathway for accelerated national and individual progress (Sukyadi, 2015), and as vital for establishing communications between Indonesians and the rest of the world across domains of politics, education, science, technology, the arts, and so forth. But behind the commitment to develop the English proficiency of the population is an ambivalence or wariness that has proved to be pivotal to success of attempts to introduce English as MOI, and to English language teaching in school curricula more generally. Coleman's (2016) image of English devouring Indonesian and local languages suggests efforts to characterize the use of English as a tool for selective use in economic development (Lauder, 2008), without compromising Indonesian languages, culture/s, and values, has failed. Lauder's (2008, pp. 13–15) discussion of Indonesia's "language schizophrenia" (Kartono, 1976, cited in Lauder, 2008, p. 14) foregrounds some of the forces at play in the attempted introduction of English MOI in the years between 2007 and 2013, specifically, tensions between the drive for modernization and a fear of dilution of cultural values, between the objective of using the national language to secure a unified national identity and the potential of English as a prestige language to entrench socioeconomic divisions in the nation.

Access to English medium instruction (EMI) school education in Indonesia, historically, was available only in international schools similar to those found in many parts of the world. Generally, these are private institutions approved by the national government but operated by representatives of foreign organizations, offering imported curricula, and catering almost exclusively to the expatriate community. However, demand by locals for the provision of EMI has made the conventional use of the term, 'international school', more complicated in Indonesia. In the late 1990s, in response to demand and with government approval, local private schools, some called international schools and others National Plus schools, began to offer EMI programs to Indonesian students (Wright, 2016). The local private 'international schools' use imported curricula leading to 'international' credentials, such as International Baccalaureate or the Victoria (Australia) Certificate of Education, delivered using EMI, and the high fees effectively restrict enrolments to the children of "extremely wealthy" (Zacharias, 2013, p. 93) local families. National Plus schools are private schools with an international orientation but less curriculum flexibility that offer an approved international curriculum either separately or in combination with the local curriculum (Hadisantosa, 2010), and using what is regarded as progressive 'international' pedagogy (Rinaldi & Saroh, 2017). Some National Plus schools prepare students for the National Examinations (Hadisantosa, 2010), and they are required to include the national curriculum elements of classes in Indonesian language, religion and civic studies, all taught using the national language, but offer the 'plus' of EMI for other curriculum subjects—Science, Mathematics, English, History, Geography, Economics, and so forth—and of substantial resources and facilities. Although National Plus school fees are not as high as the elite local private 'international schools', they nevertheless are such that students are predominantly the children of upper middle-class families. Notwithstanding, demand for English, "the highly sought commodity in Indonesia" (Manara, 2014, p. 23), and for 'international' EMI has fuelled strong growth of this private 'international school' sector.

In 2003, in what proved to be for a brief period, the government initiated the introduction into the national school system of 'international standard schools' (ISS; in Indonesian, Sekolah Bertaraf Internasional, or SBI, but hereafter ISS). An ISS was "a national school that prepares the students based on the national educational standards and offers an international standard by which the graduates are expected to have international/global competitiveness" (Sistem Penyelenggaraan, 2007, cited in Zacharias, 2013, p. 94). 'International standard' equated with teaching methods and learning materials used by schools in a globally competitive OECD member nation, in itself an approach fraught with problems in the local Indonesian context. Although numerous conditions were to be met for approval as an ISS, the requirement that EMI must be used in at least Mathematics, Science and core vocational classes "appears to be the most prominent factor separating ISSs from regular public schools" (Zacharias, 2013, p. 94). Thus, while ISSs could be characterised as essentially aiming to offer a form of content-based immersive foreign language learning to address a policy imperative to improve learning outcomes, "almost everyone in practice considers English to be the main focus of the whole programme" (Bax, 2010, p. 39). There has been a long-held belief at policy level, one that continues to sustain the attraction of private international EMI schools, that English language learners in Indonesia are at a disadvantage in comparison to learners in neighbouring countries with histories of British colonization and greater post-colonial exposure to English (Huda, 1997). The initiative was heavily funded (Coleman, 2016) and the objective was to establish at least one ISS school at each level of education—primary, junior secondary, senior secondary, and senior vocational—in all districts in the country, staffed by teachers with the English proficiency necessary to deliver the key subjects stipulated for EMI (Coleman, 2011), beginning at Grade Four in primary schools (Coleman, 2016).

In broad terms the ISS policy was "ideologically driven by the discourses of internationalization, globalization, and modernization" (Widodo, 2016, p. 135). More explicitly, the objectives were to improve the quality of education (Sukyadi, 2015; Widodo, 2016) in order to nurture the academic capabilities of outstanding students (Widodo, 2016), to develop a globally competitive education system that equipped Indonesians to communicate effectively in the international setting (Hadisantosa, 2010) in order to underpin economic growth and national development (Zacharias, 2013). It was not explicitly stated in policy documents, but the objective of being internationally competitive in the context of globalization was effectively equated with development of highly-educated English-proficient professionals across domains of business, science and technology, education, politics, and so on, and EMI was perceived to be an essential strategy in the plan to achieve this (Coleman, 2011). The initiative "surprised many observers" (Coleman, 2011, p. 91), and, by some more sceptical, it has been portrayed also as a response to the elitism and exclusiveness of the private international and National plus schools that was being publicly decried as discriminatory and inequitable (Rinaldi & Saroh, 2017)—accusations soon levelled in turn against ISSs. By the beginning of 2010, about four years after the implementation of the policy began, about 0.4% of national schools were approved as ISSs although most of these were schools operating some 'international standard' classes in addition to the regular curriculum (Coleman, 2009), and the Ministry of National Education was aiming to achieve the policy objectives of one primary, one junior secondary, one senior secondary and one vocational secondary international standard school per district, a total of 2000 schools (around 1% of national schools) by 2014 (Coleman, 2011).

3 Local Resistance

The policy objectives were not realized. In 2013, following lodgement of an application for a judicial review by the Coalition for Anti-Commercialization of Education, Indonesia's Constitutional Court determined that the 2003 legislation enabling introduction of ISSs to the national school system was unconstitutional (Constitution Court, 2012; Manara, 2014), and ISSs ceased operating in that year. A key argument against the ISSs initiative was that through the funding model and the fees charged by ISSs the government had contravened its duty to ensure through the national education system the equal right of all Indonesians to a "quality education without any socio-economic discrimination or injustice" (Widodo, 2016, p. 136). The objection was not only to the fee-paying elitism of ISSs, but to the institutionalisation of a two-tier public education system that was seen as threatening the development of regular schools and other educational initiatives, and entrenching—especially along an urban/rural divide—uneven development of education and attendant opportunities (Bruhn, 2011; see Coleman, 2011; Manara, 2014; Widodo, 2016, for further discussion of the socioeconomic context of the ISS debate). More pertinent to the issue of MOI, the use of EMI was argued to be "eroding national identity" (Manara, 2014, p. 24), reflecting a perception, perhaps well-founded, that the growing presence of English as a foreign language in the education system was in conflict with another important language policy objective, that of teaching the national language, Indonesian, already positioned as an additional/second language for the great majority of students. From a multilingual education perspective, concerns about the viability of EMI in ISSs had been voiced from the outset, although some (e.g., Bax, 2010, p. 39) argued that as "educational initiatives of this kind can often take decades to have the desired effect", what was needed was time for the shortcomings to be addressed and hopefully overcome. The ISS model expected teachers of Science, Mathematics, and core vocational subjects—and other curriculum areas in many instances of ISSs responding to parental pressure and a desire to increase school prestige (Suherdi & Kurniawan, 2005, cited in Hawanti 2014)—to teach classes using a "simplified and vague set of guidelines" (Zacharias, 2013, p. 94) that prescribed 75% use of English by the third year of implementation. The challenges for the majority of both teachers and students were tremendous; the ISS model suited elite students from internationally-oriented middle-class families living in urban centres, but not students, and their teachers, living in rural areas where English is used infrequently (Zacharias, 2013). The perspective that emerges from the research literature is overwhelmingly one of inadequacy across the requisites for successful teaching and learning.

4 Teacher Quality

Although ISSs were conceived as developing bilingualism (Indonesian/English), in the competitive environment that ensued many schools attempted to offer EMI for more than Science and Mathematics classes from Grade Four, some "enthusiastically" (Coleman, 2011, p. 96) introducing English from Grade One (Hadisantosa, 2010) and/or in other areas of the curriculum. The teaching workforce was not prepared for the task (Hadisantosa, 2010; Widodo, 2016). In 2008, for example, administration of the Test of English for International Communication to all teaching staff in ISSs by the Ministry of National Education found the competency of more than half to be in the lowest band, 'novice', and less than one percent rated in the top two bands of 'advanced working proficiency' and 'general professional proficiency' (Depdiknas, 2009, in Coleman, 2009). Even teachers of English did not perform well, and in the primary school sector another more recent analysis based on Ministry of National Education teacher data indicates the language proficiency of English teachers is generally poor across all skills (Zein, 2016). Many students, also, when faced with the realities of EMI did not have the English proficiency required for effective processing of information essential for learning (Widodo, 2016). They struggled with learning materials, were reluctant to engage in classroom interaction with teachers (Coleman, 2009), including discursive practices such as asking questions, and consequently risked either not understanding, or misunderstanding, essential concepts (Sukyadi, 2015; Zacharias, 2013). Envisioned by policymakers as effecting a change for the better in quality of teaching and learning, many teachers believed the consequences of EMI were the opposite, that it led to "decreases in teaching and learning process, (in) teachers' teaching material mastery, (in) teaching spirit of teachers, (in) students' learning achievement, and (in) students' learning motivation" (Sukyadi, 2015, p. 138). Teaching/learning materials were a source of trouble for both teachers and students, with little evidence of any analysis to determine proficiency level-appropriate subject-specific language of Science and Mathematics (Coleman, 2009). Some materials produced by university lecturers or by teachers themselves—frequently translated from Indonesian—used English vocabulary far above the level of students' proficiency (Coleman, 2009), while the same problem ensued from English-language texts from overseas programs used by some ISSs, which also did not match the local curriculum (Bax, 2010). When bilingual textbooks were used in ISS classrooms, both teachers and students relied on the Indonesian text because, Widodo (2016, p. 136) concluded, "the teachers and the students preferred using Bahasa Indonesia as a medium of instruction because it was much easier to teach and to understand a lesson." Although teachers in ISSs were provided intensive training to develop their English proficiencies, many responded strategically to the demand for English use in the classroom (Zacharias, 2013). In Zacharias's (2013) study conducted in central Java, teachers described their reliance on prepared written materials to avoid speaking English or writing English on whiteboards during teaching, on the use of on-line translation applications, such Google Translate, even during lessons, and on the practice of switching to Indonesian to explain materials and tasks written in English. The same teachers also revealed how they used much more English in classroom discourse when being observed by school or government officials, planning lessons with easy or familiar language, and equipping themselves with visual materials that included linguistic prompts. They also allied themselves with their students, acknowledged their lack of English proficiency to legitimize a focus on meaning-making rather than accuracy, and when using English often relied on the more proficient students to collaboratively negotiate meaning, in effect learning from those they were ostensibly teaching. Zacharias (2013) observes that these practices "might undermine the policy and can hamper the acquisition of English, denying the very essence of EMI policy" (Zacharias, 2013, p. 105).

5 EMI in International Standard Schools (ISSs)

Numerous studies of diverse aspects of EMI in ISSs were conducted during the years 2007–2013, and the sudden halting of the initiative meant some were published in the years following. The findings reported by Astika and Wahyana (2012) are typical. They investigated the practices of teachers in eight EMI/bilingual science classes in three senior high schools. The results indicated that the science teachers at the schools did not have sufficient mastery of English for bilingual classes. The interviews with the teachers and school principals also revealed problems with teachers' motivation to improve their English in spite of the supports provided by the school management, such as English training for science teachers delivered by invited experts who also observed and supported the teachers in their classrooms. Although the study found teachers used significantly more English than Indonesian while teaching, closer analysis revealed a majority of the English use was characterized by poor control of the forms/structures of English, and absence of complex structures necessary to deliver concepts in science. Using English for speaking was avoided. There was a preference for presenting content and tasks in written form with little or no spoken interaction using English, such as in discussions or question-and-answer sessions. Spoken English was primarily used for regulative first order pedagogic discourse (Christie, 1991) rather than teaching curriculum content. Teachers complained that the English language support provided was short-term rather than ongoing, that it targeted general English proficiency, rather than the pedagogic language of the science classroom, and that it was scheduled at unsuitable times when they had other responsibilities. Bilingual or English science books suitable for the students were unavailable, and teachers' responsibilities thus included development and evaluation of materials, evaluation of language as well as science learning, and workloads left no time to devote to development of English proficiency. The findings of this study are replicated in numerous other investigations of EMI in ISSs (e.g., Coleman, 2009, 2011; Hadisantosa, 2010; Haryanto & Mukminin, 2012; Rustandi, 2013; Sukyadi, 2015; Zacharias, 2013). Hadisantosa (2010, p. 35) offers a succinct summation of the ISS experience:

> Interviews and available research studies show that teachers are not confident in teaching maths and science using English. Students are often smarter than the teachers when it comes to English. Teachers have problems with scientific terminology as well as in classroom instruction. They might be good teachers when teaching their subjects in Indonesian, but teaching these same subjects in English is a different matter.

It would not be surprising to find the inadequacies that characterised the language proficiencies of teachers and students, and materials, led to problems with learning, both of English and the content delivered using EMI. Coleman (2009), for example, reported observing language practices in lessons, such as direct translations of materials from Indonesian to English, which he judged to be posing "substantial risks for children's learning" (p. 74), but Bax (2010) concluded the scarcity of reliable data made it impossible to determine if objectives of English proficiency and international standard outcomes were being achieved. Some local evidence suggested students in senior secondary ISSs were not achieving at the standard of their peers in regular schools in the same city (Coleman, 2009), while a year before the decision ending the ISS initiative, testing showed no significant difference in English and content knowledge between students in ISSs and those in regular schools (Sukyadi, 2015). Adopting a different benchmark, that of cost effectiveness, Fahmi, Maulana, and Yusuf (2011) examined and compared achievement in the subjects Indonesian and Mathematics of students in ISSs with those in accelerated learning programs in regular schools. Three models of accelerated programs are used, but all use the standard curriculum completed at an accelerated pace, with, in these instances, Indonesian as MOI. The findings appear equivocal, but do in fact raise questions about the use of MOI in ISSs. Students in ISSs achieved better results in Indonesian, while students in accelerated programs achieved better in Mathematics. In neither case was the MOI English, certainly a finding of significance given that the objective of ISSs is to improve the quality of education in fields, such as Mathematics, considered vital in international competitiveness.

The ISS initiative can be appreciated as an attempt to develop the academic and linguistic capital both of nation and of individuals, and certainly the program was given little time for adjustment and development, but the introduction of EMI in ISSs reinforced existing socioeconomic and structural divides based on access to English and English proficiency (Sukyadi, 2015). The best performing schools, many with already privileged student populations, were encouraged to apply to become ISSs (Coleman, 2011), and despite policy guidelines that required one fifth of places be made available to high-achieving students from less financially privileged backgrounds (Widodo, 2016), the fees levied by the newly accredited ISSs (a practice forbidden in regular government primary and junior high schools) made it impossible for the families of these students to take advantage of this opportunity (Purnomo, 2011). This, coupled with the cultural capital of wealthier, educated families who often expose children to English in the home and who have the financial capacity to provide access to private English classes/tuition (Lamb, 2011), meant students from upper middle-class backgrounds were positioned to gain the greatest benefit from EMI education in ISSs (Widodo, 2016). When ISS classes were established in schools running parallel regular programs, the obvious disparities in resources, facilities, teaching staff, class sizes, and even school uniforms, made the elitist nature of the initiative, a "considerable subsidy to the most prosperous sector of society" (Coleman, 2011, p. 104), obvious to the most casual observer, and marked English and EMI as a delineator of class, status, and power.

6 Post Cessation of ISS Schools

The ending of the ISS program did not signal the end of EMI in school education in Indonesia. EMI continues apace in an increasing number of private 'international schools' and National Plus schools, often using imported curricula (Manara, 2014). In government schools, given that English can still be used in "the circumstances that it is required for expanding knowledge of a specific subject or occupational skills" (Sukyadi, 2015, p. 125), the use of EMI in Science and Mathematics classrooms remains "pervasive" (Zacharias, 2013, p. 106), and in major urban centres bilingual classes using English and/or Indonesian MOI are still operating in some schools although no longer classed as 'international schools' (Dewi, 2017). However, it is primarily in the non-government sector of fee-levying private schools that EMI is positioned competitively as a commodity in Indonesia's education market. Although many parents choose English medium schools, including early childhood care and education institutions that use EMI (The Jakarta Post, 2014), on the basis of the arguably misplaced assumption (Coleman, 2009) that early introduction to English offers a greater chance of proficiency, the situation is more complex than pursuit of an educationally-based language learning objective. The goal of English learning and EMI is associated less with the social good of national development and prosperity and more with the private benefit of education that promises a globally competitive outlook and future, and the opportunity to establish personally beneficial international networks (Manara, 2014). English is associated with modernity, and the ability to sprinkle conversation with English is considered a mark of sophistication (Lauder, 2008). An English-medium education, furthermore, is considered by many upwardly mobile Indonesians, not just more prestigious (Manara, 2014), but superior in quality to what can be achieved through the medium of local languages, including Indonesian (Coleman, 2009). Despite evidence available in studies comparing outcomes of private and government schools—for example that of Willyarto, Werhoru, and Gea (2017, p. 179) that "the use of English in teaching has no significant effect on student achievement" when teaching Mathematics concepts—the pervasiveness of such discourses creates a strong demand for EMI schooling, and those who can afford it, particularly more economically powerful prosperous urban families, opt for English only or bilingual private schools (Asningtias, 2017; Bax, 2010).

For those seeking a grounding in English as part of school curriculum offerings, changes in 2013 to the position of English in the national curriculum, the ending of ISSs aside, differentiate government and private education even more starkly. The teaching of English as an optional subject of the primary school curriculum from Grade Four, introduced in 1993, was stopped, and the hours devoted to English in the junior and senior secondary curricula reduced (Coleman, 2016; Widodo, 2016). The decision to cease ELT in primary schools, cultural and political dimensions aside, takes place against a "chaotic ad hoc relationship between the policy of introducing English in primary schools and the school system itself" (Hawanti, 2014, p. 169) evident in widely acknowledged deficiencies in efforts. These deficiencies include lack of centrally developed curriculum, inadequate English proficiency of the majority of teachers and lack of training to teach language and/or lack of training to teach language at primary level (Zein, 2016), poor resourcing, and teaching driven by reliance on poor quality textbooks. Although, as noted earlier, observers point to the inclusion of English in some schools in the study of 'local culture' (Coleman, 2016), and to some continued use of EMI in the teaching of Science and Mathematics, the combined effect of the legal and policy decisions of 2013 have ensured that English and EMI assumes an even more powerful status as a marker of privilege and access to power.

7 EMI in Higher Education

A key motivation for the introduction of English in the school curriculum soon after independence was the preparation of students for higher education, given the national language was not yet in a position to function effectively in the academic domain (Huda, 1997). Although Indonesian quickly established itself as the default MOI in higher education (Coleman, 2016), the pressure to use English as a teaching medium is stronger than ever, and "EMI flourishes in the higher education sector" (Widodo, 2016, p. 136). Policy has focused on development of world-class universities (Fauzi, 2018), and in the absence until recently of explicit MOI policy dictates, some universities have responded to the internationalization imperative by offering programs in dual or parallel modes, identical courses distinguished only by MOI, a 'regular' Indonesian medium version and an 'international' English medium version, both targeting primarily local students but with higher fees and English proficiency requirements for the 'international' version (Dewi, 2017). Other institutions have adopted an Indonesian/English MOI bilingual model that accommodates access to English-language information and exposure to English language in use, whilst being less demanding in terms of proficiency (Simbolon, 2018). In addition, as in the school education sector, the higher education sector includes a substantial number of flourishing private institutions, in which the use of EMI is widespread (Simbolon, 2018). Whilst not explicitly a MOI policy, the status of English in higher education is evident in the requirement that since 2012 award of a Ph.D. is conditional upon a publication in an international journal, effectively a publication in English, although Coleman (2016, p. 45) claims enforcement of this has been "limited."

The 2015 announcement by the Research, Technology and Higher Education Minister that a bilingual Indonesian/English curriculum was being prepared to ensure the competitiveness of graduates in the ASEAN Economic Community (The Jakarta Post, 2015), illustrates the continued portrayal in policy of English as a tool for selective use in accessing knowledge and technology essential for national economic development (Lauder, 2008). There is uncertainty at the institutional level about the precise nature of the proposed bilingual curriculum and how and when it will be implemented (Dewi, 2017; Simbolon, 2018), and the introduction of EMI, and of English language study, appears to be an institutional responsibility. However, the political and ideological implications of choosing to use EMI are apparent to those working in the sector, as the issues raised by academics in Dewi's (2017) study illustrate: the risk of elitism and discrimination, and of devaluation of the national language because of association of English with status, to the extent that academic competence, prestige, and influence can be seen as greater in those with a working English proficiency.

EMI in higher education in Indonesia continues to be seen by policy makers (Dewi, 2017) and by students (Mirizon, Wadham, & Curtis, 2016) as a means of improving English language learning and proficiency. There is an attendant apparent confusion over the concept of content and language integrated learning (CLIL) such that an 'international' undergraduate course is seen as an appropriate setting for explicit focus on language learning (Simbolon, 2018). Institutions are also using EMI as an internationalisation strategy, but the rapid growth in the number of Indonesian's accessing EMI higher education through overseas study is seen by some as evidence that local institutions are currently not capable of satisfying the demand, in terms of neither quantity nor quality (Clark, 2014, April 4). Within institutions, there is confusion and indecision over approaches to and extent of integration of English in programs. At the vocational-based state university investigated by Simbolon (2018), for example, several departments initiated EMI in response to an institutional policy of internationalization, although MOI was not explicitly identified as a policy strategy, but the practice was stopped after four years. Several individual lecturers continue to teach using English or a mix of English/Indonesian, and most departments include compulsory English courses with program-specific orientation, essentially English-for-specific-purposes courses. Yet there is no written institution-wide policy on English; decisions about whether and/or how English is included in programs are made at the department or individual level, and some students 'learn' English through EMI delivered by content specialists, while others complete stand-alone content-focussed courses delivered by specialist English teachers.

Many of the issues that constrained EMI during the period of ISSs are experienced also in English medium or bilingual programs in higher education. Policy in the sector, from both the Ministry and individual institutions, to supply EMI or bilingual instruction is not aligned with the capacities of the teaching staff. It is concerning that some lecturers responsible for delivering EMI programs cite the opportunity to improve their own self-reported inadequate English proficiency as a benefit of EMI (Baa, 2018). Proficiency of both lecturers and students is identified as an impediment to effective learning (Mirizon et al., 2016), and while this can be characterised as a threat to the quality of what is portrayed as an internationally competitive education, it is equally noteworthy that the moment-to-moment practices in classrooms, such as regular switching between languages, have the potential to mitigate this risk and progress the learning of content (Cahyani, de Courcy, & Barnett, 2018). Research suggests students find lectures and materials in English difficult and in some cases oppose EMI as a practice (Mirizon et al., 2016), but some reports of improved proficiency (Baa, 2018) are anecdotal. It is likely that the preparedness of many students to study and learn through EMI, following the reduction of hours devoted to English language learning in secondary schools, will continue to be a problem. Arguably, the way forward, if EMI is to be pursued, is to recognize the obstacles posed by the realities of proficiency and accept and value the practices and strategies adopted by teachers and students as they negotiate the demands of EMI in classrooms. After studying a bilingual program in an Indonesian vocational university, Cahyani et al. (2018) identified pedagogic and social benefits of adopting a conception of language knowledge as a single repertoire from which features are strategically selected for effective communication (Garcia, 2011, in Cahyani et al., 2018)—a practice referred to as translanguaging, rather than codeswitching, to reflect the concept of a single repertoire rather than two or more monolingual codes. Teachers in their study drew on three languages (Indonesian, English and Javanese) in the classroom, translanguaging between them according to purpose and need. The recommendations of Cahyani et al. (2018, p. 476) are worth including here:

> Multilingual teaching strategies integrating learners' home languages should be explored more fully … Not enough practitioners know that home languages can help to maximise learning, build rapport, give support to students, and decrease student anxiety. … the present study indicates a need for institutional policy encouraging translanguaging as a pedagogical strategy for teaching in bilingual programmes, and also providing training for bilingual teachers in the effective and efficient use of translanguaging. In turn, such training would need to build on research into students' use of code-switching for making sense of their learning within the content subject as well as in developing proficiency in the target language.

8 Moving Forward

At this point in time, Indonesia remains an outlier in the phenomenon of efforts to embrace multilingual education practices that recognize the value of local languages as MOI during schooling. In contrast to some neighbouring countries, such as Cambodia, the Philippines, Thailand, Timor-Leste, and Viet Nam, which have developed policies of including non-dominant local languages as MOI in school education (Kosonen, 2017a), Indonesian policy—in principle—excludes local languages as MOI from schools. The complexity of language ecologies in Indonesia, the tremendous diversity of local languages, and the varying applicability of them to literacy education, complicates efforts to restore local languages as MOI in schools, as do discourses that reinforce perceptions of local vernaculars as marking the uneducated and lacking prestige (Asshiddiqie, 2008), but policy-makers focussed on development and international competitiveness could benefit from looking at the practices of other nations. South Korea, for instance, admittedly advantaged by a much less complex language ecology, has relied largely on the national language as MOI and has led the world in international rankings of school education and emerged as a prosperous developed economy (Coleman, 2009). Indonesia, with language policies oriented to pursuit of national identity, and struggling with the ideological implications and 'language schizophrenia' of the introduction of English, languishes much closer to the end of the same rankings.

The demand for English has endowed the language with "a symbolic value that the ability to use this language leads to a number of profits or economic advantages in a certain 'imagined' market (in this case, the believed 'global market)" (Manara, 2014, p. 26). This commodification has installed it as a marker of a sharp divide in Indonesia's education market between public and private education. The question of English as MOI is enmeshed in desires to improve the quality of English teaching and learning and beliefs that EMI provides an advantage to learners and its use in 'international curricula' in private schools associates it with opportunities to take advantage of the promises of globalization, as well as enjoy the prestige and social status attached to proficiency in the language. Despite encouragement of English MOI in higher education, the practice of EMI is ostensibly proscribed in the system of government National schools—but given free rein in the private 'international' school sector—and the hours allocated to English learning in the curriculum have been reduced in high schools. Such a situation would appear to potentially both constrain the opportunities for graduates of government schools whilst privileging those from private schools in the context of EMI in higher education.

Use of EMI is not necessarily based on understandings of language learning or pedagogic principles, and early introduction as practised in the private education sector before students have the necessary academic language proficiency could be counterproductive to learning (Hapsari, 2012). But in present circumstances, without greater exposure to English in the national education system, introduction of bilingual or EMI models in higher education can only entrench the advantages of students from privileged socioeconomic backgrounds (Abduh, 2018) and undermine aspirations of national and social unity. Indonesia's objectives of improved quality of education and of the nation being equipped to participate productively in the global economy, in which the capacity to communicate effectively in English is seen as essential, might be better achieved if EMI was not misunderstood as a convenient way of simultaneously achieving both these objectives. Perhaps the concentration in national school education on using the national language as MOI and building the quality of ELT to prepare students for participation in EMI in higher education is the most productive path for the nation as a whole after all. While socioeconomic inequality will continue to allow elite groups to access private education and EMI 'international' curricula, the option of decoupling of development objectives and English proficiency at the school level, as argued for in similar settings elsewhere in the world (Brock-Utne, 2012, 2016), is supported by evidence that questions the success of (what proved to be) the ISS experiment in achievement of improvements in the quality of education and in English language learning through EMI. Similar uncertainty applies to EMI in higher education, and what is needed is a model of bi/multilingual education that can pedagogically accommodate both local language/s and English to achieve learning outcomes at all levels of education that exceed those achievable through use of a monolingual MOI.

References

Abduh, A. (2018). *Adopting bilingual education in Indonesia*. Retrieved from http://australiaindonesiacentre.org/adopting-bilingual-education-in-indonesia/.

Asningtias, S. (2017). Revisiting English as a global language. *Indonesian Journal of English Teaching, 6*(1), 137–148.

Asshiddiqie, J. (2008). *Perlindungan Bahasa Daerah Berdasarkan UUD 1945 (Protection of local languages based on the 1945 Constitution)*. Paper presented at the Pembelajaran Bahasa dan Sastra Daerah dalam Kerangka Budaya (Regional Language and Literature Learning in Cultural Frames Conference), Yogyakarta.

Astika, G., & Wahyana, A. (2012). Studi Kasus Pembelajaran MIPA Bilingual di Tiga SMA RSBI di Jawa Tengah (A Case Study of Billingual Science Learning in Three International Standard Senior High Schools in Central Java). *LITERA Jurnal Penelitian Bahasa, Sastra dan Pengajarannya, 11*(2), 227–242.

Baa, S. (2018). *Lecturer perceptions toward the teaching of Mathematics using English as a medium of instruction at the International Class Program (ICP) of Mathematics Department of the State University of Makassar*. Paper presented at the Journal of Physics: Conference Series.

Bax, S. (2010). *Researching English bilingual education in Thailand, Indonesia and South Korea*. Kuala Lumpur: British Council East Asia.

Benson, C. (2016). Addressing language of instruction issues in education: Recommendations for documenting progress (Paper commissioned for the Global Education Monitoring Report 2016, Education for people and planet: Creating sustainable futures for all). Retrieved from http://unesdoc.unesco.org/images/0024/002455/245575E.pdf.

Brock-Utne, B. (2012). Language policy and science: Could some African countries learn from some Asian countries? *International Review of Education, 58*(4), 481–503. https://doi.org/10.1007/s11159-012-9308-2.

Brock-Utne, B. (2016). English as the language of science and technology. In Z. Babaci-Wilhite (Ed.), *Human rights in language and STEM education: Science, technology, engineering and mathematics* (pp. 111–128). Rotterdam: Sense Publishers.

Bruhn, K. (2011). The internationalization of education in Indonesia: Comparative look at the RSBI Project in Daerah Istimewa Yogyakarta and West Sulawesi. In *Proceedings of the IGSC III* (pp. 145–155). Retrieved from http://igsci.pasca.ugm.ac.id/archive/v2.0/assets/files/igsc-03-033-katherine-bruhn.pdf.

Cahyani, H., de Courcy, M., & Barnett, J. (2018). Teachers' code-switching in bilingual classrooms: Exploring pedagogical and sociocultural functions. *International Journal of Bilingual Education and Bilingualism, 21*(4), 465–479. https://doi.org/10.1080/13670050.2016.1189509.

Catalano, T., & Hamann, E. T. (2016). Multilingual pedagogies and pre-service teachers: Implementing "language as a resource" orientations in teacher education programs. *Bilingual Research Journal, 39*(3), 263–278. https://doi.org/10.1080/15235882.2016.1229701.

Christie, F. (1991). First and second order registers in education. In A. Ventola (Ed.), *Functional and systemic linguistics: Approaches and uses* (pp. 235–256). Berlin; New York: Mouton de Gruyter.

Clark, N. (2014, April 4). Education in Indonesia. *World Education News & Reviews*. Retrieved from https://wenr.wes.org/2014/04/education-in-indonesia.

Coleman, H. (2009). *Teaching other subjects through English in two Asian nations: Teachers' responses and implications for learners*. Paper presented at the Access English EBE Symposium, June 2009, Jakarta.

Coleman, H. (2011). Allocating resources for English: The case of Indonesia's English medium international standard schools. In H. Coleman (Ed.), *Dreams and realities: Developing countries and the English language* (pp. 87–111). London: British Council.

Coleman, H. (2016). The English language as Naga in Indonesia. In P. Bunce, R. Phillipson, V. Rapatahana, & R. Tupas (Eds.), *Why English?: Confronting the Hydra* (pp. 42–48). Bristol, UK: Multilingual Matters.

Constitution Court. (2012). *Putusan Mahkamah Konstitusi Republik Indonesia tentang Sistem Pendidikan Nasional (Constitution Court's Decree on National Education System)*. Jakarta: Constitution Court.
de Lotbinière, M. (2013, November 13). Indonesia to end teaching of English in primary schools. *The Guardian*. Retrieved from https://www.theguardian.com/education/2012/nov/13/elt-diary-november-indonesia-english.
Dewi, A. (2017). English as a medium of instruction in Indonesian higher education: A study of lecturers' perceptions. In B. Fenton-Smith, P. Humphreys, & I. Walkinshaw (Eds.), *English medium instruction in higher education in Asia-Pacific* (pp. 241–258). Cham, Switzerland: Springer.
Djojonegoro, W. (1996). *Fifty years' Indonesian education*. Jakarta: Depdikbud.
Fahmi, M., Maulana, A., & Yusuf, A. A. (2011). *Acceleration or internationalization? A cost-effectiveness-analysis of improving school quality in Indonesia. Working paper in economics and development studies*. Retrieved from http://repec.economicsofeducation.com/2014valencia/09-14.pdf.
Fauzi, A. M. (2018, January 1). New initiative for Indonesian higher education toward world-class status. Retrieved from https://qswownews.com/new-initiative-indonesian-higher-education-toward-world-class-status/.
Fillmore, N., & Handayani, W. (2018, March 28). Language matters: Language and learning in Bima, Indonesia. Retrieved from http://www.devpolicy.org/language-matters-language-and-learning-in-bima-indonesia-20180328/.
Hadisantosa, N. (2010). Insights from Indonesia. In R. Johnstone (Ed.), *Learning through English: Policies, challenges and prospects. Insights from East Asia* (pp. 24–46). Kuala Lumpur: British Council.
Hapsari, A. (2012). English bilingual education: The challenge of communication and cognition aspects of content language integrated learning (CLIL) In Indonesia. *Journal of English and Education, 6*(2), 12–20.
Haryanto, E., & Mukminin, A. (2012). Global, national, and local goals: English language policy implementation in an Indonesian international standard school. *Excellence in Higher Education, 3*(2), 69–78. https://doi.org/10.5195/ehe.2012.66.
Hawanti, S. (2014). Implementing Indonesia's English language teaching policy in primary schools: The role of teachers' knowledge and beliefs. *International Journal of Pedagogies and Learning, 9*(2), 162–170. https://doi.org/10.1080/18334105.2014.11082029.
Huda, N. (1997). A national strategy in achieving English communicative ability: Globalisation perspectives. *Jurnal Ilmu Pendidikan, 4*, 281–292. https://doi.org/10.17977/jip.v4i0.1298.
Kompas. (2016, August 4). Jadikan Bahasa Daerah sebagai Pengantar (Make local language the language of instruction). *Kompas*. Retrieved from https://acdpindonesia.wordpress.com/2016/08/04/jadikan-bahasa-daerah-sebagai-pengantar/.
Kosonen, K. (2017a). Language of instruction in Southeast Asia (Paper commissioned for the 2017/8 Global Education Monitoring Report, Accountability in education: Meeting our commitments). Retrieved from http://unesdoc.unesco.org/images/0025/002595/259576e.pdf.
Kosonen, K. (2017b). Language policy and education in Southeast Asia. In T. L. McCarty & S. May (Eds.), *Language policy and political issues in education* (pp. 477–490). Cham, Switzerland: Springer.
Lamb, M. (2011). A Matthew effect in English language education in a developing country context. In H. Coleman (Ed.), *Dreams and realities: Developing countries and the English language* (pp. 186–206). London: British Council.
Lauder, A. (2008). The status and function of English in Indonesia: A review of key factors. *Makara, Sosial Humaniora, 12*(1), 9–20.
Manara, C. (2014). That's what worries me: Tensions in English language education in today's Indonesia. *International Journal of Innovation in English Language Teaching and Research, 3*(1), 21–35.
Media Indonesia. (2015, August 27). Bahasa pengantar picu putus sekolah di daerah (Language of instruction triggers school dropouts in regions) (p. 12). Retrieved from https://acdpindonesia.

files.wordpress.com/2015/08/media-indonesia_p12_bahasa-pengantar-picu-putus-sekolah-di-daerah.jpg.
Ministry of Education and Culture. (2013). *Peraturan Menteri Pendidikan dan Kebudayaan Republik Indonesia No 81A tahun 2013 tentang Implementasi Kurikulum (Regulation of Ministry of Education and Culture of the Republic of Indonesia No 81A 2013 on Implementation of Curriculum)*. Jakarta: Berita Negara Republik Indonesia.
Mirizon, S., Wadham, B., & Curtis, D. D. (2016). Teaching mathematics and science in English at a university in Indonesia. In J. Orrell & D. D. Curtis (Eds.), *Publishing Higher Degree Research* (pp. 127–136). Rotterdam: SensePublishers.
Paku Alam IX. (2008). *Kebijakan Pembelajaran Bahasa dan Sastra Jawa dalam Kerangka Budaya Jawa sebagai Muatan Lokal Wajib (Policy on Javanese language and literature learning in a Javanese cultural frame as a compulsory local content)*. Paper presented at the Pembelajaran Bahasa dan Sastra Daerah dalam Kerangka Budaya (Regional Language and Literature Learning in Cultural Frames Conference), Yogyakarta.
Purnomo, S. H. (2011). English teaching and 'RSBI' schools. *Jurnal Linguistik Terapan, 1*(1), 54–57.
Rinaldi, I., & Saroh, Y. (2017). The rise of National Plus School in Indonesia: Education for parents and government. *Lingua Didaktika, 10*(2), 194–205. Retrieved from http://ejournal.unp.ac.id/index.php/linguadidaktika/article/view/7322.
Rustandi, A. (2013). Meaning negotiation between teacher and students in a fledgling International Standardized School. *International Journal of English and Education, 2*(3), 539–553.
Simbolon, N. E. (2018). EMI in Indonesian higher education: Stakeholders' perspectives. *TEFLIN Journal, 29*(1), 108–128. https://doi.org/10.15639/teflinjournal.v29i1/108-128.
Simons, G. F., & Fennig, C. D. (Eds.). (2018). *Ethnologue: Languages of the World: Indonesia* (21st ed.). Dallas, TX: SIL International. Online version: https://www.ethnologue.com/country/ID.
Somba, N. D. (2017, April 26). Papua students learn local language. *Jakarta Post*. Retrieved from https://acdpindonesia.files.wordpress.com/2017/04/jakarta-post_papuan-students-learn-local-language.jpg.
Suara Pembaruan. (2014, September 25). Anak yang diajarkan bahasa ibu lebih cepat paham konsep (Children taught in mother tongue understand concepts faster). Retrieved from http://sp.beritasatu.com/nasional/anak-yang-diajarkan-bahasa-ibu-lebih-cepat-paham-konsep/65512.
Sugito. (2008). *Pembelajaran Bahasa dan Sastra Daerah dalam Kerangka Budaya sebagai Muatan Lokal Wajib di Propinsi DIY (The learning of regional languages and culture in cultural frames as compulsory local content in DIY Province)*. Paper presented at the Pembelajaran Bahasa dan Sastra Daerah dalam Kerangka Budaya (Regional Language and Literature Learning in Cultural Frames Conference), Yogyakarta.
Sukamdi, & Mujahid, G. (2015). *UNFPA Indonesia Monograph Series: No. 3, Internal migration in Indonesia*. Jakarta: United Nations Population Fund. Retrieved from http://indonesia.unfpa.org/en/publications/monograph-series-no-3-internal-migration-indonesia.
Sukyadi, D. (2015). The teaching of English at secondary schools in Indonesia. In B. Spolsky & K. Sung (Eds.), *Secondary school English education in Asia: From policy to practice* (pp. 123–147). Abingdon, UK: New York: Routledge.
The Jakarta Post. (2014, September 26). Pupils learn best in local languages, say experts. *The Jakarta Post*. Retrieved from https://www.thejakartapost.com/news/2014/09/26/pupils-learn-best-local-languages-say.html.
The Jakarta Post. (2015, August 27). Bilingual education key to student success. *Jakarta Post*, p. 4. Retrieved from https://www.thejakartapost.com/news/2015/08/27/bilingual-education-key-student-success.html.
Widodo, H. P. (2016). Language policy in practice: Reframing the English language curriculum in the Indonesian secondary education sector. In R. Kirkpatrick (Ed.), *English language education policy in Asia* (pp. 127–151). Cham, Switzerland: Springer.

Willyarto, M. N., Werhoru, D., & Gea, A. A. (2017). *The use of English in learning mathematics for Grade 7 junior high school.* Paper presented at the Educational Technology (ISET), 2017 International Symposium on Educational Technology, 27–29 June 2017, Hong Kong.

Wright, S. (2016). *Language policy and language planning: From nationalism to globalisation* (2nd ed.). London: Palgrave Macmillan.

Zacharias, N. T. (2013). Navigating through the English-medium-of-instruction policy: Voices from the field. *Current Issues in Language Planning, 14*(1), 93–108. https://doi.org/10.1080/14664208.2013.782797.

Zein, S. (2016). Pre-service education for primary school English teachers in Indonesia: Policy implications. *Asia Pacific Journal of Education, 36*(sup1), 119–134. https://doi.org/10.1080/02188791.2014.961899.

Tony Walker (Ph.D.) is a Research Fellow in TESOL and LOTE in the School of Education, Deakin University, Australia. He worked in Australia as an English teacher and language teacher educator for many years, and continues to publish in the field and to work with teacher educators in Asia as an international consultant on academic writing.

Indika Liyanage (Ph.D.) is Associate Professor in TESOL and Discipline Leader (TESOL/LOTE) at Deakin University, Australia. He is also an Honorary Professor at the Faculty of Education, Sichuan Normal University, and Researcher at the Research Centre for Multi-culture, Sichuan Province, People's Republic of China. He has been an English language teacher educator and doctoral supervisor for many years. He has published widely and worked as an international consultant on TESOL in the Pacific.

Suwarsih Madhya (Ph.D.) has been an English language teacher educator since 1977. With a range of experiences in international cooperation (through her posts as Attache for Education and Culture, Indonesian Embassy, Bangkok, 1995–1999; Head of the Bureau for International Cooperation and Public Relation, Ministry of National Education, 2003–2005; member of the Governing Board of the Unesco Institute of Education, Hamburg, Germany, 2001–2004) and in international organizations (Asia TEFL, ICSEI, APRACSI), she now views language teaching from multi-perspectives by relating it to other important matters such as character education, identity formation, international cooperation/collaboration and world peace establishment. Her research interest is around teacher and instructional developments with emphasis on autonomous learning and also in intercultural learning. Her newest article is "Instilling character values through a local wisdom-based school culture: An Indonesian case study". She is currently involved in the production of an online standardized test of English proficiency (TOEP) for national use.

Sari Hidayati is a senior lecturer in English Education Department, Yogyakarta State University. She completed her M.A. in Applied Linguistics at Griffith University, QLD, Australia. Her current roles include developing syllabi and teaching subjects of Academic Writing, Literature in Language Teaching and English for Specific Purposes. Her teaching and research interests include Foreign Language Writing, English for Academic Purposes, Teacher's Reflective Practice, and Teacher Professional Development.

vi

Printed by Printforce, the Netherlands